The Armor of Love and Hope

A Memoir by Doris Mercado

FLORICANTO PRESS

Floricanto Press
7177 Walnut Canyon Rd.
Moorpark, California 93021
(415) 793-2662
(800) 523-3175

www. FloricantoPress. com

ISBN:13: 978-1494245993
"Por nuestra cultura hablarán nuestros libros. Our books shall speak for our culture."

Roberto Cabello-Argandoña, Editor

For privacy purposes, the names of my mother, my siblings, and some other individuals have been changed. The events and the places at which they took place are real.

To Bob,
May you gain
much resilience!
~~Dois~~ Mercado

The Armor of Love and Hope

Hugs can do great amounts of good, especially in children.
Diana, Princess of Wales (1961–1997)

Dedication

This book is dedicated to all the impoverished, orphaned, and suffering children in the world.

\

In Memory of

Doña Blasina Negrón López, "Mama Blas,"
and
Diego Maldonado Flores, U.S. Korean War veteran

Contents

Introduction

Chapter 1 Pearl of the South

Chapter 2 Meeting Mama Blas

Chapter 3 Jayuya, Indigenous Capital

Chapter 4 Doña Blasina Negrón López, "Mama Blas," February 2, 1896, to July 1993

Chapter 5 Torments

Chapter 6 Hurricanes David and Frederick, August 30 and September 4, 1979

Chapter 7 Visit from New York

Chapter 8 You All Behave

Chapter 9 "Take Care of Them"

Chapter 10 The Abandonment

Chapter 11 Graduation

Chapter 12 Last Letter

Chapter 13 Revelation

Chapter 14 Precious

Chapter 15 From Paradise to Hell

Chapter 16 Reunification

Chapter 17 Father's Help Attempt

Chapter 18 Homeless

Chapter 19 Nightmares

Chapter 20 Light

Chapter 21 Father

Chapter 22 The Meeting

Chapter 23 Mother

Epilogue: In Their Own Words

Acknowledgments

About the Author

The Armor of Love and Hope

Introduction

Remember, you were born naked.
—Mother

Jayuya, Puerto Rico; a midsummer's day in the early 1980s, during one of our visits to the river, in one of the most memorable moments I can recall. I sat by the shore with my beat-up feet in the water. The coolness was refreshing; my guard was down, my chin up, and I inhaled the pure forest breeze. I admired the greenery and generous peace this sanctuary offered. The other kids' voices echoed as they splashed in the water amid this secret paradise, calling, "Dori, look!"

We exchanged smiles while they swam. Their faces took on angelic forms, displaying how happy and safe they felt then.

The kids raced against each other, swimming as fast as they could. The splashing of the water sounded crisp and harmonious. As I reflected, *we are okay,* I looked at my four brothers and one sister; and Marcos, my youngest brother, smiled with me as if he could read my thoughts. I felt I was part of their happiness, and instantly my love for them armored me in a way that made me better able to face the world.

Like me, all five kids resembled Mother in some way: they all had olive skin, medium lips, and thick hair. The funny thing was that they balanced each other out. Marcos, or "Mitch," the innocent chatterbox and lover of our ancestors, the Taínos Indians, was seven. Jonas, "Chiqui," the pure, sentimental nature lover, was eight. Veronica, "Vera," age ten, was the stubborn and feisty one. Alejandro, "Titus," the funny daredevil, was twelve. And Franco, "El

Lobo," the optimist, a personable yet fearless cowboy, was age sixteen. If you looked for trouble with Franco, that's exactly what you found.

I, Doris, was fourteen.

Some days we laughed at each other: "Hey, kids, you have to let me cut your hair; you look like apes!"

Other days weren't too funny. We loved Christmas holidays, but I hated the kids' anguish on Three Kings Day at finding no gifts waiting in the morning. Franco, our tireless vigilant, was their consoler: "Don't worry, man, maybe there were too many kids without shoes, and they ran out."

Having Mama Blas, our grandmother, as a role model was a virtue. She herself was an orphan and sole survivor, a fierce woman who took pleasure in teaching us life values, ethics, and spirituality. Mama Blas was a highly sought-after medicine woman, a farm manager, a seamstress, and a mother. "Speak the truth and offer no explanations," she taught us.

One morning, the six of us watched Mother pack and leave us. Four days later, we watched Father do the same. Surviving became our art. Dreaming and hoping for better days helped us maintain radiant faces when we hurt and gave us new strength to go on when we were broken. Going to school assured us of a new tomorrow. Church offered us healing, forgiveness, and new hope. Miss Serra, one of my teachers, taught me this about poverty: "It doesn't matter how old your uniform is. As long as they're cleanly pressed, your clothes are as good as mine or anyone else's." I was proud to share her lesson with my siblings. Afterward, I pressed our uniforms humbly.

During our three years of abandonment, our bond to our house in Jayuya became sacred. Inside its thick walls, we felt loved, we were free, and we belonged. It was our precious little heaven. Upon graduating high school and earning a full scholarship to the University of Puerto Rico, I knew the effort had paid off—and I was ready for more.

1. Pearl of the South

La Baldorioty, my first home, was within walking distance of the city of Ponce, Puerto Rico's vibrant downtown. Ponce, also known as Noble City and Genip City, includes several neoclassical structures dating back to the seventeenth century and that have been declared national treasures. Our diminutive two-and-a-half-room wooden house was supported by stilts and had a zinc roof with dark walls and creaking floorboards. The kitchen spared room for a small refrigerator and counter space that fit a two-burner electric stove, coffee cans, and cornflake boxes. We were fortunate to have a shower and a flushing toilet outside. The house squeezed in two parents with an army of eight children.

Mornings were never pretty scenes. My older siblings—Lorena, Victor, Josue, Naomi, and Franco—fought to use the bathroom first; Josue and Victor always prevailed, owing to their size and strength. They'd stir up Mother's temper with their constant complaining. "Mom, I got up first and Victor kicked me out of the bathroom!"

There was only one hairbrush, and the fighting turned

physical whenever someone took too long with it. Then there was the fighting for socks; and by the time everyone was out the door, Mother had also given them a few licks because they drove her crazy.

I began kindergarten at age four. By then, Mother had taught me how to read using the local newspaper. She'd have me sit on the floor in the same spot every afternoon; I'd flip through the pages while Mother assisted, reading some of the harder words until I learned them. In first grade, reading my age-appropriate books always felt innocent and harmless by comparison. I was soon ready to trade my schoolbooks for the newspaper; I loved the excitement of the real world. I remember on one particular occasion, while practicing my reading, I came across a graphic photo of what seemed to be a dead body covered by a white blanket. I well remember the headline associated with it: "MAN CHOPPED WIFE INTO LITTLE PIECES." I felt sorry for the lady who had died. I don't know how long I stared at the picture, visualizing her agony. Every afternoon, I read every single line in the newspaper, and Mother would tell me, "Doris, read me my horoscope. Remember, it's the one with the little crab, Cancer."

I'd flip through the pages carefully until I found the horoscopes; I remembered they all had a symbol. I read at a slow pace, and Mother loved to listen. She took to heart whatever the daily horoscope predicted. I'd start with "Cancer, June . . .

"It's all right—skip the date."

The newspaper gave me a glimpse of worldly dangers, and I looked forward to reading about new happenings, Mother's horoscope, sex scandals, and other stories. Too early, I came to understand that some topics were unsuitable for my age. One day, I asked, "What is pregnancy? What is an affair? What is romance?"

"This is it, no more." Mother snatched the newspaper away and never allowed me to read it again. For a while, I insisted on knowing the answers to my questions, but Mother told me I was too small.

Schoolbooks replaced my dramatic daily readings. The headline "MAN CHOPPED WIFE INTO LITTLE PIECES" popped back into my head every now and then, and for a long time, I kept thinking about that particular story.

Now that the newspaper was forbidden fruit, I'd stare at it where it lay on the table every day after school. Temptation almost took over sometimes and more than once I tried to read it despite Mother's wishes. But I held back—even though I had faith the newspaper could teach me all I needed to know about the daily happenings on the island. I knew my age-appropriate readings in school weren't realistic, and I didn't buy what they were telling me. I'd look at other kids in my classroom and wish I could be as mesmerized as they were while reading, but only the newspaper did the trick for me.

Beyond this point, I was fascinated by writing. I was absolutely intrigued as I watched Mother write in the black-covered notebook she had titled *My Life*. I was fascinated by the way she sat there in the living room, back straight, lifting her chin up, looking away for a second or two; then her fingers would rush through the lines, pencil flying. When she was done, she would shut the notebook hard and put it on top of a tall dresser.

Curiosity almost killed the cat. I sometimes stared at her notebook, almost drooling. I wanted so badly to read what she had just written, though I questioned my own urgency to do so. Eventually, I figured out that if I climbed on a chair, I could reach her notebook. Mother saw me staring and knew exactly what I was thinking. "You are not to touch my notebook, all right?" she shouted. "You don't touch other people's belongings without permission. It's disrespectful!"

She'd set aside her own sharpened pencils, and we were not to touch those either. So I nodded and stayed away, and aside from noting the journal's title, I never flipped through its pages like I wanted to. Occasionally, she'd write a daily reflection or poem on a single sheet of paper and leave it on top of our little dining table. I'd read it, but without touching. I remember she once wrote something like, "A laborer gets up and looks forward to a fruitful day—but what if there isn't enough for him to do?"

Father respected her writing, and he was also a fan of the practice. Once in a while, he'd also share a note or a single phrase, just as Mother did. He'd smile brightly, displaying pride in his written creations. Unlike Mother, he preferred pens in various colors. According to his mood, he'd pick a particular pen and sit down, back straight, reminding me of my fellow students.

I got home from school earlier than my siblings, in the early part of the afternoon. While the house was quiet, Mother would park her old Singer sewing machine by one of the windows and work on fulfilling sewing orders. She made women's dresses, suits, and school uniforms, designing styles using newspaper sheets. When her customers came in, she'd make suggestions, using her newspaper designs; shawl-collared suits were a favorite. Her clients' approval of her finished pieces was her ultimate joy.

Watching Mother create new garments was thrilling, though we weren't allowed to approach her sewing area beyond a certain point. Sometimes she worked while listening to music; other times she'd work in complete silence. She aligned the fabric evenly, with so much care. She'd clear her throat before initiating the cut, and then her manly right hand would lead the cutting. The scissors made a hissing noise as they sliced through the cloth. Then, keeping the fabric even, she'd sit and began sewing, pedaling away to run the machine. Whenever she needed to pause, she'd stand up, one leg on the floor, one leg on top of her chair; she'd pick up the sweat dripping from her forehead like a man, mopping it up with her right thumb before flinging it across the room but away from her sewing area, drying her thumb on the bottom of her short dress as the pedaling continued.

Every now and then, she'd happily glance at the garment as the fabric took form, then say, "Ah-ha!" Mother would smile in approval as she turned the new garment inside out to inspect her own sewing. She'd take a deep breath; then, turning her sweaty cinnamon face to Veronica, Alejandro, and me, she'd pierce us with her sharp black eyes and shout, "You work hard, you all hear me?"

I would tremble and stare at her without answering. Then she'd move on, placing the finished garment on her lap; next, the hemming commenced. It almost looked like cursive writing. Then came a sizing comparison to the original clothing sample, and final but careful ironing, which elegantly stamped her sewing style into the garment. Finished pieces were hung up high, and her customers were excited when they walked in and saw their new garments. Sometimes she'd let me have small remnants of cloth to play with; other times I'd fall in love with certain fabrics. I remember one in particular, a polyester white with horizontal navy blue stripes. She made me a jumpsuit from the nice material; and boy, did I love my jumpsuit! I remember wearing it to church.

Sometimes she'd sew at night, and we'd fall asleep to the *taka taka taka* of the old Singer.

My mom, Lina Torres, was born and raised north of Ponce. Her parents owned a sixty-three-acre coffee plantation between Ponce and Jayuya, where they also sold oranges and other fruits by bulk. Mother was the youngest of fourteen children; she grew up Catholic and loved numbers, fashion, cosmetics, reading, and writing.

Mother loved doing business, too, and was a careful listener. Unlike Father, she often showed her temper and brandished her right fist at us when she felt upset or threatened. She took good care of her skin and hair; she did her own facials on a weekly basis, applying her own homemade rice facial mask. She also took care of Father's skin; macho man he was, he actually enjoyed the pampering, and his complexion was clear. She also plucked his eyebrows. It was hard to tell the difference, though, because his eyebrows were quite thick.

Across from our house was Cacho's Store; its jukebox played Héctor Lavoe songs around the clock. His songs made you love life. Downtown Ponce was within walking distance; so was the art museum, which had been founded by our beloved, most admirable former governor, Don Luis A. Ferré.

The fire station was another favorite location. There were always people at the ice cream stop, too, and *piragueros* rolled their ice carts around. I loved the raspberry flavor. My favorite thing, though, was *maví,* a drink made from fermented bark. Father loved *guarapo,* a drink made of sugarcane.

Almost every Saturday, newlyweds posed by Plaza Las Delicias for wedding pictures. I recall our city as one with many friendly, happy faces, ours among them.

Father, aka Papi, Mercado, Clidin, Quique, and Barrabás, always woke up cheerful, humming or whistling to his own tunes. Most people in Ponce knew him as Mercado. Sometimes Mother teased him by calling him Barrabás, and he didn't mind it at all. He had a natural deep voice, and every morning he'd repeat over and over, "Hey, everyone, it's time to get up, let's get going."

He'd open all the windows and turn on the radio or TV, then undertake his morning ritual of shaving and showering. He kept a trimmed mustache and a clear medium complexion and had large, happy aquamarine eyes.

He read the newspaper daily and paid special interest to historical events. He was dramatic, often shouting out interesting things: "Lina, you have to read this! 'FIRST PUERTO RICAN GIRL TO WIN THE MISS UNIVERSE PAGEANT,' 'HERMAN BADILLO, FIRST PUERTO RICAN TO SERVE AS VOTING MEMBER OF THE UNITED STATES CONGRESS.'"

His eyes sparkled like diamonds at those times. Mother dropped whatever she was doing and read the newspaper articles. Father saved his favorites; he kept a collection of magazine and newspaper clippings and enjoyed returning to and talking about his stories.

Traveling was Father's all-time favorite pastime. He was a spoiled firstborn of three—and a revered miracle child after a nasty accident at age five. He had been hungry, and so he reached up and dislodged a boiling pot of milk on the stove. It spilled over his chest, causing third-degree burns. After several months of recovery, he spent most of his early years traveling with the Mercado Castellar Rodríguez clan around the island, then back and forth from Puerto Rico to New York. His father, Domingo Mercado, "Mingo," was in the sugarcane business. His mother, Petra Castellar, "Doña Tato," worked for a brassiere company and sewed her own garments as well. Both spoke English fluently, and so did my father.

He loved the singer Donna Summer but was Jackie Gleason's biggest fan, coincidentally sharing his body frame, protruding eyes, and thundering voice. He turned heads anywhere he went and loved meeting people; he was outspoken but had a kind demeanor. He began his first job as a police officer in Ponce at age twenty.

He married my mother in the Roman Catholic Church, marking his first introduction to religion. Mama Blas (Mother's mother) loved him profoundly, but a lack of religion didn't fly with her. So he married my mother on the condition he'd learn how to pray and become Catholic like the Torres Negrón family. Mama Blas taught him how to pray, and Father was baptized and received first communion on his wedding day. I was born eight years later, a middle child of thirteen.

I've never known another Puerto Rican as addicted to rice and beans or bread as Father was. With the exception of an occasional dish of spaghetti and meatballs—he was a meat lover, too—he was content to eat rice and beans every single day. Mother protested about the repetition, telling him, "Hey, Barrabás, you eat too much rice and beans."

Dad scowled. He was a happy, easygoing person; but when it came to rice and beans, he was a spoiled *jíbaro*. He had such a terrible sweet tooth. Anything—from sugarcane to donuts, ice cream to milkshakes, caramels to all sorts of pastries—was fair game.

On Sundays, we walked to Parroquia San Conrado, our first Roman Catholic Church. I'd stare at the little old ladies wearing their *mantillas*. Some of them appeared sorrowful as they prayed, bowed down until Mass began. They made church a soft musical place prior to Mass, with their hissing and whistling bead prayers. I'd stare at their colored rosaries and wrinkled hands. Some had fine fingers, and some had crooked fingers with long, thick fingernails. Their hands appeared to map their toil in life. Their urgency in handling the rosary beads had me absolutely intrigued. I wanted to know what was going on or what was about to happen. Why the sadness, and why couldn't they speak up? I remember asking, "Mother, why do they whisper?"

"Shush. It's called prayer. When you speak with the Lord, no one else needs to listen but Him."

After Mother taught me about prayer, I came to love the secrecy and the urgency of pleas to the Lord. I'd stare at the old women in their *mantillas* while conducting my own private talks with Him.

"Lord, please tell the Three Kings we can't wait for gifts. Lord, I met Mama Blas; I want to see her again! Lord, Daddy got hurt at work. He can't walk—please make him better."

"Hosanna in the highest" was my favorite line of the entire Mass; my heart rejoiced when I heard it.

Some evenings, Dad would take us for rides. "Hurry up and eat so we can go for a ride, hurry!" The car was packed tight with Lorena, Victor, Josue, Franco, Naomi, Alejandro, Veronica, and me. Sometimes we went downtown; other days we went to the beach. Wherever we went, strangers saluted Father. "Hey, Mercado, how are you doing?"

Back then, almost everyone in Ponce knew my father's family. Dad took pride in introducing us, and we were always excited to meet new people. My father lived his life as if parading through an eternal carnival, always happy, making friends, joking, and moving forward without a worry in the world.

2. Meeting Mama Blas

I was four when my parents took me on a car ride to visit Mama Blas in Jayuya. She was Mother's mother. Jayuya, Puerto Rico, is also known as the Indigenous Capital, or Coffee Land, or Tomato City. In terms of elevation, Jayuya is one of the island's highest towns. I had never seen so much vegetation or so many curvy roads and precipices.

The high country was dense, the drive seemed dark, and it appeared we drove in a spiral. The seemingly never-ending drive made me dizzy and sleepy. The air was cooler and smelled like freshly picked coffee.

Driving in the high country entailed certain tactics, particularly beeping the horn and pausing before approaching tight curves. The roads were extremely narrow; we'd occasionally drive by a few crucifixes by the roadside, and my parents would make the Catholic sign of the cross. "Look, someone died there; maybe they lost control. Who knows," Father would say to Mother.

He also made sure I didn't miss anything.

"Doris, look, there's a waterfall!" Or "Look at the horses."

I'd keep staring, not wanting to miss anything. Suddenly, the high country turned colorful with flamboyant trees: banana, orange, and mango. Children played by the side of the road. *Lechoneras,* pork restaurants, hosted little packs of cheerful people enjoying a fiesta atmosphere. Well-dressed men gathered outside; they stood straight and tall like stallions, shiny hair pulled back, faces bright with friendly smiles. The smell of roast pork was succulent, inviting.

Further along, young men dove from a huge boulder

into a stunningly beautiful river. Golden-complexioned women with braided black hair carried baskets alongside the road and waved at us as we passed. Coffee fields and fruit trees lined the road. I loved the bright red and orange tones of the coffee beans.

After a long drive, we finally arrived at Mama Blas's place at La Pica in Jayuya. A tall rosewood tree divided her property from the main road. A blue cement house, larger than ours, sat with majesty amid green vegetation. This type of structure was commonly known as a hurricane home. Built in the 1950s, it was intended to endure winds of up to Category 5. It had immensely thick walls, and the windows were protected by storm shutters.

The green mountain views from the front door extended for miles and miles. The property included a four-acre coffee plantation; the rest was planted with other fruits and vegetables.

An Indian-looking elderly woman with watery eyes greeted us at the door. She walked slowly, as if she and time were old friends. I had never seen anyone with such prominent features. She had coppery skin, deep-set eyes, a small forehead, and high cheekbones. Her brilliant white hair was pulled back in a bun. She wore a long black dress that swept the floor to either side as she walked. Our eyes met. Mother brought me close to her, holding on to my shoulders, and said, "Mama, this is Doris."

The old woman reached out, cupping my face in her hands.

"You are my granddaughter, but I am your mother too," she informed me.

She smelled like sage and amber, and her hands were silky and warm. Blas then kissed my forehead and smiled at me as if we were the only two people in the house. I stared at her and smiled back. Her eyes were dark and intense, which gave me pause. We owned such a moment together. I could read her—the humbleness, her generosity and fairness. She made a statement of authority with even the most diminutive body movement, yet she seemed vulnerable, at least to me.

The house was neat but somewhat dark. It was hard to tell anyone actually lived there. The furniture was bulky, the tables decorated with doilies. The living and dining rooms boasted cream and gold linoleum, a famous flooring choice in Puerto Rico back then. A huge painting of the Madonna of Perpetual Help hung on the living room wall. The dining table had a marble top with a mahogany base and bulky chairs and was presided over by a painting of the Last Supper.

In her bedroom, she kept a porcelain statue of Our Lady, a crucifix, and tons of half-burned white candles on a table on the left side of her bed. To the right, there was a second table with a water bowl, and a third table across the room held multiple glass bottles with dark liquids. A large armoire with double mirrored doors dominated one side of the room. Her bed was perfectly made with white cotton linens; peace flowed around it, and her scent of sage and amber added a pleasant touch. Then there was the sewing room—Blas also had an old Singer—and tons of children's clothing. In addition, the house had two other small rooms, which appeared empty.

She lived alone. Her husband, Teyo, had died years before at age eighty-six, when my mother was pregnant with Franco. The kitchen had a little window over the sink and dried herbs hung upside down against the wall. I remember staring out the open window and admiring the view, as a gentle breeze caressed my face. A nearby door led out to the herb garden. The house had a complete bathroom with a flushing toilet inside. It had two exits, one from the kitchen and another leading outside. As Father made the rounds of the house, Mama Blas told him, "Hey, Clidin, see if you can get me some bananas and yucca."

"Of course," Father responded with merry eyes, then grabbed a machete and went off onto the farm for bananas and yucca for Mama Blas.

Mama Blas smiled at me, her face softly turned to one side and I felt her warmth.

"Come on, little one, I'm going to make you something in the kitchen."

Excited, I followed her. She stepped outside and picked herbs, while chatting to my mother; they talked in a different dialect than I was used to, and I couldn't understand a single word. Mama Blas's thick little hands moved quickly in the kitchen after she brought the herbs indoors. The aromas were exquisite. Father reappeared, laden with bananas.

"Well, look at that, a good batch!" Mama Blas said happily.

After delivering the fruits, he went out again and kept making little trips back and forth to the farm for various items. Blas was excited as she inspected the bananas and vegetables.

"Hey, Blas, there's tons of yucca," Father said after one of the trips, while wiping sweat from his forehead with his handkerchief.

We had stepped outside to pick more herbs; Mama Blas's face glowed like gold against the sun. She picked a few tiny leaves, which smelled exquisite, then glanced at Father and said, "Hey, Clidin, you know casaba is my favorite, right?"

Father chuckled. She was all excited and looked forward to making one of her specialties, casaba bread. She made it from yucca root; it was an original recipe she had grown up

24

with, and it dated back to our Native ancestors.

Father's shoes were muddy when he came back indoors. He talked to Mother and Mama Blas in turn while looking at me with raised eyebrows, smiling.

Later, Mama Blas served us a tasty and comforting bean soup. After we ate, she headed to her rocking chair. Partially lifting her skirt, letting her small feet swing, she leaned back and rocked. As her lips moved in silent prayers, she rocked herself into a partial nap. I simply couldn't take my eyes off her. I wanted to stay with Mama Blas and share her peaceful surroundings forever.

When we left her house, I kissed her aged face with teary eyes while she cupped my face in her hands again. She let me go while caressing my hair and whispering prayers. I smiled and professed my love for her with my eyes. Her aged face lit up with a tender smile. Mother assured me we'd come back to visit Mama Blas again.

I enjoyed this particular memory, her scent, and a humility I had never seen before—plus her coppery velvet skin and eyes that looked straight into you, piercing but righteous. I embraced Mama Blas in my heart as if she were my own child, clinging tight to the warmth she'd unconditionally given me. As our car took off for Ponce, I fell asleep to the sweetest of memories, inhaling them almost as if they were the breath of life.

Day and night thereafter, I thought about her, talked about her, and waited to see her again. It almost seemed she lived a whole world away, but my love for Mama Blas pulled me like a magnet.

Our house in the city was extremely loud, with constant baby cries, boys shouting and running around, and the music or TV always playing. We fought like cats and dogs, and Mother's constant supervising, chore assignments, and alerts about eating or showering punctuated our lives and kept us on our toes. The kitchen sink was never empty of dishes, and the clotheslines were literally owned by our babies; cloth diapers and baby sheets always hung there, drying. Meanwhile, the tiny house was stuffed with piles of clothing, schoolbooks, and shoes. It looked like a mobbed mess.

We'd just walk over things and find our way around as well as we could. Father was like our singing fat lady. He'd get home from work with his loud, happy voice, cheering everyone up and giving us each a warm smile, his happy, glowing emerald-blue eyes buying into our rascally behavior. He handed out kisses, tickled our feet, and played with us on the floor, making roaring sounds. We felt loved. We were happy. Life was just dandy.

Later on, my brother Jonas was born, anemic and sickly. A year later, Marcos was born with pneumonia and spent his first month in the hospital. Marcos was my parents' tenth child, and they were devastated by his illness. Then there was the pressure of caring for skinny, fragile Jonas, in addition to the eight of us who were of school age. I don't know how they managed. By then, I was six years old and could read Mother's tiredness, sadness, and constant worry about both boys. It took a toll on her as she made her daily visits to the hospital, and for a while, her sewing came to a halt.

During Marcos's hospital stay, tension filled our home, and my parents no longer smiled the way they used to. Our family trips to the beach and downtown ceased. When Marcos finally came home, we kids were glad to meet him. He had chunky little legs, fair skin, almond brown hair, and aquamarine eyes like Father. After his arrival, a lot of visitors came by to see him and offer gifts.

Marcos and Jonas both remained fragile for a while, but they eventually recovered and grew healthy and strong.

In time, Mother returned to her sewing. Once the boys were well, Mother shopped around for a new house for a while but was unsuccessful in finding a suitable one for our family. She loved nearby Aibonito, also known as the City of Flowers. Aibonito celebrated a flower festival every year in June. Mother's birthday was also in June, so it was definitely the place Mother preferred to visit and enjoy on her birthday.

"But they want too much money for a mere two hundred square foot home," Mother vented to Father. She was very disappointed; she had always longed to buy the house of her dreams.

My parents then discussed the possibility of moving into Mama Blas's house in Jayuya. The house had more space than ours, but it was an hour away from Ponce. Living in Ponce had its advantages; our schools were within walking distance, and downtown was two miles from home. Moving to Mama Blas's house in the high country would mean a complete change of lifestyle.

I was excited about the idea of moving. I loved my school but couldn't wait to see Mama Blas again. I could tell we didn't have enough space in our old house in Ponce. In the mornings, I woke up to find my big sister Naomi's feet in my face; and on cold nights, she'd wrap herself up like tamale in the single blanket we shared. I'd freeze until she fell asleep, whereupon I could sometimes manage to steal the blanket back, little by little.

I especially hated our fights over the solitary hairbrush every morning. Horrified by Mother's threats, I'd beg Naomi to hurry up with the hairbrush, but by the time Mother made her give it up, it was getting late—usually too late. I'd just tie up my uncombed hair, and out I'd go. On several occasions, though, Mother grabbed me right by my ponytail, wiggling my head.

"Where do you think you're going with uncombed hair, huh?"

A few licks followed, which encouraged me to brush my hair in about two seconds flat. I needed help brushing it, because it was thick and long, and I got used to not brushing it too often; eventually, the less I combed my hair, the happier I felt about it. It was just too arduous. Whenever I was home, I was enthusiastic about running back and forth helping with babies and chores and playing outdoors, so having neat hair was not a priority.

3. Jayuya, Indigenous Capital

Entre punta y punta cabe una vieja sienta.
(Between every single stitch an old woman can sit.)
—Mama Blas

In the summer of 1972, we moved out of our bubbly little home in Ponce to the city of Jayuya. Located north of Ponce, it's the location of Tres Picachos, one of the island's highest mountains. Tres Picachos has three peaks (hence the name) and soars to 3,952 feet. I was seven and very excited about our move. Our family had ten children by then, plus my parents, plus Blas—thirteen altogether, which seemed to be our lucky number.

Moving to the Indigenous Capital brought Mama Blas, serenaded nights, prayer, fear, religion, superstition, and vampire and ghost stories into my life. Praying the rosary was one of the first things we learned after we arrived. We sat around in a circle and prayed the rosary with Mama Blas every morning before school and every evening at six. In her spare time, Mama Blas enjoyed talking to us in

29

riddles.

"When praying, never fall asleep without completing prayers. You may as well cut yourself in half! An ox cannot work the land alone; the effort is so great it breaks its back."

I'd just stare at her.

"When speaking the truth, offer no explanation."

The more she talked, the more confused I was. "No explanation?"

"Yes. Do not explain, and do not use excuses. Excuses are a liar's way out."

Other days, Mama Blas scared the living daylights out of us with her dismaying horror stories. Mostly they were about vampires and ghosts, but she also introduced us to other forms of evil.

"When siblings fight, hell's gates swing open," she told us. And "Never answer the door when there is a single knock . . . it is not Jesus."

I'd never been so scared in my life. Thanks to Blas, I became a light sleeper. Father, a city boy, found Blas's teachings most intriguing and fascinating. He was very fond of Blas, and she returned his adoration. They enjoyed each other's company, and she looked forward to hearing about his day after he came home from work. Father soon became Blas's most faithful student. He made Blas laugh out loud; her round little stomach bounced when she did.

We enjoyed our new life in underpopulated Jayuya, where the nights were made melodious by the singing frogs, or *coquíes*. We were accustomed, though, to Ponce's electrifying energy. We had nothing in common with peace and quiet. We were loud and proud, and happy to bring along our bubbly city atmosphere to El Campo, the high country. El Campo was a world apart; it was dark green and cool and quiet. The people, the Jayuyanos, were kind and happy yet seemed as if they'd invented humility.

"Don't be fooled by a Jayuyano's humbleness," Mama Blas warned us. "Before being taken for a fool, I'd already have you pinned down by your tail, ha!"

Mama Blas's "ha" was as threatening as her entire statement. Humbleness, then, was our newly acquired trait, in the Jayuyano way. We adapted well to our new surroundings, especially when Mama Blas gave us permission to go out into the coffee plantation, where we played and picked fruit. The plantation had an abundance of tree ferns, vines, philodendrons, and bromeliads perched on trees at which to wonder. We were eager to wander around and choose our favorite spots. The mango tree located on the east side of the farm was Mother and Father's favorite. Mother thought it was the perfect spot to build a house, because the land there was flat and the view of the coffee plantation was picturesque. The boys enjoyed it as well. To the west were bamboo trees, which made melodious noises when caressed by the wind.

On the north side of the plantation was a little brook with a miniature waterfall, which came in handy when we needed water. It was adorned by helicons and tons of vines and morning glories. On the south side was my favorite place: the "horse's back," a high, flat hill that was, in fact, shaped like a horse's back. It was Blas's favorite as well; there on the peaceful, flat peak, the air was cooler and the coffee trees were tall and perfectly aligned. We could see a good portion of the farm from up there but weren't allowed to cross beyond it. I couldn't stop staring at the deep, green mountain views and other houses out in the distance.

To the west was a second brook surrounded by steep slopes. Coffee trees do well on such surfaces. Then there were the orange and pomarrosa trees (the latter is also known as pommerose or Malay apple). Banana, avocado, and guava trees also abounded, as did passion fruit, guanabana, and anones, among several other fruits and vegetables.

Marcos was a baby then, and Jonas was a toddler. Three more children were born later; we were a total of thirteen. By the end, we were a party of sixteen—sharing long, colicky nights, with food disappearing before our eyes, dishes piling up like magic, and laundry multiplying out of control. There was always a new little one taking baby steps, a toddler finding his or her way around, or a preschooler learning to ride a bike. It was great fun as our place got tighter and noisier. Every time Mother gave birth to a new baby, we waited anxiously to hold him or her; and Mother only let us hold the new baby for a few seconds each. Everyone waited his or her turn; we all wanted to be introduced.

For political reasons, Father quit his job as a police officer to become a truck driver for La Rovira Corporation in Ponce. My father was lucky to obtain a job that matched his personality in every sense. He was in bliss, driving around constantly to places on the island he'd never seen before. He worked for Rovira for many years and made lifetime friends while he was there. His closest friend, Ramon, also known as Cara de papa, or "Potato Face," loved stopping by our house to hang out with Father on the weekends.

Father liked to give his friends weird nicknames; only very rarely did he call them by their given names. El Pestañú, for example, was a funny-looking guy; his eyebrows were so thick, it was distracting. Every time he visited us, we hardly paid attention to what he said but just kept staring at his eyebrows. I'd try hard not to laugh. Franco used to hide and laugh nonstop, as if someone had tickled him.

El Gago, a guy who stuttered badly, was Franco's favorite. Any time El Gago tried to share stories with Father,

Franco walked away, laughing and holding his stomach. Father seemed pretty engaged in his conversations with El Gago and understood what he was saying. Father's friends tended to share his personality; they were always happy and pleasant. They loved trading truck-driving stories, too. Father was especially fascinated by La Piquiña de Cayey, one of the island's most treacherous roads. La Piquiña's steepness was a real challenge for trailers. He'd entertain his friends by sharing, "You know, there's a riddle about La Piquiña." Father's eyes lit up. *Subiendo por La Piquiña, ñia ñia que se va 'pa atrás*. Heavy trucks that didn't have enough power gave up and made a *ñia ñia* sound going backward. I'd never seen a road so high and steep. My God, it was hilarious when the truck gave up; I had to start from the bottom all over again," Father said, laughing out loud.

Every day he got up no later than five in the morning; sometimes he'd leave the house as early as four. He loved heading out for a new day's journey, delivering crackers to different places around the island. He'd bring us Rovira crackers every now and then. He'd walk into the house with a can of crackers on his shoulder, smiling as we all ran toward him. Sometimes he wrestled with us on the floor or tickled our feet until we laughed so hard we couldn't breathe.

Our mornings remained war zones but were most interesting with Mama Blas's presence. We'd stare at her as she got up solemnly, rosary in hand, murmuring morning prayers and giving thanks to God. She'd wave at us to join in her prayers. She prayed for world peace, for the departed, and for *los necesitados,* the needy. She'd then step outside, bow down, and kiss the ground.

Her prayers to the Lord seemed the richest offering I could imagine. After her morning prayers, Mama Blas would have a cup of cappuccino while we ate our breakfast.

Then she'd help us get ready and comb our hair one by one. The gentleness of her hands and her loving touch felt like a gift. My hair felt so neat and even; I'd never worn my hair up, and I felt special when she fixed it this particular style. We were fortunate to grow up around so much love.

Once we were ready to leave the house, she'd have us pray the Our Father and to our guardian angel. She'd then give us her final blessing: "May the Lord guide and keep you." Then, after waiting a few seconds, she'd look up as if waiting for some signal. Nodding, she would say, "*Vayan, se pueden ir ahora*. Go on, you can leave now."

Afterward, I felt almost as if we were accompanied by some sort of guide, a guardian angel indeed. We were forbidden to leave the house without her blessing, and there were no exceptions; trying to find an excuse was even worse. Admitting to being sorry was better than saying, "I forgot."

You see, Mother's "Oh, you forgot?" was followed by a whipping with the belt. "This shall remind you for the *next* time."

Mama Blas was furious when we failed to follow her rules, but she never hit us.

§ § §

I had loved learning to read the newspaper and attending first grade. Second grade was rough, as I adjusted to life in the high country.

Third grade was the worst of all my primary school years. In the mornings, Mother would hit me on the head with her knuckles for not finding my school socks. I didn't know where to look for them. Then her threats: "If you miss the bus, you'll see what awaits you." I'd become frantic as I searched through piles of clothing for my socks. I had no idea how I passed from third grade to fourth grade. I didn't learn anything.

It took us a while to adjust to catching school buses. I, for one, found getting up earlier to wait for them difficult. Mornings in El Campo were chilly. I missed walking to school—not to mention visiting our lively downtown Ponce, our trips to the beach, and Cacho's jukebox overplaying Héctor Lavoe songs.

The Jibaritos of Jayuya resembled our ancestors, the Taínos. They had copper complexions, lustrous black hair, almond-shaped eyes, high cheekbones, and hawk noses. They stared at us, and we stared at them; I was astounded by their beauty. I was excited to meet new friends in our new home—but they called us aliens. Some of the girls even called me "Freckle Face."

Still, I made three of my best friends ever in Jayuya: Liz Perez, Aby Reyes, and Mary Rivera. Liz resembled the Taíno. She was a classy, humble, sweet girl—and she liked Franco. The feeling was not mutual: "I can't have a girlfriend, I'm too young," said Franco. Liz and I went to school together from second to eighth grade. Sadly, in eighth grade, her mother died, and days later, her grandmother died as well. The family soon moved to San Juan. I missed her greatly but never saw her again.

Nighttime in the high country was provocative; we were treated to a sky full of stars, serenaded by *coquíes*, and caressed by a soft breeze, which carried its own exotic melody. Naomi and I loved looking at the stars; I believed if I were tall enough, I could touch them. We were excited any time we saw shooting stars. We loved a bright night lit by a full moon, but I didn't like seeing my shadow on such nights; it was like someone was following me. We'd try to laugh, stepping on our shadows, but the night was dense, and many times we'd get scared and end up running into the house.

The Armor of Love and Hope

When bedtime arrived, Mother clapped her hands, which alerted us of her final dispatch. "*Vamos, todo pájaro a dormir.* Let's go, all birds to their nest, let's get going," she'd say.

Anyone who tried to hang back would get a whipping with the belt. Mother, Blas, and Father would sit in the living room for their nighttime chats, and Blas would always share her macabre stories. The living room was divided by double wooden doors, which Mother closed, but their whispering failed at times. Father would sometimes laugh out loud; Blas would sometimes say "*Hmmm*" in a malicious tone; and Mother's loud "Jesus!" made us tremble. I'd hang on to Naomi, and Naomi would hang on to Lorena. Veronica was too young to worry; she'd fall into a sound sleep.

Blas's suspenseful stories were perturbing.

"Never forget to bless a *fogata,* a fire pit; or else the devil will bathe in it. The front door most be closed by seven to keep evil from entering, and don't sweep the floors; you're sweeping the Lord's blessings. Baptize children right away. The incessant cry of an unbaptized child means they have one foot in hell!"

Naomi and I shared a small bed in Blas's bedroom. When Blas was done with her nighttime stories and came to bed, under an aura of tranquility, I'd watch her loosen her hair so it cascaded below her waist. Gently she'd comb her snow-white tresses by candlelight. Her hands moved in the same slow pace as the burning candles. When it was combed to her satisfaction, she'd part her hair into two white strands cascading down her chest, almost touching her knees. She'd then braid her hair, small thick hands moving quickly but gently. Once done, she'd take off layers of clothing while whispering prayers. I was absolutely perplexed as I stared at the glowing rosary beads and candles, while trembling in the dark.

Mama Blas freshened up with her own handmade herbal scents, one of the last touches before bedtime. Softly lying down, tucking in her sheets, Mama Blas would next commend her soul to the holy family: "*Jesús, María y José, en voz descanse el alma mía.* Jesus, Mary, and Joseph, may my soul rest under your protection." She never went to sleep without doing so. She prayed with so much authority, faith, and strength that she made me believe evil really existed and that she had in fact embarked on a quest to conquer it and keep it away.

Blas looked like a baby tucked under the splendor of her white sheets. Sometimes she'd blow out the candles; other times she'd let them burn while we slept. Many times I'd fall asleep quickly, but other times, I'd stare at the glowing candles and think about the magic that light and prayer seemed to offer.

One afternoon, while driving home from work, Father stopped and picked up an injured owl from the road. The owl scratched Father's left forearm severely, but he brought it home and cleaned its wound. Father kept the owl for several days; then he released it back into the wild, right by the mango tree where he liked to hang out. Every now and then, early in the evening, the owl would stop by the mango tree, at the same spot where Father had released it.

"Hey, doing better, ah? Hey, kids, come here, look who came for a visit. Walk slowly."

The owl would stare at Father for a few seconds and then vanish into the wild again. It made Father's day when this happened; we were astounded by its beauty and by the fact that the owl seemed to have developed a bond with Father.

Coffee flowers were my absolute favorite. They're pure white, very delicate blooms, splendid against the dark green of the foliage. As a child, white was my favorite color, so the time when the trees bloomed was always one of my favorite times of the year. Coffee season was a happy time; the farm glowed with the red-orange beans, so bright against the greenery. Grandma Blas hired coffee pickers to carry out the harvest; then she'd sell a portion of the coffee and keep the rest to use year round. Coffee processing was a four- to five-day process. Mama Blas preferred a light roast, but she also made a darker roast, which Mother preferred. The grinding of the toasted beans was great fun, and the smells were exquisite. Oh, how I cherished Mama Blas's smiling face over a fresh cup!

Doris Mercado

4. Doña Blasina Negrón López, "Mama Blas," February 2, 1896, to July 1993

"Prayer should be accompanied by light, because God is light," Blas said, as she lit her candles and began her daily rituals.

I was mesmerized by the way she lit her candles, one by one, pausing as if she commanded each one to undertake a particular task. Her lips moved softly, in silent prayer. As the dark room was lit by golden flames, the solemnity of her prayers became irresistible. I'd sit still and pray with her, almost feeling as if I were being watched. It intrigued me to feel how the peace settled on us and how she managed to accept its grasp. I wanted to get to know her. I wanted to be like her.

Blasina Negrón López was named after Saint Blas. She was orphaned when Cyclone San Ciriaco struck the island in 1899. It was recognized as "the last hurricane of the nineteenth century" and accounted for well over three thousand deaths, making it one of the most devastating hurricanes in Puerto Rican history. Blas was placed in an orphanage and later adopted. Her adoptive family taught her about sales, farm work, sewing, and other skills that were considered important for making a living. Blas was a devoted Catholic; she was illiterate but knew numbers and did accounting by heart.

She began to work at a young age, married young, and before long had three children. Blas made her own dresses—round neck, quarter sleeve, a slim, tight waist, ankle length. She kept her hair pulled back in a bun and had a "what you see is what you get" look. Blas was not easy to intimidate; her petite frame camouflaged a fiery temperament. When she got mad, even my father put his tail between his legs. Her demeanor was strong; she was a careful listener and studied a person closely when talking business.

Aside from making her everyday garments, her specialty was children's clothing. She made baptism outfits for newborns and special-occasion dresses for girls in an array of styles. She loved pastel colors and had a special taste for quality fabric. Blas also made quilts from scratch. She crafted small flowers out of fabric, ironed them to perfection, and attached them one by one to create the upper layer of the quilt. The finished product was heavy and colorful.

In the early years of her first marriage, her husband died in a car crash. She'd then wake up at four every morning and walk miles to La Plaza in Ponce to sell children's clothing to support her family. Blas later met my grandfather, Teyo Torres; his parents were from Madrid, Spain. They married, and as a wedding gift, he bought Blas a sixty-three-acre property on which they worked together for about forty years. Blas hired the farmworkers and provided them with lunch. Teyo handled the business dealings with the coffee and fruit buyers.

They had ten more children. The second youngest was Lina, who died in a house fire. My grandmother then became pregnant one more time and gave birth to a fourteenth child in honor of the lost one; they named her Lina as well, and in the fullness of time she became my beloved mother.

Blas and Teyo prospered but noticed many of the people around them struggled—so they built a house next to their own especially for the needy. They allowed families to stay for as long as they needed to, until they got back on their feet, and often invited them over for dinner. People in the neighborhood called my grandparents the "Compassionate Riches." At one point, word came from Spain: my grandfather's father was sick, but he didn't feel it was an opportune time to return to Spain. He never went back.

Blas celebrated her birthday each year by building a campfire in honor of Saint Blas, shouting, "*¡Qué viva San Blas y la Candelaria!*" La Candelaria was the acquired saint name. When we were living with her, she had us shout along with her for several minutes.

She was well known as a medicine woman; she mixed her own herbs, which she used for curing different physical ailments. Some of her medicines consisted of teas, massages, hot herbal treatments, and other mixtures she applied directly to open wounds. She treated people with health problems ranging from the common cold to stomach problems, burns or cuts, muscle sprains, strains, some fractures, and severe headaches. Mama Blas also made her own sweet pea coffee, processing the peas just like coffee beans; she did the same with garbanzo beans.

She was particular about her hair accessories; she carefully preserved her hair grips, rolling her hair in a bun which stayed intact all day long. Grandma's favorite suggestion for living a good life was, "Start the day early if you want to be fruitful."

Hurricane season always made Mama Blas melancholic. Every time a storm or hurricane was announced, she'd become sad and agitated. Sometimes she'd talk about hurricanes Santa Clara and San Felipe. She expressed great sadness about losing her parents. She'd pause as if trying to remember something else, her eyes dimming in horror. I'd never seen anyone as sad as she was at those times; she seemed to be trying to reach out for something far away. Whenever this happened, Mother would warn, "Mama doesn't feel well. Don't ask her questions."

During those times, Mama Blas talked mostly to Mother, and then only in bits and pieces.

"The ripping wind, people's screams . . ."

Sometimes she changed her dialect to the one only she and Mother spoke, but we could read their expressions. Blas had witnessed something truly horrific. Then Mama Blas would let out a loud, agonizing cry that pierced my heart. "Mama, don't cry!" we'd hear Mother say to Blas. Those days turned gray and dull and held a heavy feeling of loss as we listened to Mother comforting Mama Blas. Occasionally, Mother would emerge from Mama Blas's room to cook for us. She'd remind us to stay outside and play quietly—Mama Blas was sleeping. On a few occasions, I'd see Mother emerge from behind the house with watery eyes. Because we were forbidden to ask questions, I assumed Mother cried from seeing her own Mother mourning her loss. The topic of hurricanes and bad weather was almost too sacred to talk about.

During these times, Father looked somber as well. It was even harder to see Father sad; it was very unlike him. We understood Blas's sadness over losing her parents and siblings, and maybe being unable to remember them after all this time. I wondered what they had looked like but dared not ask any questions. Patiently, we waited for Blas to feel better again.

I loved Blas's cooking; she made the best potato balls ever. One time Naomi tempted me to take two extra potato balls without permission. I felt horrible when Blas searched for them and tried to find out who took them, and I felt guilty about it for the longest time. But Naomi had threatened me with bodily harm if I said anything, so I held my tongue. Afterward I behaved extra nicely, in hope of somehow paying for the theft. The potato balls were so tasty—but if our grandmother had found out I had stolen them, and who had suggested it, we would both have been severely punished.

Mama Blas hated Halloween; she prayed incessantly every October 31. I couldn't help but laugh at her superstitions. "Halloween is the devil's and witches' feast day," she'd tell us. "Black cats gather and take part in evil cults. Dracula existed—he enticed women to go to his castle, and he killed them."

She'd then entertain us with horror stories and advice. "Once upon a time, there were two brothers who fought constantly. Their fighting turned fatal: one killed the other, and then killed himself. But even after death, they continued fighting. They'd be seen sometimes, still fighting, rolling through the woods in a ball of fire . . ."

"Once, three relatives were digging up the ground looking for a supposed inheritance. They could not find it, because one had adverse intentions . . ."

"There was a woman who could not stop crying because she had lost a child. A white dove appeared, drenched, unable to fly. The woman asked the dove, *why are you all wet?* The dove replied, *Because of your tears; they keep me from flying.* The lady, astonished, stopped crying, and the dove flew away."

"Mother Goose feeds her babies until they ask, *Give me more.* Once they ask for more, she replies, *Go get your own!* When you're in danger, yell the name of the Lord and you will be saved. When stranded, the best place to spend the night is a cemetery. It's a sacred resting place. Don't spend the night in a church. It gets filled with souls who are in need of praying for; they will not let you rest!"

43

"Don't you let yourselves get infected with the disease of judgment or the pestilence of hate; don't preach about love, because love comes from the heart and is manifested in deeds. Hypocrites preach about love, oh under grand invitations and smiles, yet they stab you in the back the second you turn around. Do for others what you can; be generous. Even if you are wronged, pay the bad with good. Your goodness will be your reward."

Her voice echoed throughout the house as she made these pronouncements. In a way, she was our home professor. She tested me repeatedly with the same phrase. "An ox can't work the land alone. Tell me, Doris. What does it mean?"

"Mama, I don't know what you're saying," I'd answer.

"Once again: an ox can't work the land alone. Think about it and let me know when you have the answer."

She'd then glare at me with piercing eyes, pick up her skirt, turn around, and walk away. I'd be puzzled, trying to understand what she meant as I went about my day. Later, she would demand, "Doris, did you think about what I said? What's the answer?"

"Oh, Mama, I don't know, I give up," I'd say, frustrated.

"Very well: an ox can't work the land alone, because if it tries, it breaks its back. The effort has to be equal, in pairs. In a marriage, the effort must come from the man *and* the woman, not one person alone," she'd say firmly, staring straight into my eyes.

"I understand," I'd answer, blushing. What I didn't tell her, though, was that I understood my mother was working much harder than my father. Mother's ambitions weren't enough, because while she was doing all she could, Father wasn't helping as much as he needed to, and Mother was the one breaking her back in the marriage.

5. Torments

I was seven when I made First Communion, whereupon Mother told me, "You've reached the age of sin, so you shall be accountable for your actions. You are no longer a little kid, but a *manganzona,* old enough."

Overnight, I went from bubbly and happy to extremely shy. I became horrified of Mother's black eyes and her manly hands and didn't understand the beatings I now received.

"Lord, please make it stop," I'd plea at church, forgiving her Sunday after Sunday; but the shyness settled in.

Mama Blas's intercession was a real relief; she'd help us look for things and comb our hair. To make things worse, a crazy boy named Genaro began to pull my hair every day at school. I'd leave for school each day with perfect hair: Mama Blas applied oils and pulled my hair up into a bun. I'd return home with my hair down, messy, sometimes with headaches, and no sign of the hair grips with which Mama Blas had sent me to school. Both women questioned me, but I was afraid to tell them what had happened for fear they wouldn't believe me—and for fear of punishment. Mother was suspicious, and threatened, "If I hear you're letting someone hit you, I'll hit you twice. If anyone hits you, you punch them back, hard!"

I figured Mother should have been a boxer. Her right fist delivered heavy force and guaranteed damage. "Listen, I want you to learn how to defend yourself," she commanded. "Close your fist like this, use all your strength, and punch *hard.*"

Then she'd throw a few sample punches. Frankly, I was

more afraid of her demonstrations than of Genaro. She had me practice, but I didn't have the heart to punch anyone.

Her temper often made her right fist fly, especially when Father didn't take her seriously. While cooking one afternoon when I was nine, Mother said to Father, "Barrabás, there's no more white rice."

"Oh, really? Make black rice then," Father teased, laughing.

It happened in a flash. This was the first time I saw her fist do real damage and was horrified when I saw blood dripping down over Father's right eye. His face was frozen in a cold smile of disbelief as he reached for his handkerchief. Mother looked him straight in the eye, mumbled something, and continued moving about the kitchen.

In school I was finally relieved when my teacher, Ms. Bianchi, caught Genaro pulling my hair in her classroom. She hit him several times on his arms with a yardstick, and every day, she'd have me sit in the first row so she could keep an eye on him. Eventually, the freak stopped pulling my hair. Ms. Bianchi also defended me from the group of girls who called me "Freckle Face." They'd laugh at me and walk away anytime I tried to sit with them for lunch.

"You keep teasing her, and watch—she'll grow up to be a beautiful girl," Ms. Bianchi said to them. Her kindness helped me regain my self-esteem. Finally, I had someone standing up for me! I wanted to do well in her class just because she loved me.

Trying to keep up with chores while fearing Mother was horrid; I'd shiver as she inspected dishes, taking the ones she claimed were still dirty and saying things like, "Look at these baby bottles—see, they still have traces of milk on the bottom!" Then she'd hit me over the head several times with a bottle. I'd have to rewash the bottles with a burning skull and no energy left to do homework. I'd fall asleep in the classroom and was always worried about catching the bus back home in the afternoons.

In fifth grade, I got lost in all my subjects and was ashamed to ask for help. I knew I could do better, but my desperation and fears incarcerated me in shyness. I wanted to get away from it all, but I couldn't, especially not at home.

"Doris, go prepare new bottles. Do the dishes. Give the kids a bath."

By the time I went to bed, I'd fall in a comatose sleep and wake up tired. Trying to listen and learn in school was like watching TV during storm season; the connection came and went.

I loved my Mother, and I thought maybe I'd gain her favor by helping even more. I could see she was often overwhelmed, trying to keep up with her sewing orders while caring for the babies. I missed seeing her happy and believed if I helped her more, she wouldn't hit me as much. At age nine, I asked her to teach me how to cook, and she did. Mother seemed pleased with my eagerness, and I felt consoled—to a point.

Soon Father began to arrive late from work, sometimes staying out an entire weekend, which infuriated Mother.

"I am the man *and* the woman in this house. You don't wear the pants in this family," Mother told him flatly.

I also understood all about our financial struggles and whenever Mother could afford to go shopping, she'd tell us, "There isn't enough for all, but I'll do my best." Once, upon returning from a shopping trip, she told us, "Doris, Franco, I couldn't buy you shoes. It will have to be next time." Alejandro, Veronica, and Jonas were excited; however, their new shoes came with a warning: "If I see you laughing at your brother or sister because they didn't get shoes, I'll take them away, do you understand?"

Our siblings nodded and couldn't wait to wear their new shoes. Franco and I had to continue wearing our old, broken shoes until Mother could afford to go shopping again. She'd tell us, "Children, study and educate yourselves, so you don't have to live like this."

I recognized her efforts and understood her frustrations, given Father's lack of support. Wishing I could help her, I asked Mama Blas about teaching me how to sew, so Blas had me make a hem. When I was done, I handed her my finished work, and she chuckled loudly.

"Entre punta y punta cabe una vieja sienta. Between every single stitch an old woman can sit." I had no idea what her comment meant until Mother clarified that my stitches were far too wide for a hem. We all laughed out loud then.

Every now and then, we had certain visitors, aside from people who came seeking Mama Blas's remedies. Doña Belén—aka *la bruja,* the Witch—was one of Blas's old friends. According to Blas, her house was "deep in a mountain, near a river." She'd visit Mama Blas for spiritual counseling. The first time I met her was when I headed to the front door to answer a soft, "Doña Blas, are you home?"

I remember staring deep into her dark eyes, feeling almost hypnotized. She was petite, shorter than me, about five foot one. She had deep dark eyes, her head was covered with a black bandana, and she wore black clothing; her left hand rested above her stomach, her right hand holding onto her bandana, her back slightly hunched. She had tiny hands and feet. Her oval, coppery face and hands were the only exposed parts of her body. Mama Blas had a good ear, so she'd greet Doña Belén as she arrived; then she'd say to us, "Go on, kids."

We already knew what that meant and quickly vanished

into the farm. Blas was most hospitable, offering Doña Belén a cup of mint tea.

"Mint tea will make you feel better," Blas would say.

Doña Belén would give a soft nod, accepting a cup. I couldn't help but hang back and stare at Doña Belén, for her presence was mysterious, and I was curious about the reasons for her visits.

"Doris, if Mama Blas sees you, bad trouble awaits. Now go on," Lorena scolded me.

I'd disappear quickly. We all feared our older sister, just as we feared Mother, and didn't question any of her commands.

Doña Belén had been accused of witchcraft in the past, just as Mama Blas had been. The accusations against my grandmother lacked any foundation, of course; she insisted she never practiced witchcraft and believed in prayer and counseled people about faith, and sometimes used herbs to cure ailments. The bottom line, as Blas recounted, was that a certain woman had tried to put a spell on Mama Blas, and it hadn't worked. Then her accuser argued only another witch could possibly break the spell.

Her accuser turned out to be Doña Belén.

Once her name had been cleared, Mama Blas forgave Doña Belén and became her spiritual counselor. Doña Belén confided to Mama Blas about her encounters with the devil and also shared some of the results of the rituals she'd performed with undisclosed parties on certain nights of the week, at midnight. Mama Blas consistently counseled her to refrain from witchcraft, and Doña Belén appeared attentive and calm while Blas whispered this and other things to her.

As it was, hardly anyone in the neighborhood talked to Doña Belén; as a matter of fact, people used to hide in their homes and close the doors whenever she passed by.

Every time Doña Belén left our house, Mama Blas swept the floors with a special herb broom, then sprinkled holy water and said a special prayer to keep away evil. She'd pray for Doña Belén then, because she knew Belén would never stop practicing black magic. Mama Blas was very concerned about her. Sometimes I'd overhear Blas's conversations with Mother about Belén.

"Hey, did you hear Doña Belén?" my grandmother would ask my mother.

"No, Mama, I didn't hear her."

"She said the devil is in love with her—and how she took part in some dark worshiping and dancing, and she was able to fly. She said she kept flying, way beyond the oceans."

"Jesus, Mary, and Joseph," Mother replied.

"I told her to refrain from such things," Mama Blas said.

Then there was Cruz Cabra, a local *jamón* (unmarried old man). He was tall and skinny, with black eyes lurking beneath thick eyebrows. His face was thin, with a long, curved nose and pointy chin; he reminded me of Blas's witch stories. His mental state wasn't clear, but he was accused of being the neighborhood pervert. He'd appear out of nowhere, hissing like a cat and grinning, showing two green teeth. "Mother, Cruz Cabra is bothering me!" I'd yell. I swear Mother had wings. I could never figure out how she managed to appear so instantly anytime one of us screamed.

"What is it you're looking for?" Mother would demand.

"Just a drink of water," he'd say.

"You have less than one second to get off my property. I swear I'll make you swallow your teeth!"

Mother had a mean closed fist, and when he saw it, Cruz Cabra ran for his life. I was truly scared of him. He enjoyed scaring little girls in the neighborhood.

Pablo El Bobo was a degenerate. He was a hunchback with oily black hair hanging down over his forehead, almost covering his eyes and fair skin. He drooled constantly. He'd start masturbating any time young girls went by his house. As with Cruz Cabra, Mother didn't let her humble look fool Pablo El Bobo; she let him see some of her monstrosity. Both creatures left us alone shortly. Oh, they couldn't avoid us entirely, but both took a detour through the woods any time they saw any of us walking to or from home. I never saw them together, but they were disgusting.

Mariana Jorgi was one of Mother's loyal customers; she worked for a local bank in Jayuya. Mother was concerned every time she dropped by because her fabrics always had holes in them.

"Ms. Jorgi, the holes in your fabric . . . I'm afraid there are rats in your home," Mother would tell her, concerned.

Ms. Jorgi never gave up on Mother. "I have faith in you, Lina. Just do whatever you can. I appreciate it."

I was paying close attention to this particular conversation and couldn't help but walk over and take a glance.

"Mother, that's disgusting, don't touch it!"

"Doris, get out of here this instant," Mother said, looking at me with fiery eyes.

She then apologized to Ms. Jorgi. I felt sorry for Mother, so I hid behind the living room door and watched as she unfolded the partially eaten fabric.

After Ms. Jorgi left, Mother grabbed me by the ear when I least expected it, twisting it several times. "The next time one of my customers comes here, you stay away! This is none of your business, and don't forget to respect them!"

My ear hurt—and boy, did I stay away from her customers after that. Any time Ms. Jorgi (or *any* of

Mother's customers) stopped by and called, "Señora, are you home?" I'd vanish like the devil runs from the cross.

During a summer vacation, I was almost eleven, and I'd been playing in the woods. Mother had been calling me, but I didn't hear her, so when I walked into the house, she was upset.

"Doris, I've been calling you. Why didn't you respond?"

"Mami, I did not hear you!" I answered desperately.

She was accustomed to hitting us with the first thing she grabbed: a peeled tree branch, an extension cord, or sometimes she'd remove one of her flip-flops. This time, she was wearing wooden clogs. She grabbed me by one arm, took off one of her clogs, and smacked me over the head with it. I felt a loud hammering noise, and everything went dark. Father's high-pitched yelling brought me back. I couldn't make out his words; I just remember opening my eyes and seeing Father picking me up. Later I woke up lying in bed, with a gigantic headache. The back of my head, all the way down my shoulders, was drenched with blood; I couldn't get up.

I remember looking into Mama Blas's sad face at some point. Her small hands, handling strong herbal scents, helped me drift into a deep sleep. I don't know how long I slept, but I figured, vaguely, that I had been in bed for a day. The second day, when I opened my eyes, my head hurt as if it were being crushed. I still couldn't get up. I looked at Mama Blas and tried to read her, but she tended me in silence. I knew I had a serious injury.

Blas stayed by my side for long hours. I was not taken to a hospital. At one point, Mother entered the room, and I could hear Blas whisper something sadly. I felt my grandmother's hands carefully lifting one side of me, showing Mother my wound. I remember Mother's sigh; but she left the room without saying a word.

Grandma continued curing me with her herbs, applying new mixtures whenever she felt it was necessary. After the first week, I could stand, though my head throbbed when I did. The headache continued through a second week. I remember not being able to brush my hair for a month. Slowly I began to move about again, and the pain eventually faded.

At one point, Blas lashed out at Mother. "Talking is simple! There's no need for hitting! You're going to kill them!" Blas's tone was thunderous; the house echoed with her wrath and power.

Mother's tone was high but defiant. "They're *my* kids. I'll do as I please!"

"*El que abusa de un niño no tiene escape*. There's no escape from child abuse," my grandma threatened. Then she gave the biggest sigh I've ever heard. By then, we were all hiding, trembling.

"This is cruelty." Blas paused and then lashed out at Mother again. "Mark my words, woman, you shall remember this day! They will all leave you, one by one. In your old age, you won't have anyone around—including me. I'm warning you: one day I'll leave and never come back."

It was devastating to hear Mama Blas's threat to leave, and I thought, if she left, this may be our end.

§ § §

School life took a new turn for me; suddenly I loved my writing assignments. My teacher, Ms. Rosales, was extremely kind to me; she made me laugh. Seventh grade turned out to be the best of all my school years. I felt like royalty when I received a B in more than one class; the last time I'd been this happy, I was in kindergarten! My life had taken a dramatically good turn—or so I thought at the time.

I was recruited as a runner for track events, which marked the end of the bullying I'd suffered. Suddenly I became one of the most popular students in school, just because I was an athlete. I felt like a celebrity every day during breakfast and lunch, as many students called out my name so I could sit with them. I didn't take my popularity for granted, though, and continued battling my fears when I boarded the bus to go home at the end of every school day. Every single afternoon, after two o'clock, I'd fall into a suspenseful, cold sweat as I pictured Mother waiting by the kitchen door, staring at me, smiling in contempt, balancing a toothpick in her close lips. Oh, how I dreaded her menacing look!

When Mother learned about my success at track, she seemed impressed, and for a while, the beatings decreased. On various occasions I attended track events in San Juan, Ponce, Utuado, Villalba, and Arecibo. I'd smile at her and tell her how I'd won first place, and how fast I'd run. I'd write to Grandma Tato in New York and share my victories with her. But all too soon, Mother no longer had time to hear about my accomplishments. "Oh, yeah, there are dishes in the sink waiting for you."

I was encouraged by my good grades and popularity, and I'd stay up late at night doing homework. My fingers rushed down line after line, writing swiftly, and then, one night, the curtain that served as the door to my room opened suddenly.

"What in the world are you doing, *muchachita*?"

Mother snatched up my notebook and began reading; my heart started beating fast, for I remembered all too well how she'd treated my writings in the past. Then she looked at me, and for the first time in a long time, I saw a pair of sad eyes barely able to look into mine. Her shoulders dropped and her chest lifted; Mother gave me back my notebook and whispered, "Hurry and finish, and go to sleep." She turned around and left quietly.

When I passed to eighth grade, Mother appeared pleased when she received my report card. She laid it on the dining table for Father to see. "Wow," Father said, and chuckled. Mother gave me a Mona Lisa smile. I was relieved to see her happy, and I felt happy and sad at the same time. I didn't want the school year to end, because I hated vacation time. It left me with the reality of being reintroduced to Mother's wrath.

I was almost twelve and remember one day returning home from school to learn that there was no running water. This occurred quite often in the high country, I don't know why. When everyone was home from school, Mother told Franco, Alejandro, and me to get ready to go to the brook for water. She gave us buckets, and we headed out.

I was nervous because the ground was slippery. Mother helped us fill our buckets with water, but said, "Spill your water, and you'll see what happens."

I remember looking at Franco, and we both got nervous. Carrying water uphill on one shoulder was hard. There were many leaves on the ground, and the water was heavy. I struggled because I couldn't see the ground. I climbed slowly but didn't have anything to hold on to. I slipped and nearly lost my balance. I managed not to fall, but I did spill some of my water. Mother had been walking behind me and immediately whipped me with a tree branch. The branch hit the left side of my face. I was caught off-guard, when I suddenly felt an intense burning and let out an instant loud cry. I don't know how I managed not to drop the bucket, but I didn't; I stumbled in agony until I regained my balance and somehow made it back home.

After we got home, when I turned around, Mother stared at my face and sighed. "That's what you get for not being careful," she said.

I stepped inside the house and headed straight to the mirror and was completely horrified when I looked at my face and saw my left eye red and swollen; the skin beneath it had come off. A bright red line slashed across my face, almost in an X shape, starting at my forehead and continuing down over my left eye, over my nose, lips, and left cheek. I had other small cuts on the right side of my forehead and cheek, but they weren't as severe. I didn't wash my face that day; I didn't know how.

The following morning, Mother forgot the "don't go to school" pattern we usually followed when any of us were severely beaten. When I got off the bus at school, Genaro laughed at me, saying, "What happened to you? Were you playing with a cat?"

He kept walking, laughing, as I stared at him coldly. I went into my classroom, and my teacher, Ms. Rosales, immediately noticed my facial injuries.

"Doris, what happened? Are you okay?"

I was still shy; I just stared at her without answering. Ms. Rosales left the classroom and came back with another teacher, who stared at me for a few moments and then left. Just before lunch, I was called out of the classroom to meet with a social worker. As I sat down, I was shaking. Once I got a good look at her, I almost fainted; I think I threw up and swallowed my own vomit. The social worker resembled Mother: same body frame, skin tone, long black hair, and manly looking hands. She stared at my face while taking notes. I began sweating.

"What are those marks on your face?" the social worker asked. Fearing Mother, I couldn't answer.

"Doris, when you get home from school every day, what do you usually do?" she asked.

I still couldn't answer. The social worker stared at me with a poker face, tactless and cold.

"Do you do your homework, Doris?"

She didn't bother to ask if I was okay and didn't assure me I'd be safe. Determined to protect Mother, I let the tactless social worker hear what she wanted to hear.

"I eat supper, shower, then do homework."

My answer was sufficient; after she took some notes, I was dismissed. Ms. Rosales walked me back to the classroom. I wasn't questioned again, but as I went home at the end of the day, my heart raced. Once I boarded the bus, I sat by a window and stared away into the distance. I wanted the beatings to end. I didn't know what would happen if they didn't.

When I got off the bus, I spotted my brother Alejandro and walked home with him. He was all smiles, walking in little bounces, whistling and making bird sounds. When we approached our house, Mother was waiting by the kitchen door, wearing a black bandana, a toothpick in her mouth over closed lips—usually a sign it wasn't going to be a good day. My chest tightened as we entered the danger zone. As we approached the house, Alejandro paused, almost in reverence, and said, "A blessing, please."

"May the Lord protect you," Mother replied.

Alejandro vanished into the house, and suddenly I was in front of her.

"A blessing, please," I said, and as I lifted my head, the image of the social worker popped into my mind. Just as Mother opened her mouth for her blessing, her eyes shifted to my facial cuts, and her reply was delayed. I copied Alejandro's walking bounces, pretending I was cool, and walked right by her and into the house.

I dropped my book bag in my room and changed out of my uniform. My mind was racing, as I hoped my plan to conceal my suspiciousness worked. I felt different and thought about what the consequences might have been if I *had* talked with the social worker. There was too much at stake—too many children to be hurt. I didn't want to cause Mother any grief.

"Hey, Mom, can I eat? I'm hungry!" Jonas yelled.

"Me too," added Veronica.

"What's for dinner?" Alejandro rushed to ask.

"Whatever you're served is what you'll eat. How many times have I told you not to question me?" Mother said.

Suddenly there was a swarm of kids waiting for dinner. My knees were weak as I resurfaced from my room to join everyone. The kids stared at me in silence, without questioning; they knew Mother had hit me the day before, plus we were used to seeing each other bruised up or cut. I became nauseated as her face turned my way while she stirred the pot of rice. Her silence and mystery made me shiver, more so than any scary movie I'd ever seen, more so than Blas's horror stories.

I don't know how I had the stomach to execute my plan, but I walked right up to her and started working by her side. I took out bowls and plates and silverware for everyone to use. Mother seemed pleased; her face relaxed as she began serving dinner.

"Hey, Alejandro, you pass the plates. The first one is for Franco," Mother said.

I gave her plates, and she piled on the food, and Alejandro delivered the plates until everyone was served. We all ate, and she seemed serene. I wanted to forget about the meeting with the social worker. I finished eating, and while I stood by the kitchen sink drinking water, Mother put a little bottle in my left hand.

"Here, go put this on your face," she whispered.

I put my glass down.

"Yes, Mother," I murmured, then vanished to the bathroom to apply the ointment. When I emerged, I handed the ointment back with a "Here, Mother" and headed to the kitchen. Dishes were piled in the sink in a perfect pyramid. Without hesitating, I went straight for the stack.

Pleased, Mother let out a loud, "Hmm," then said, "Naomi, look at her. She's younger than you—and you're lazy. Doris, don't do the dishes. Let that lazy bum do them."

"It's all right, Mother, I can do them," I said, while preparing the lather. I began washing the dishes.

Nodding, Mother said, "What can I do without your help? Those older ones, including the men, they're lazy."

I felt her closeness at that moment and realized I had an opportunity to talk with her, to tell her I could do much better without the beatings. But I feared her too much; I couldn't do it. I kept my face down as I battled my feelings. Then I felt pity for Naomi, because Mother began eying her. Although I had managed to stay off Mother's radar for this one day, I wished for strength.

After I finished the dishes, I was cold and drenched from my waist down. Mother hovered around me like a guard. As I dried my hands and arms, I saw that the clotheslines were full and went out to bring in the laundry, fold it, and put it away as fast as I could.

"Mother, I'm done," I said, as I stood in front of her, waiting for the next chore assignment.

"You've done more in one day than these lazy bums have done in a month," Mother growled. "Go on. Take your shower and do your homework."

I felt relieved as I went off and showered. I tried to do my homework afterward but was tired—as I lay in bed, reflecting on the day and the macabre-looking social worker, I realized I was exhausted, but I was also glad to feel a little safe for once. At the same time, I was sad because I loved Mother no matter what.

I fell asleep . . . but soon came awake, unable to breathe, because someone was holding a pillow over my face! I screamed and fought. I couldn't see who it was; the person was much stronger than I. Just when I couldn't take it any longer, as I started getting weak, the pillow was pulled away. Horrified, I gasped for air.

"There you go, Missy." Naomi laughed sarcastically.

I began weeping and coughing and called out for Mother. She stormed into the room, demanding, "What's the matter?"

"Naomi pressed a pillow against my face!" I cried. "I couldn't breathe!"

"It's not true, she's lying!" Naomi said angrily.

"It's true! I was lying down, and she pressed the pillow . . ."

My face was burning red, my cuts inflamed. Mother took a good look into my eyes as I cried and coughed—and then, deliberately, gave Naomi a severe beating. Father came in later, and Mother mentioned Naomi, saying, "She's vicious; she tried to suffocate the other one."

"What!" shouted Father. "*Mira que sinvergüenza, ah pues castígala más.* How fresh, punish her more, then!"

Naomi then went to bed crying, furious at me. I lay on my bed trembling, without turning my back to Naomi, who slept in the same room. The next day she muttered, "You're stupid. I was only playing."

I stared at her, not believing a word of it. Naomi went on, "Mother is so lenient with you—she barely hits you. She hits me more, and she used to hit Lorena even *more.* You're the lucky one. She likes you better than me. I don't care. It doesn't even hurt. I only cried so she would stop hitting me. I skip class in school and don't care if the school tells her."

I forgave Naomi, but her rebel spirit scared me. I knew she'd only get more beatings if Mother learned she skipped classes. Naomi repeated the pillow game on a few other occasions, and after I cried and caught my breath, she'd tell me, "You're stupid, I'm only playing," and laugh devilishly. I'd get mad at her but didn't tell Mother again, because Naomi would have been severely punished.

I wished fervently the good old days would return. The good old days, when I first learned how to read and write; the good old days, when we went to downtown Ponce, with the ice cream stops; and the days when Mother greeted us with a bright smile of love as we came home from school.

In her good moments, Mother talked to us about things like hard work, education, and honesty. I liked her good days and worked extra hard for acceptance. I wanted her to see I was good, that I was understanding and cared.

Whenever we went out, whether to the hospital or church, we were accustomed to people staring, sometimes asking Mother how many kids she had. She wasn't shy in answering, "I have thirteen children, all legitimate."

The "legitimate" remark sent a "legal" and "true" message that portrayed a woman's morality, demanding respect. Asking about legitimacy was common—almost standard procedure at doctor's appointments, schools, or anywhere. When she made this pronouncement, Mother's tone was menacing and relayed the message that she would not tolerate mockery. She'd pause and contemplate the person to whom she was speaking, and she wouldn't blink or breathe until the person answered back.

§ § §

Boarding the bus to go to school was salvation. I could escape for a while and be with my friends, who seemed to have happier existences. My friend Aby especially had a careless happiness about her. The way she walked, in happy little bounces, wiggling her long ponytail sideways, made me happy, too. She always wore new uniforms, and her socks remained intact all day.

"Your house—it's very loud, Dori," Aby said once.

"It's a zoo, actually; the boys play baseball with my Father sometimes. We fill an entire pew at church on Sundays. Aby, you should see how people stare at us anytime we go to church or the store. People always look dismayed, especially when Mother says we are thirteen, all legitimate . . . whatever this means," I said.

"My God, I have five sisters, plus my mother and grandmother, and that's enough," Aby said.

At home, I began to defend myself by venting to Mother when I wasn't too afraid to face her.

"You always hit us!"

"It seems someone is looking for trouble," Mother would reply.

"All you do here is hit and hit!"

One day, she hit me with a knife. I was proud of myself for facing her down. I became convinced that for me to accomplish anything, it would have to be away from home. I was often tempted to run and call for help, but then I thought about the consequences: what if something happened to her? I didn't have the heart to hurt her. No matter what, she'd always be my mother, and I would love and respect her.

We could tell when Mother wasn't feeling well. During her pregnancies, the purple varicose veins on her legs swelled up. I didn't dare tell her she needed rest, though Blas sometimes would. Blas would take care of us then, saying, "Your Mother doesn't feel well. Don't make noise; just eat your food."

Doris Mercado

Every year during coffee season, Mother worked hard picking and selling coffee. She had five of us work with her, and we loved it. The coffee cherries were bright red, and I thought they were beautiful. We earned enough during this period to buy new school uniforms. Uniforms were expensive; she'd tell us, "This time I was able to buy uniforms, but you'll need to wait for new shoes."

I understood but stared at the other kids in school who *were* wearing new shoes. I had faith I'd be wearing new shoes just like them, sometime soon.

Every new school year, I dreaded any bullying to come. I was also sick and tired of hiding my bruised extremities, nursing a sore skull that couldn't take one more hit from Mother, and dealing with my painful shyness. The new readings and chapters we were assigned seemed foreign to me. I'd try to read and understand, but it didn't work. I began to disconnect myself from homework and started to write, as an escape. I'd pretend I was into the subject but instead began to write my own stories. Writing became a joyous adventure; I created my own safe place and felt that no one could hurt me there. I returned to my stories every day, until the day when I got home from school and found Mother waiting for me, brandishing several pages of my writings in her hand.

"What is this?" she demanded.

I'd always saved them and kept them with me, but this time I forgot—and my world of secrets had been discovered by Mother. Father stood by Mother and frowned.

Mother grabbed me by my hair and slapped me several times in the face. She then ripped up all the pages I'd written and threw them in the garbage. In so doing, she made me feel my writing was evil and bad and perverse; so writing then became a secret—a malicious but good secret. I began to crave writing; I felt I'd explode if I didn't write.

I'd write and erase, and sometimes I tore up the pages I'd written. I knew if Mother read them again, I'd be seriously punished—but the writing itself made me feel better. I didn't know how else to deal with the reality of my mother and the pain she inflicted over and over again.

Sometimes when she caught me looking at the marks she'd made on my arms or legs, she gave me ointments to treat them. Other times she just sneered.

"Yes, take a good look—and remember for next time."

As if I could forget.

§ § §

Mother found out Lorena had a boyfriend. She gave her a severe beating, even going so far as to bang Lorena's head against the walls, making crackling noises. Lorena's screams attracted neighbors. They stood out on the main road and looked at the house, as I looked back, afraid. I remained outside with my siblings, away from the house, away from Mother.

Days later, Lorena ran away and never came back. I was twelve. I remember Mother crying and trying to find Lorena, but no one knew where she was. We found out later that Lorena had gotten married. Because of our age difference, I viewed Lorena as one of my caretakers; she was also quiet and shy. She had a clear complexion and long, reddish hair; she resembled Mother.

With Lorena gone, I felt exposed and vulnerable to Mother. It wasn't long before Victor left, too. One day I came home from school and the house was filled was arguing voices. This prompted me to slow down and almost tiptoe in an attempt to remain unnoticed. It turned out Mother and Victor were arguing. He was a high school senior and wanted to get married. Mother did not approve of his desire to marry before finishing school.

"You have two months until you graduate! You should be thinking about college. Marriage is a huge responsibility."

"I don't care," answered Victor. "I can drive trucks to support my family."

"You're too young to start your life with hard labor—it will ruin your life," Mother pleaded. Their argument soon spun out of control, and Mother tried to punch Victor—but he jumped out of the living room window to avoid her fist.

"You hit us like we're savages!" he shouted. "I'm getting married whether you like it or not!"

Then he got in his car and left for good, running away like Lorena had. Josue was gone by then, too, but he'd obtained permission from Mother to live in New York with one of our aunts. Josue made his life in New York and never returned to the island. Out of all my siblings, he most resembled Father, with the same copious body hair and the same ever-happy personality. The boys called him "Tarzan."

We didn't see Victor for many months, until he came back to visit with Mora, his pregnant wife. They both looked very happy, and we were happy to see them. Lorena also visited with Mother later, and Mother made peace with Lorena and Victor.

6. Hurricanes David and Frederick, August 30 and September 4, 1979

Late in August 1979, I was thirteen and had started tenth grade. News that a Category 5 hurricane was heading our way generated a lot of energy and prayer in our home. We received word from Mother's sister Nicia, who invited us to stay at her house in Hacienda La Carmelita in Ponce until the hurricane had passed. Mother accepted the offer and began packing right away. While Mother packed, Mama Blas had us join her for a short yet fervent prayer.

"Children, say the Our Father so the Lord can have mercy!"

While we prayed, Mama whispered her own prayers, hands clasped; with such solemnity, it seemed she was talking face-to-face with the Lord.

On August 29, a gray, rainy day, eleven of us packed into Father's car and headed out for the sixteen-mile ride to Aunt Nicia's house. Her place in Hacienda La Carmelita was all wood with a zinc roof, located in the central region of the city, five hundred meters above sea level. It had a balcony and storm shutters and sat gracefully on a hillside, supported by stilts. The location had the glorious nickname Cerro Maravilla, "Wonder Peak." This part of the island was cooler and offered a generous view of the city of Ponce, including the uninhabited, tiny island Caja de Muertos. Toro Negro forest made for wonderful views as well.

On the trip, Mother and Blas shared the passenger seat. Mother held Sergio, who was a toddler. Franco, Alejandro, Naomi, and I sat in the backseat. I held Veronica, and Naomi held Jonas. Raquel and Marcos sat on the floor in fetal positions by our feet.

The ride was tight, but we laughed at the younger kids sitting on the floor. Upon our arrival, sore from the long ride, we settled quickly into one of the bedrooms. It was divided from the living room and the dining room, forming a C shape, with double wooden doors at each end. I loved Nicia's house, and this was my favorite room.

The room was arranged for all of us to weather the storm, including Nicia and Mama Blas. I don't know how thirteen people fit in one room, but we did. The room seemed dim inside because of its natural, dark wood walls. It had a dark wooden dresser in one corner and nightstands at each end; one held candles, while the other held a *ponchera,* a large water bowl. Underneath one of the beds was a *escupidera,* a ceramic bowl used for urination. When the bowl became full, the urine was tossed out the window. I thought it was disgusting. There were two extra mattresses on the floor, in addition to two regular-sized beds and three chairs.

In the early afternoon of the next day, August 30, the cloudy sky grew darker. Mother had us go one by one to use the latrine outside. Shortly after, the air became dense. Heavy rain came quickly, and a whistling wind arrived, sending the trees into a rough dance. Nicia, Mother, and Father rushed around closing all the windows, and Father helped with the storm shutters. I peered through a crack in the wall and saw how the wind bent the trees back. Then the vegetation began to fade under a dense gray fog and heavy rain.

"Doris, come on!" yelled Nicia. We were all directed into the C-shaped room, and Nicia locked its doors behind her.

Nicia, Mother, and Mama Blas sat on the chairs, listening to the staticky news about the hurricane on a little radio. To their left, the youngest children, Sergio and Raquel, shared one of the beds; both soon fell asleep.

Naomi, Veronica, and I shared one of the mattresses on the floor, to the right side of the women. Father shared a mattress on the floor across from the women with Franco, Alejandro, Jonas, and Marcos.

The rain fell hard, with the rolling resonance of a herd of horses approaching, the howling wind filling the brief intervals between stampedes. Nicia turned up the volume and listened to a last-minute alert.

"*Alerta, noticia de última hora, El Centro Meteorológico de los Estados Unidos, ha anunciado un incremento en la velocidad del Huracán David, se estima ha aumentado a 175 millas por hora.* The U.S. National Weather Center has reported Hurricane David has strengthened to 175 mph."

Upon hearing the alert, the women made the sign of the cross and held hands. Veronica, Naomi, and I remained still. Father cried in horror, "Dear Lord, Jesus Christ!"

He sat with his back against the wall, embracing Jonas and Marcos under his left arm and Alejandro and Franco under his right.

We heard objects being whirled up in the air and tree branches breaking off and falling. The doors shook with a constant but loud thud. The house made a clinking sound as it shook and the candles appeared to burn faster than before. Marcos and Jonas emitted loud cries, but Father kept them calm. The women mumbled desperate prayers. Mama Blas led the beads, and Mother and Nicia answered. Nicia's hands shook. The air was cold and held a damp, earthy scent.

The rain made an astoundingly loud noise as it fell against the zinc roof. We sat still in the darkened room, vaguely illuminated by the golden glow of the candles, listening to the mad wind and the incessant, high-pitched pleas of the women's prayers. Veronica and the boys eventually fell asleep. Naomi and I listened to the hurricane and the women praying. Mama Blas's hair-raising prayers rose above the thundering wind and rain, almost equally defiant. Tapping her chest, she recited, *"Bramando, viene el enemigo, bramando viene como león. Manso llegue a mi corazón, como Jesucristo llegó al calvario con su santísima pasión.* Fierce approaches the enemy, fierce as a lion. May he reach my heart meekly, as Jesus Christ reached Calvary during his sacred passion."

Father reacted, rubbing his arms, *"Uy, tengo los pelos encrespaos, Jesús, María y José.* Ugh, I've got the worst chills. Jesus, Mary, and Joseph."

I was frightened and held on to Naomi. Mama Blas's tone, while reciting this particular prayer, carried an exorbitant amount of suspense. She stood up, back straight, holding on to her beads, occasionally wiping sweat from her face. She glanced at us and Father occasionally, in fear.

At times, I didn't know if we were going to make it. The house shook severely; it almost felt like we were on a rough train ride. The wind sounded as if it were cracking a gigantic whip. It whipped, whistled, roared, and threatened. Blas's prayers continued.

"Tres divinas personas, Padre, Hijo y Espíritu Santo, líbranos del mal. Ángeles de los cuatro vientos, norte, sur, este, y oeste, apacigüen esta tempestad, y líbrenos del mal. Holy Trinity, Father, Son, and Holy Ghost, deliver us from evil. Angels of the four winds, north, south, east, and west, calm this tempest and deliver us from evil."

The women continued their incessant praying. Blas's face became somber with horror at times, but she maintained a firm grip on the beads and didn't cease from praying. Eventually I fell asleep but was awakened on and off by Mama Blas's perpetual pleas.

"Los tres clavos de la cruz, vayan delante de mí y me quiten del peligro. The three nails of the cross, may they

protect me and deliver me from any dangers. *Ruega por nosotros, vuestros devotos hijos ahora y en la hora de nuestra muerte, amén.* Pray for us, your devoted children, now and at the hour of our death, Amen."

The following day, we woke to a silent morning accompanied by a cool breeze and a mist of rain. A fresh scent made its way through the house. When we looked out, we saw many trees had been knocked down, and all the orchids that had once surrounded the house were gone. The road was a river of mud; the bare, clayey ground around the house looked slippery and mucky.

In general, the vast land around us looked wet, sad, and uncombed.

As the day went on, it remained cloudy, and the misty rain didn't dry up. We weren't allowed to go outside; kids who needed to pee were referred to *la escupidera.* I hated the idea and couldn't stand the repugnant smell of the urine, nor its orange color.

Mother was worried about our house.

"The news warned of severe floods."

Mama Blas refused to eat and kept praying while peering out the window, observing the weather. Sometimes she gave me the creeps with her *"Por mi culpa, por mi culpa y por mi gran culpa. Por eso ruego a los santos y a ustedes hermanos . . .* For my sin, and my sins, and my very own sins, I plea to all saints and you, my brothers and sisters . . ."

I don't know how she managed to stay up and pray for so many hours. She'd stare out in the distance, with conviction, muttering, "Hmm, it's not time yet."

Mama Blas's words were never questioned. Nicia, Mother, and Father listened and took her feelings to heart.

On this day, there were no signs of birds, chickens, or any other small animals around the house, which was unusual.

There was silence, except for Father's conversations with Franco and Alejandro and the playful noises of the little ones—Marcos, Jonas, Raquel, and Sergio.

Later, the adults gathered in the living room to talk about the hurricane. Blas remained on edge. Besides losing her entire family during Cyclone San Ciriaco, she had also lived through Hurricane San Felipe in 1928 and Hurricane Santa Clara in 1956, which also turned out to be quite devastating.

This time, she appeared to fear more for us kids than for herself. Naomi was the oldest still at home at that time; Sergio was the youngest.

Mama Blas walked around the house, praying silently. As she made her rounds, I followed her, keeping her company. Every now and then, her piercing eyes would soften, her face blooming in a gentle, tender, warm smile. She'd hold my face in her warm, thick hands, making me feel how much I was loved. I'd love her in return, as always, as if she were my own little child. She was all I ever wanted, all I ever needed. The rain continued for a second, third, and fourth day. On the morning of September 3, Mother declared, "We'll go home tomorrow."

She appeared extremely worried about our house. She began packing, but soon Father called everyone to the living room.

"My Lord, everyone, hey, Blas, come here, there's another hurricane approaching!" Father leaped to his feet as the news came in.

"*Alerta, Alerta, noticia de última hora, El Centro Meteorológico de los Estados Unidos, ha anunciado un segundo Huracán, Federico, categoría 4, se avecina en dirección a la isla.* The U.S. National Weather Center reports a second hurricane, Frederick, Category 4, is heading straight for the island."

The Armor of Love and Hope

"*Mamá, anunciaron otro huracán se llama Federico.*
Hey, Blas, another hurricane is heading our way. Frederick.
I've never lived through anything like this," Father cried
out.

Mother, Nicia, and Mama Blas were very frightened. In
fact, I had never seen my mother or grandmother look so
scared.

Too bad for me, I got my very first period—but I didn't
dare tell Mother. I was scared and decided to use the
latrine on my own. I didn't know how periods worked but
assumed that if I went to use the latrine, it would stop.
Since it would be a mere latrine visit, I thought I'd have
time before Hurricane Federico hit, so I snuck out without
permission.

The rain was very cold, and most of the trees were
down; a good portion of Nicia's farm was visible as a result.
The ground was extremely slippery and smelled strongly
of mud. I realized my mistake as my feet were instantly
slimed with mud and leaf litter. It wouldn't be an easy trip.
I walked slowly, hanging on to coffee tree branches, until I
made it to the outhouse.

The smelly thing was dark and damp. I left the door
open for light—and as I was trying to do my business, the
wind abruptly slammed the door shut. I screamed and
jumped so hard I almost fell in. I then let out a second
scream and tried to reach for the door. I couldn't see a
thing and couldn't even find the wall. My feet began to slip,
so I decided to kneel down on the damp wooden floor and
crawl.

I could hear the wind and rain whipping around again.
I let out another frantic cry as I reached for the wall but,
instead, found the smelly hole again. The wind began
howling, and I didn't know if I should stay where I was
until the storm had passed or try to reach for the wall

again. I was terribly cold, and the menstrual pain didn't spare me much energy. I decided to try for the door again. After a minute or two of slow crawling, I reached a wall.

I inched along, pushing on the wall, hoping to find the door. The darkness, and the rushing sounds of the rain and wind, sent me into a state of despair. I wanted to believe it was all a dream. I continued, inch by inch, until the wall moved a little—I'd reached the door. I had to push hard to get it open because the wind was terribly strong. It was a relief to see light fall into the outhouse and to breathe clean air. I stuck my hand out the door so that if it banged shut again, it wouldn't close completely.

Exhausted, I left the latrine; but the rain was pounding down hard, and I didn't know how I'd make it back. The wind's force was menacing, but I walked against it, slowly, with my face turned to one side, hanging on to the coffee trees. When I was about halfway back, I heard Mother shout my name in a frightened voice. I looked up and saw the house, with the women staring out of one of the windows. I couldn't make out what they were saying; they all seemed to scream and wave at the same time. I pushed on.

I stopped and hung on to a small tree as I looked up again to see how far I had to go. Suddenly I slipped and fell, and one of the women screamed loudly as I slid down the slope. I scrambled, and my feet hit a rock, bringing me to an immediate halt. The rock was sharp and cut the bottom of my right foot; it began throbbing, but I managed to get up again.

I sensed Mother's fear then; I looked up to see her open the door and rush toward me. Just as the winds crescendoed into a truly threatening roar, I took the chance of running on the muddy trail and managed to scramble back to the house and crawl up onto the cement steps, exhausted.

"Doris, give me your hand," Mother ordered.

Her voice echoed oddly, torn away by the wind. Mother's strong arm reached out; I stretched for her hand, and we touched. Her hands were dry and warm, and her firm grip lifted me bodily up and into the house.

They closed the door quickly, and just when I thought I'd get a severe beating, I heard, *"Caripela, quién te dio permiso 'pa ir afuera?* You fresh, who gave you permission to go outside?" Mother demanded. Everyone stared at me; Father's face was so serious I was horrified, and I just kept my head down.

Nicia saw my distress and mumbled something to Mother; then she ushered everyone except Mother and Mama Blas back into the C-shaped room. When they were gone, Mother asked, "Why didn't you tell me?"

I didn't answer. I didn't dare tell her it was because we hadn't grown up telling her things. In fact, no one had ever told me I'd get a period. Feeling ashamed, I replied, "I just went to the latrine because I thought if I did, it would stop."

Mama Blas looked sad; so did Mother. I felt bad for not telling her because she was too punitive. But truthfully, I was afraid to talk to her about anything. Mother helped me clean up and taught me how to wear feminine hygiene pads.

The heavy rain continued after Hurricane Federico touched down, making a screeching sound, as if trying to perforate the zinc. Sometimes it sounded as if someone were dragging a bunch of tin cans across the roof. This time, we were really scared, vulnerable, and at the Lord's mercy.

"Doris, why did you go outside?" Naomi asked me, as we cowered beneath a wall of sound. "You could have died."

Frightened, I told Naomi about the ordeal of almost falling into the disgusting latrine and my difficult journey back to the house—but I didn't tell her about my period. I fell asleep to the sound of the thunderous wind and rain and the prayers of Mama Blas, Nicia, and Mother.

The following morning was dull and silent, and we couldn't differentiate between the damage caused by one hurricane or the other; the trees were almost all flat, the plants were ripped from the ground, and everything smelled woodsy and muddy. The orchids had completely vanished, along with all the other small plants and flowers. Nicia's orchids had once been sold locally for weddings and other special events; they were so dense and thick that from a distance, they looked like a huge, colorful blanket on the ground. Before the hurricanes, her property had offered astonishing, vibrantly colored vistas of vegetables, fruits, plantains, and banana trees. Now much of the vegetation was gone, and Cerro Maravilla spoke to loss and the cry of the poor.

The time had finally come for us to go home; the rain and winds had ceased, and eventually, the golden sun made an appearance. Our seven days at Nicia's house were truly days to remember.

"Good luck, Lina, I hope the house held up okay," my aunt told Mother as we left.

I felt awful to see Nicia stay behind alone in her house, as we headed back to ours. I could sense my parents were greatly concerned about our little home's fate—and they had reason to be. Our house had been flooded. There were at least ten inches of mud inside the house, all the way through. It was a horrific, disgusting, and devastating sight.

"My God, I don't even know how to begin!" Mother cried after surveying the damage. Poor Mama Blas placed one hand on her chest and looked like she might have a stroke. Mother discussed with my father the possibility of taking Mama Blas back to Aunt Nicia's house, and she eventually won the argument, so Father reloaded my grandmother into the car and took her back.

"Wait up, Dad!" yelled Franco, Father's buddy. Franco climbed into the car, and off they went back to La Carmelita.

The water came out of the faucets brown and orange, at first. Mother spent long hours thereafter hosing down the floors in the entire house, and we helped clean up, throwing out my parents' magazines, books, papers, ruined photo albums, clothing and shoes, and even Sergio's crib—which amounted to almost all of our belongings. The stench of wet cement and mud was repulsive and made the air hard to breathe, and we had trouble sleeping at night. The house held on to the repugnant smell for a long time.

Tree branches were strewn throughout our yard, and many of the coffee trees were flattened. Overall, the property looked sad and broken. We didn't know what we were going to do or what was going to happen, but then a government representative stopped by to assess our losses. Several days later, we were fortunate enough to receive a government stipend, which Mother used to pay for the most urgent things we needed.

Weeks later, after the ground had dried, Mother tried to go out onto the farm and tie up some of the coffee trees, but it was a laborious process. She truly had a green thumb, but it would take long weeks of hard work to save the trees. We couldn't afford to hire someone else to do the work. The farm was never the same, and the coffee never grew as abundantly afterward.

Merely a few years after living with Mama Blas, she'd had enough. It wasn't our presence she disagreed with but rather Mother's way of raising us. I was sad when she gave a stern warning she'd soon leave. The bickering continued back and forth. Father often wasn't home; on this particular day, I didn't know how much longer I could live under this constant aura of pain and fear.

Mama Blas called Franco and sent him on an errand. A while later, Mother's brother Monce showed up. Blas had gathered most of her belongings while she waited for him and soon had them loaded into Uncle Monce's truck. The way she then boarded the truck, chin high, back straight, holding her skirt as she climbed in, I knew she wasn't coming back. She left her own house to get away from her own daughter.

I missed Mama Blas and felt extremely vulnerable without her love and advocacy. I went from shyness to enduring and wishing I were invisible to Mother. For a while, I just tried to work hard while staying off her radar, a strategy that failed most of the time; but the less I bothered Mother for anything, the better life was for me, even if it meant enduring sore limbs and nauseating headaches. It didn't take me long to start venting against my misery, though. Not too long after Blas left, I started threatening, "I'll leave this house!"

That was the first time Mother broke the broomstick on my back; my skinny bones felt demolished, but it felt good to dare to say I'd leave. This helped me set my heart on leaving, as I saw there was no other way out for me.

Mother favored the boys. Anything they did seemed to amuse her; and they were lazy, especially Alejandro. They were allowed to play whenever they wanted and were never assigned chores. Only the girls worked at home—I wasn't allowed to complain and was never excused from chores.

In late 1979, after Mama Blas left, Naomi met a guy named Diego. We giggled and bonded with him almost immediately. Mother liked Diego, and we did, too. Naomi was a tall girl, and she shared the Taíno look: a round face, high cheekbones, soft mocha skin, and deep black eyes. She had straight black hair that hung below her waist to her rump. She also had a distinctive black mole on her left cheek and was quite outspoken. Diego adored her.

"Doris, I'm going to tell you a secret," he told me one day. "Don't tell anyone, but I'm going to marry your sister." I kept his secret.

"Hey, kids, have you done the drive around the island?" he asked us all on another occasion.

I didn't know what he was talking about, and none of us answered, so Mother did. "No, they don't do too many outings."

"Well, Doña Lina, it's good for them! You have to let them go out," Diego insisted, as he looked my mother in the eye.

I glanced at the boys, smiling with closed lips. Marcos chuckled, then Jonas. Franco laughed and said, "I'm ready!"

Mother just made an "uhum" sound to Diego and looked down.

"Come on, kids, everyone, let's go!" Diego yelled enthusiastically. I was extremely shocked when I heard Diego say, "Hey, Doña Lina, you too, let's go!"

We'd never gone out on a trip like this. I was trembling with anticipation as Mother smiled shyly and said, "But there's so much to do here."

"Don't worry. We'll have fun!" Diego said.

I couldn't believe it when Mother came with us. We all sat in back of the truck; Mother sat next to Naomi, while holding Sergio. Diego drove us via Route 184, and the mountain views were breathtaking. We stopped by Cayey, at one of the island's most popular *lechoneras,* and all had fresh roasted pork. We were back home by nightfall, and even Mother had enjoyed herself.

Father didn't like Diego. Mother gave Diego her approval to marry Naomi—but Father would not. In fact, he wasn't happy with the idea and forbade Naomi from ever seeing Diego again. He argued with Mother repeatedly about it and resented that Mother stood by her decision regardless. He then began to bully Mother with insults, sneeringly calling her a *mapriola,* a matchmaker.

Diego was truly a gentleman. He continued treating us with the same love, and I noticed he was in fact aware my father didn't like him. He'd share with my mother how she wanted Naomi to have a nice wedding and that he'd incur all expenses, but Father never accepted him.

One afternoon, when I came home from school, Father had a long face, and Mother appeared to have been crying.

"Naomi ran away," she told me.

I broke down myself. I'd so looked forward to seeing Naomi and Diego get married. Soon Diego sent word they *were* getting married, but Father wouldn't let us attend their wedding. After Naomi left, Mother changed our room assignments. Most of the kids slept in Mama Blas's room. I kept the cozy, small room by the kitchen that had belonged to Lorena, then Naomi. I saw Mama Blas shortly after. By that time, she was living with Mother's sister Honora.

"Do good," she told me. "You *are* good. Make your mother happy."

I missed her and longed for her blessings and her hugs, but I tried to follow her advice.

§ § §

Once Naomi and Diego had married and settled, they began to visit us, and Diego soon made peace with Father.

Diego could read me, though, and knew something was wrong.

"I'm concerned—is Doris okay?" he asked the family one day. Naomi and Father heard Diego's question, but Mother did not. He said to me, "In your eyes, I see sadness. Hey, what are those marks on your arms?"

I pressed my lips together and looked at him fearfully. I think he knew what was going on. He didn't judge Mother, though, and was always kind to her and us. He made me feel I could talk with him, though I never told him about how Mother treated me. Their visits were healing events, and Mother appeared happy when they were there. Seeing her happy was a relief; it was precisely what I wanted, and I didn't want to ruin it. During one visit, Diego asked, "Doña Lina, can I take the kids just for a little ride again?"

Franco, Alejandro, Marcos, Jonas, Veronica, and I were happy every time Diego mentioned a ride.

"Oh . . . the boys, sure, you can take them."

"Doña Lina, I'm taking the girls, too. It's good for them to get out of the house. I'll come back soon, don't worry."

I ran to the truck; I didn't dare look at Mother. Diego had all of us sit in the back, and we couldn't stop smiling as he took us on a long drive; we enjoyed the views and the fresh breeze. On different occasions, he'd drive us to different places across the island. After visits by Naomi and Diego, Mother was quiet and withdrawn. It appeared she missed them as well. Naomi leaving promoted me to Mother's right hand. One morning, Jonas and Marcos woke up sick. I was thirteen.

"Doris, get up and get ready," Mother commanded. "You're going to take the kids to the hospital with your Father."

Father's involvement with sick children was limited to such hospital visits; and even then, he didn't get involved much. This was especially true of my Mother's hospitalizations for childbirth. Visiting Mother after childbirth, according to him, was not "a man's thing."

"Mother, I don't know where I'd be taking them! I don't want to go!" I protested.

I didn't tell her I was afraid of taking the kids with just Father. I didn't know what I needed to do when we got to the hospital. Mother didn't care; she just ordered, "Shut up and take them to the hospital with your Father, as I just told you. Now move it."

I did as Mother ordered. When we arrived at the hospital, Father stopped by the emergency entrance and didn't bother to get out of the car. I helped the kids out of the car alone and stood waiting with them, waiting for Father to get out.

"Go take them inside," he scolded.

"Dad, you have to come into the hospital with us!" I had no idea where I was supposed to take the kids.

"Just take them inside and tell them they're sick!" Father shouted. "Now move it!"

Shaken, I escorted the kids inside. I found the place packed with people—some sitting, many moaning. There were three pairs of double doors, and I didn't know which way to go. The foyer was noisy and smelled like rubbing alcohol. A lady wearing white came out of one of the doors.

"They're sick," I said to her, pointing at the boys.

"Very well, be seated and take your turn. Someone will call you shortly."

I had no choice but to have faith in the nurse. I didn't understand what "taking a turn" meant and how we could be called from among so many people sitting and waiting around. I found a place and said, "Let's sit here, guys," to Jonas and Marcos, who were unusually quiet.

After a little while, the same nurse called me and asked

our names. I gave the boys' names, but she asked, "Where are your parents?"

"Mother is at home taking care of more kids, and Father is outside," I answered.

"Leave the kids here and go get your father," said the nurse.

I went outside and found him sitting in his car.

"Dad, they want you to go inside."

"Don't tell them I'm here!" he said angrily. "Now go back inside."

I thought he was going to hit me, so I walked back into the hospital and reported to the nurse, "He doesn't want to come in."

The nurse consulted with a doctor. I stared at them while they mumbled together and called yet another doctor. The kids were obviously sick, so they decided to treat them. One doctor gave me several prescriptions, saying, "They need to take these medicines immediately."

I nodded and walked out with the boys, and we all got into Father's car.

"Here, Father," I said, handing him the prescriptions. "The doctor said the kids need to take these medicines immediately."

"Bah, nonsense, I'm not stopping anywhere," Father said stubbornly.

I stared at him in disbelief as we began the drive toward home.

"Father, please!" I insisted. "The doctor said to stop by the pharmacy! They need the medicine, they're very sick!"

But he refused to listen and never even took the prescriptions from me. When we got home, I handed them to Mother.

"What did the doctor say?" she demanded.

"The doctor said they need to take medicine. He wanted

to speak with Father, but he didn't want to get out of the car and made me go into the hospital by myself," I said.

Mother became very upset. "How could you just sit in the car and let them go in alone?" she shouted at Father.

Father was clearly angry with me for telling on him, but I didn't care. Mother then yelled at him, "They need their prescriptions! You're not the one who sits up all night taking care of them!" Her voice thundered through the house.

It felt incredibly good to be off Mother's radar, and I didn't feel sorry for Father at all. He mumbled a word or two in response but refused to go back to get the boys' prescriptions until the following morning. Marcos stayed sick, and Mother was irate, blaming Father for his delayed recovery.

A couple days later, I came home from school to find Marcos wheezing severely. Mother rushed back and forth through the place, looking for a certain remedy Mama Blas used for asthma. When I asked for my blessing, Mother gave it, and then said, "Doris, get ready to go to the hospital."

"Mother, I'm beat," I said. I had been running that day. In a rough tone, she ordered me to go anyway. I got upset, as I knew I'd end up taking Marcos into the hospital by myself, so I told her, "He should do it! He's their father!"

Mother grabbed the broomstick and, as usual, began hitting me on my head, upper back, and arms until it broke in half. It felt like all the bones in my back were broken, but she forced me to get up and leave right away without even changing my school uniform or eating supper. I was very hungry, and my sore body felt heavy as iron. With one hand resting on my right hip, hair messy and limbs destroyed, I walked slowly as I left the house, though I felt as if I, too, needed to see a doctor.

Again we arrived at the hospital; Father stopped at the

entrance and didn't bother to walk us inside. "Go and tell them he's not getting better," he demanded. I scowled at him and helped little Marcos out of the car. The poor kid could barely walk himself.

This time, I knew where the waiting area was located and went directly there, telling them, "My little brother isn't feeling better."

"Where are your parents?" a nurse with a serious demeanor asked.

"My father is outside. He told me to bring my brother in by myself."

"Go tell him we need to speak with him. He needs to come inside."

I sighed and, feeling extremely sore, walked outside. I couldn't help but look at Father with shame as he blasted music on the car radio. "The nurse said you have to go inside. She wants to talk with you."

"Why did you tell them I was here?" he yelled. "Go back and tell them I'm *not* here."

I walked back inside and said to the nurse, "My father doesn't want to come in."

"This boy is very ill. The doctor says we need to admit him."

"I'll be right back," I said, then walked back outside—disgusted, tired, and mad as a dragon.

"Marcos is very ill and they want to admit him!" I roared at my father. "I see you're very comfortable, but come inside if you care!"

Father's chest flattened and his eyes widened. I didn't care; I turned around and went back inside. I was aware this kind of talk toward my father was disrespectful, and woe is me if he reported this to Mother. I dismissed my concern and continued into the hospital.

My brother was admitted immediately. I sat on a chair

by his bedside, keeping watch. Someone had to. Marcos was extremely pale. He was on an IV and had fallen asleep; I soon began to fall asleep myself. Minutes later, one of the doctors escorted Father into Marcos's room, where they discussed my brother's condition. My stomach could barely handle Father's repetitive laughter, which probably derived from his embarrassment at staying outside while he sent me to do his job for him. When the doctor told Father Marcos needed rest, I jumped in and said, "Father, go home. I'll stay with him."

He shot me a look of surprise, yet again, and I pierced him with my eyes. After a few minutes, Father left the room quietly. I was still very upset with him because he'd seen Mother hit me with the broomstick, and he knew I hadn't eaten supper. I was having cold sweats from my own pain—my back felt demolished—but I didn't dare to ask Marcos's doctor for help.

When Father returned to the hospital the following day, Marcos was cleared for discharge. I was proud to say, "Father, you can take Marcos home. I'm going to school now." He didn't say anything, so I walked back to school from Jayuya Hospital.

I was tired, sore, hungry, and craved a shower. I had no books with me nor anything to write with. My first stop was the principal's office. I explained how I'd spent the night at the hospital with my brother; I was then allowed to go straight into class. I didn't care the school day was almost over by then. I'd had no breakfast or lunch, but school had become my only resting place. I told my coach I couldn't practice because of my fatigue—but what I wanted to say was, "My mother beat me with the broomstick, and my back is killing me!"

From age eight through fourteen, the beatings intensified so that my body was constantly in the process of healing. I loved school, but otherwise, life just got harder and harder.

7. Visit from New York

I literally stretch the fabric to make them uniforms, but it isn't enough.

Not only do we live in poverty, but in scarcity, which is evil.

—Mother

In 1981, Antonio Garcia, also known as Toño Bicicleta, the island's most notorious criminal, escaped from prison for the third time. People referred to him as Toño Bicicleta because, according to the news reports, "He has never owned a car, and his preferred mode of transportation is a bicycle."

People would tell all kinds of tales about him, and local bands wrote songs about him. He had been accused of murder, rape, and kidnapping. He became an island sensation as people's curiosity grew, wondering how he managed to escape prison over and over and how he moved about when he did.

Because of his popularity, Toño Bicicleta was also a scapegoat, accused of committing many other crimes. He was, indeed, the talk of the island.

The same year, Father's mother, "Tato" Petra Castellar, came to visit us in Jayuya. Tato had been born and raised in Ponce but moved to Brooklyn in the late 1950s, after my parents married. Tato's unannounced visits every few years were a mini-vacation for us. There was so much love and excitement then! We enjoyed the never-ending chats about family, with updates as to who had married, who had had children, who had moved to the States, and, of course, how many children Mother had now.

The Armor of Love and Hope

Tato made her own baby-doll dresses: knee-length, sleeveless garments with pockets on the sides. The style and length, along with her accessories, complimented her petite figure. She loved wearing head wraps, hoop earrings, bangles, and long, gold chains. She was a big fan of sandals, too. Overall, Tato was a complete rascal, always displaying a careless but cheery look, and had an electrifying personality. Shouting a loud "Ah-ha!" was part of her grand arrival, and we knew her distinctive voice instantly. The stampede of kids (Franco, now sixteen; Alejandro, twelve; Veronica, ten; Jonas, nine; Marcos, seven; Raquel, five; and me, fourteen) ran to and surrounded Tato, while the little ones (Sergio, three, and Uma, two) hung onto Mother's legs.

It was astounding to hear such a big voice come out of such a small woman. Tato had a small frame and small, delicate hands. I wondered if she'd ever done dishes in her life. Her hands were soft, her fingernails carefully manicured. She had jet-black hair and a light, clear complexion, which made an interesting contrast with her brilliant aquamarine eyes. She projected a pleasant but comical aura and cursed a lot but laughed incessantly. The way she smiled at us, no words were needed; we could feel her love and warmth.

"It's been a long time," Mother greeted Tato. We kissed her one by one, asking for the traditional blessing: "*Abuela, la Bendición*. Grandma, a blessing!"

Her eyes sparkled with joy as she placed her hand over our heads, one after the other: "*Que el Señor los bendiga y los proteja*. May God bless and protect you."

Lorena, Víctor, Josué, and Naomi were out of the house by then, but there were a couple of new faces for Tato to see: Sergio and Uma. In awe Tato cried, "More children!"

"They're the last ones," Mother said.

"Lina, how many are there now?" asked Tato, almost in dismay.

After contemplating Tato's question, Mother replied, "Thirteen. I have thirteen children; six girls and seven boys."

"Thirteen children, my God," Tato cried.

Mother's tone softened, "There were major complications with Uma. Just like with Raquel . . . another breach birth. I don't know how I made it. All I remember saying in my heart was 'my God' when the doctor grabbed a pair of forceps . . ." Mother paused.

Tato nodded as a gesture of empathy. Then, glancing at the nine of us around her, she laughed, "It's good to be back on the island!"

Tato had arrived with Uncle Pello and two of our cousins, Carmin and Kenny, while we were eating dinner.

"Everyone, please have a seat," Mother said, but she didn't need to say a word to us. We were trained to read her body language. We quickly moved out of the way and let the visitors sit at the table with Father. We were too happy to care where we had to sit. Some of us sat on different spots on the floor; others sat outside on the bare ground. While Father entertained them with stories, memories, and laughter, Mother quietly approached us one by one, confiscating our silverware.

"But Mother, what I am going to use?" I asked.

"Eat with your hands. This is just for the visit," she scolded. In no time, Mother was in the kitchen turning empanadas in the frying pan.

Soon enough, all of our visitors were savoring and complimenting Mother's cooking. Tato confused the boys with each other, but we were used to watching Mother clarify who was who.

"The skinny one is El Lobo, Franco. He's now the oldest

of the boys, he's sixteen. He's Daddy's boy; ahead in his class, but loves car racing. The dark one is Alejandro, he's twelve, and we call him Titus. He's also into car racing."

"They look like twins, Lina." Tato's jaw dropped as she stared at Franco and Alejandro.

Mother chuckled, "The blonde one is Jonas, 'Chiqui.' He turned eight a couple of weeks ago. He loves the outdoors, and he's always exploring. The short, round one is Marcos, 'Mitch.' He's seven. Marcos is passionate about the Taínos—he loves learning about them. The youngest boy is Sergio, he's three. Quite a character but doesn't like to eat."

Tato laughed. "The girls . . . I know Veronica and Doris," she said.

"Doris takes care of the kids and does almost every chore," said Mother. "Her birthday is coming up in November, she's fourteen. Veronica is ten—she's shy but loves drawing. Raquel is five, a complete chatterbox. She can entertain a whole room of people, telling one joke after another. The youngest one is Uma, she's fourteen months."

"What a collection of good-looking faces," Tato said and sighed loudly. Her face reminded me so much of my Father's, with its bright, generous smile and constant, happy look. She winked as she smiled at us.

Tato had brought several boxes containing shoes, clothing, and other things. After dinner, she directed us, "Hurry, open them!" She laughed out loud as we did.

"New shoes!" the boys screeched.

We had never seen so many shoes! We were overwhelmed by the smell of new clothes. We raced back and forth, trying on new shoes and clothing and thanking Tato. Mother always did the final sorting, so everyone got an equal share.

While we emptied boxes, a strange dialogue took place

between Tato and my parents. Kids weren't allowed to intrude into adult conversations, so I was able to catch just bits and pieces, such as "Life would be better for all of them . . ."

When I heard this, I stopped what I was doing, stepped behind the kitchen door, and listened, contemplating the tone of Tato's voice and the serious looks on my parents' faces. The atmosphere in the house changed, seeming to grow heavier. Tato continued, "They can go to schools there."

Mother listened with an erect posture, chin up, looking straight into Tato's eyes, studying every word that came out of her mother-in-law's mouth. She'd contribute an "uh hum" occasionally. Father mumbled, and unlike Mother, his eyes were content, even fascinated by their discussion.

I looked around at my siblings. Before I could open my mouth to call Veronica, Mother appeared out of nowhere, grinding her teeth.

"Doris, what are you doing here? Have you no respect for visitors? Go outside before I lose my patience."

A chill swept through my entire body. I turned around and left without making eye contact with Mother; making eye contact while being reprimanded was considered disrespectful.

Despite knowing Mother's threats were serious, I couldn't resist the temptation to go back to my listening spot behind the kitchen door and start eavesdropping again. My heart raced, but once again, I listened.

"It's the best thing to do. The situation will only get worse. If Honora wants the house so badly, things aren't going to change," Tato said.

Mother seemed confused and overwhelmed when Father said, "I have to agree. Things aren't going to change—plus, the economy is better in the States."

91

I knew Mother loved the house and didn't want to leave it. And in fact, my grandparents, Teyo and Blas, had expressed their wish for Mother to inherit it. But I knew Mother's sister Honora was interested and had been pressuring Mother about it for quite a while.

I remember, during one of her first visits, her saying, "Lina, it's better to sell." Honora's sporadic visits weren't exactly concerned about our welfare.

"Sell? My father never said anything about selling," Mother said to her sister. "And where would I go with my children?"

The sound of Mother's desperation gave me chills. I was twelve at the time, and I despised my Aunt Honora from that day on. I understood that Blas's house, this place that was "soon to be ours," was simply a temporary home for us. It looked like Honora would eventually get the house, so Mother gave up the illusion of inheriting it herself.

"My children," she told us bitterly, "when you have something and someone aches for it, don't keep it; let them have it. Let them eat it, even. Remember you were born naked. Do well unto others, because those who do wrong shall fall by their own weight."

I suppose I understood Honora's greediness, but I also understood Mother's anger. Mother walked as if she bore the weight of the world on her shoulders. Feeling almost hopeless as she did, having only a temporary home, was just one more pressure for her to bear. Father, however, didn't take the matter too seriously.

"This property is ours—don't give them the satisfaction of getting it. Teyo and Blas clearly *said* the house is ours. Your sister doesn't want it. She just wants money."

Mother shot him a serious yet hopeless look. "If I could, I'd buy something new and leave this place, but my customers don't want to pay much. Sewing isn't easy, and people want things fast too. What I make isn't enough," she said.

Mother worked hard and saved every penny she could. But caring for nine children and a husband was extremely demanding. The laundry was especially bad. It had to be done by hand; it took Mother several hours of washing and hanging clothes to finish up. Father's work clothes were the worse to wash, but all the cloth diapers, sheets, whites, and other baby clothes were too much to handle at times. Our clotheslines were always filled with laundry. Luckily, baby diapers dried quickly, as did the cotton sheets, given the breeze and warm temperatures.

Rainy days were torturous, though, because they meant we had to stretch the use of the diapers. There was one line near the house that didn't get wet from the rain, but it still took a long time for the diapers to dry on wet days because of the dampness.

I was inspired by Mother's tireless spirit and helped as much as I could. The babies still stayed ahead of me, especially in terms of wetting and pooping their diapers. It almost seemed they timed my chores and arranged to make things as difficult as possible. It all got to be too much sometimes. Whenever I thought I could go away to rest for a while, someone had to be changed or cared for.

Mother's life was far from a walk in the park, which was the reason I had dedicated myself to helping her, at least, as much as I could. She struggled to take care of the nine of us kids, while simultaneously doing enough sewing work to make ends meet. Although Father worked as a truck driver, he didn't bring in much.

Each school year, Mother pointed out, "Every year it's the same thing. I literally stretch the fabric to make them uniforms, but it isn't enough. We don't live in poverty, but in scarcity, which is evil."

In the conversation with Tato, she repeated this remark. Taking a deep breath, she then said, "It's better to leave the island. The future of my children worries me."

As the secret conversation went on, I grew increasingly disturbed. I was a high school junior and didn't want to go anywhere! Suddenly I realized Mother was walking my way. I tried to take off as fast as I could but felt as if I were running in slow motion. Luckily, she didn't seem to notice me; I felt a strange relief as she called, "Everyone, come on inside, it's getting dark."

We were all inside the house when Mother said to Father, "I could take Sergio, Raquel, and Uma, while you stay with the rest until I find a place. Doris could take care of the kids until I get settled there. She knows how to cook and do things around the house."

My nervous system jumped to full attention, wondering if taking care of the kids meant the end to my school days. My knees began to shake, and before I could absorb what I had just heard, Mother announced, as if it were settled, "Everyone, I'm leaving for New York on Monday, and I'll take Raquel, Sergio, and Uma with me. It's time to move on to a new start for everyone and hopefully look forward to a better future."

There was chaos as all the kids began shouting to one another about Mother's announcement. The kids' reaction was as if hitting a light switch: we all lit up and reacted in our own ways to the electrifying news.

Now, our house was never quiet, but right then it sounded like a drunken social club. It was a good thing we didn't have close neighbors. I can't imagine how anyone could have stood our noise, especially at nighttime— though the colicky nights were the worst indeed. It was also a good thing the house didn't have glass windows; the kids' screeches would have cracked every single one of them.

"What?" I said now, staring at Mother and Tato in horror. Tato smiled brightly, like she'd just hit the lottery. Me, I didn't think any of this was funny.

"Are we moving to Nueva York for good?" Franco asked.

"Will we go live in a new house?" Alejandro shouted, chuckling and celebrating.

"We're leaving?" Jonas demanded.

"Yes, we're *leaving,* we're *leaving!*" Alejandro shouted, jumping up and down.

The giggles were nonstop.

"Why? Where are we going?" Marcos asked.

The little ones stared at everyone, while Veronica and I stared at the boys and Tato, aghast at the news and their reaction to it.

"Okay, enough!" Mother yelled. Tato just laughed eyes wide.

"We're moving, but not immediately," Mother told us. "Your Father and Doris will stay with you until I find us a new place in New York. I have to find a place big enough for everyone. Then all of you will come."

I trembled. "Why can't I go with you? I don't want to stay behind!" I said.

"I want to go, too," Veronica chimed in.

"You can't go; there aren't enough plane tickets for you all. No more questions. You all heard what I said, and that's final."

Horror and fear took over me.

"Mother, why do I have to stay with Father and the kids?" I asked plaintively.

Her answer was a shout that made my ears ring and my whole body tremble. "Because I say so, I don't have to give you any reasons! You'll do as you're told!"

It had been a long time since the house had echoed with

so much chaos, but I was too upset to care—and I wished I wasn't a part of it. But once I made eye contact with Tato, her cheerfulness touched my heart. She moved over on the couch so I could sit next to her. She hugged me and I felt loved; oh, I felt safe. We watched TV and shared laughs, as Uma danced to every TV commercial.

As bedtime approached, we were dispatched from the living room. I could hear my parents giving Tato updates about the older kids.

"Victor is a father, and Lorena is a mother. They and Naomi are all newlyweds. Naomi's husband, Diego, fought in the Korean War. He's a Borinqueneer. Older than her, but I approved the marriage," said Mother. "He is a good husband; I've never had anyone love my kids like he does. He comes here and takes them for long rides."

I'd give anything for the house to remain this joyful, but Mother was about to leave, and I had to take over all her responsibilities and household tasks. The idea scared me. I didn't know how we were going to make it. I was dying to learn more about their plans, but intruding on adult conversations was grounds for serious punishment, for disrespecting my parents and my grandmother.

I wondered what Mama Blas would think about us moving. She was still living with Aunt Honora. Blas was well aware of Honora's interest in the house.

The following morning, Tato clarified with Mother the day and time of the flight to New York. As for me, I was overwhelmed. I just couldn't process the thought of Mother leaving us and the house she loved behind. We had never been apart, except for the times she delivered a new baby. Tato informed Mother, "I'm going to Ponce to spend some time with the rest of the family. We'll come back early

Monday morning and go straight to the airport."

As Tato began her good-byes to all the kids, my stomach turned. I walked outside and sat behind our house next to a lemongrass bush. I sat hugging my knees and heard my name called.

"Doris! Where is she, have you seen her?"

Eventually, they gave up calling me, and she said a final good-bye to my parents and the rest of the kids, saying, "See you Monday."

My heart pounded, and cold sweat dripped down my face. My heart sank in sorrow as I heard the kids chorusing excitedly, "Bye, Grandma, bye-bye."

After the car took off, I waited a while and then, drying my tears, I slowly emerged from behind the house. My body felt cold and light. Mother soon spotted me.

"Where were you?" she demanded.

Outside," I said, and kept walking toward her without any expression on my face; then I paused. "Mother, I want to go with you."

"No, Doris. I already told you there aren't enough tickets."

She looked serious as she prepared for the trip, her lips closed tightly, her manly hands moving fast, sorting and picking out articles of clothing. It was awful to see Mother pack her clothes; gradually, I felt the separation begin.

Later, Mother sent the boys to the homes of Ms. Jorgi and her other customers to inform them she was leaving for a while. She cleared her sewing area and returned some finished garments and materials. My chest tightened as I watched Mother putting away the old Singer sewing machine, gently folding its table as if in meditation. Her manly hands caressed the remaining fabrics, as if saying good-bye to her sewing.

As always, Ms. Jorgi had implored her for one more

garment, but Mother's no was final and emphatic. Once the sewing area was clear, a hideous feeling of abandonment swept over me. I prayed and hoped with all my strength she'd change her mind. I tried to be strong, but the reality seemed harsh. I couldn't see how things would work without Mother.

I'd give her bitter and upset looks occasionally, and Mother would just threaten me with, *"Ten cuidado con esa cara.* You better watch that look on your face." Her threats didn't change the way I felt. I kept wondering how Mama Blas felt about Mother's move, but Mama Blas lived seventeen miles away in La Carmelita, with Aunt Honora.

8. You All Behave

On a Monday morning in late July 1981, I was awakened earlier than usual by the exquisite aroma of our coffee. The cool morning breeze danced its way around the house, birds sang, and the golden Puerto Rican sun rose over the edge of the world.

I could hear heavy objects being moved around and the opening and closing of zippers. I pulled up my blanket and tried to sleep a little longer, but my efforts were thwarted by incessant whispering and noises in the kitchen and living room. Curiosity made me get up. Half asleep, I emerged from my bedroom, a tiny living space divided from the rest of the house by a curtain, and headed to the living room. I saw several pieces of luggage lined up in the living room beside the front door, which was wide open. There was a bag on top of the table, packed with bottles and diapers.

Mother came out of her room and handed me Uma and her bottle. As I held Uma, the little one smiled at me. She looked like a new doll, with sparkling honey eyes and soft cinnamon skin. I smiled back. Her tiny hands clutched the bottle tightly. Her hair was fragrant from baby shampoo and was picked up in a tiny bun, but a few golden curls cascaded on either side of her face. Her little body's warmth and innocence gave me comfort.

Minutes later, Raquel emerged, wearing a *pique* dress. Raquel had pretty black eyes and straight black hair. Sergio was also dressed up in navy blue pants and a long-sleeved white shirt.

"Doris, watch the kids, so they don't go outside and get dirty," Mother called to me as she moved objects in her room. So I sat in the living room, surrounded by my younger siblings, and watched.

Mother came out of her room holding a small black comb and headed to the mirror. I stared at Mother as she divided her thick black hair into strands, her hands moving gently but fast. She parted her hair on the side and styled it up in a twist. Father walked in and said, "It's almost time."

Mother glanced at Father, then rushed into her room. I smelled Mother's perfume on the air, and my heart said, *This is it*.

I felt like hanging on to my little siblings and never letting go. A new feeling of *Mother is leaving us* swept over me. I had never been so scared or uncertain in my life.

Within minutes, all the rest of the kids were up, but there was silence and tension in the air. Mother reminded Veronica and my four brothers to brush their teeth while she served breakfast. My body trembled as I held Uma, and I stared at Mother as she served us small dishes of oatmeal and filled cups with coffee.

"Everyone, breakfast is served," she announced, like it was some ordinary day.

While the kids took seats in the dining room, Mother took one last walk through the house, making sure she hadn't forgotten anything. Then she made last-minute touches to her hair. Her cinnamon skin contrasted sharply with her bright red lips. I bit my tongue but wanted to say, "Oh, Mother, please don't leave us! I'll help. I'll work hard, just as you taught us!" But I didn't have the strength or courage to speak.

She continued mumbling last-minute instructions to Father until, all of a sudden, a new car pulled up in front of our house: Grandma Tato had arrived. Father and Mother headed out, talking with each other; the little ones and I followed. Tato smiled at my little siblings as they approached, saying, "Well, look at you, all dressed up. Are you ready to go bye-bye? We're going away in a big airplane."

My siblings and I just stared at her.

"Well, it's time," Tato said to my parents.

My stomach turned horribly. My parents never said good-bye when they left to go somewhere, only telling us, "You all behave." Not saying good-bye meant we would see each other again, and soon. Grandma Tato hugged my father, and I felt like running away. Then she came to me and gave me a strong hug and a kiss. She smiled and gave me another kiss; along with an *I love you* with her eyes. I felt special and happy and loved her back, begging her with my own eyes, *Can I go?*

But she only gave me her blessing and then walked over to the other older kids, who were lined up, watching. One by one, she gave them a hug, a kiss, and the accustomed blessing: "*Dios le bendiga y le proteja.* May the Lord guide and protect you." Finally, she got into the car. We remained speechless and motionless, all our eyes fixed on them as Tato told us, "See you soon!"

The others then climbed in, one by one. Mother was the last one to get into the car. She settled into the backseat with Uma, Raquel, and Sergio. As the car moved toward the main road, Tato blew us kisses and waved. Mother rolled down her window and called, "You all behave!" Raquel's and Sergio's little hands looked like small fans rapidly waving their good-byes. They were too young to know any better. As the car slowly moved away, we kept waving back and remained outside until we couldn't see the car anymore, until the dust that had been lifted from the road settled again.

The house was immediately filled with silence, feeling enormous and empty. I didn't know what to say or do; the feeling of separation was too heavy to bear. Time seemed to stand still, the minutes dragging slowly into hours, and the hours seemed everlasting.

Father didn't go to work and stayed with us the day Mother left. I could barely breathe, and my chest hurt. I could almost see Mother's hands quickly moving about the kitchen, making coffee and breakfast. A pot of oatmeal remained on the stove, still warm, and her coffee cup with her lipstick on it was still on the table. The scent of her perfume, which the breeze slowly blew around the house, made us miss her even more.

We were quiet, and all we could hear was the sound of the brook, the soft breeze caressing the trees, and the birds singing. At one point I glanced into Mother's room and stared at Uma's crib, which was still set up, some of her toys scattered around it. Veronica joined me, and the look in her eyes scared me.

"What are we going to do?" she asked mournfully.

"I don't know," I replied, in anguish myself. I hoped Mother would change her mind and return. But not a single car approached our house for the rest of the day. The boys spent the day outside with our father. I could hear Marcos and Jonas sobbing.

"Come on, don't cry, you'll be seeing her soon," Father reassured the kids.

Nighttime on this particular day felt teeth-gnashing. I looked often toward the main road, but the night, as they say, was *negra como boca de lobo,* dark as a wolf's mouth. Still, I stared out the window at the horrendous dark, hoping the new car would emerge bearing my mother. I waited and I waited, but the darkness just looked back at me, and the fog came in and eddied about.

All I felt was emptiness, nothingness. Over the next few days, I wondered how I'd be able to keep up with all the chores. The house was messy already. I wondered what I would say to everyone at school. What if they found out Mother wasn't living with us now? What if the school calls a social worker, like the time Mother hit me with the tree branch and I had marks on my left eye? What if the investigator decided to remove us from our home because we weren't safe without Mother? The more I thought about our situation, the more questions I had. *What if something happened?*

I woke up early the next morning and called out to the other kids to get up and get ready for school. It was the first day of the new school year. We left the house together but walked to the bus stop with heavy steps. As we approached, I heard familiar voices.

"Doris, did you have a good summer?"

I didn't reply. My brain was too busy to process anything other than *Mother left us*. The memory of her leaving seemed to drain me of strength.

I thought about her last words, "you all behave," and about my little siblings waving their good-byes. What if someone found out?

I glanced at Jonas and Marcos, who stood across the street, waiting for their bus. They looked like two little statues, standing side by side, petrified. The short pants of their school uniforms exposed their skinny, scraped legs.

I looked at the pretty girls waiting with me at the bus stop. I wished I could be as careless and normal as they. Their faces held perpetual happiness, their hair was neatly combed and tucked into perfect high ponytails, and their uniforms were well tailored and tight at the waist. I wanted to be as happy as they were, but Mother's leaving made me feel abandoned and inferior. I didn't feel as pretty as the other girls, either. I was concealing a horrible secret, and it made me feel dark.

Veronica and I had combed our hair but left it loose. Veronica's jet-black hair was thicker and longer than mine, with spiral curls cascading below her shoulders. It was arduous to comb in the mornings, but we did our best.

To make things worse, my school bus arrived first to take me away from those I loved. After boarding, I stared at my siblings until I couldn't see them anymore. This was the most horrific of all my school days. Mother had taken a part of me away with her, and my mind remained blank for most of the day. Gym class revived me a little; it almost made me forget my motherless home and vulnerable siblings.

I couldn't sleep easily that night or any night thereafter, fearing a break-in. What would happen to us? What if we got taken away? What if we got separated and I couldn't see my siblings again? What if my classes turned out to be too hard to handle? For relief, I'd pray the rosary the way Mama Blas had taught me, wishing and hoping for a miracle to occur.

In school, I dreaded hearing any teacher–parent meeting announcements. "Dori, what if my teacher asks about Mother?" Marcos asked me once.

"No one should know, Marcos. I think it's best we don't tell anyone. Remember how Mother doesn't like anyone knowing our business," I replied.

I was mortified and didn't feel safe. I doubted we were going to make it. Father was harsh and expected me to know things. He didn't bother to teach me anything though. The day after Mother left, I burned the rice at dinner, and he shouted, "Stupid!" Then the boys laughed, repeating "Stupid, stupid!" He threw the rice away and told me to cook it again.

I scraped the burned pot until all the blackened rice was removed. By the time I'd cooked all over again, it was late in the evening, and he didn't bother to say thank you.

The following day, we headed out to school as usual, but Father stayed home. He'd stopped going to work. I was concerned for our well-being. My jaws hurt from grinding my teeth at night.

Only two days had passed, but it felt much longer. The mornings were rough. I'd get up first, fix breakfast, and keep a close eye on the time. Dad didn't encourage the kids to get up and go to school. Every morning I had to yell loudly at them so they would get moving. I decided that although Mother wasn't home, I'd follow her routine of rising at six in the morning and starting coffee and breakfast, announcing, "Everyone, time to get up and go to school!"

The kids got up quietly, but Father had a long face when he did. After getting home from school, I'd say, "Marcos, Chiqui, Vera, everyone, don't forget to change out of your uniforms and hang them up so they don't get dirty or wrinkled."

I'd change my uniform as well and then go straight to the kitchen to cook. Father waited outside with the boys until dinner was ready. It was a relief to see how he kept them calm. The smells of herbs seemed to soothe them, so I'd pick fresh cilantro or oregano and make my own version of *sofrito* from scratch. Yellow rice with beans and fried chicken was their favorite. Dad, of course, was obsessed with rice and beans. Slowly, we all adjusted to our motherless home.

"Dinner ready yet?" Jonas asked me on the third day, as he hung around the kitchen.

I replied, "Jonas, dinner is *not* ready, unless you want to eat raw meat, just like cannibals do!"

He stared at me, eyebrows lifted, looking paralyzed. Then he relaxed his eyebrows, smiling. "Cannibals are happy people, because they don't have to wait!" We both laughed, and even Father laughed out loud. Jonas was shy, but he'd come out with the funniest remarks sometimes.

Once dinner was ready, I served the meal at the table and then vanished to eat mine outside. Veronica followed me. Dad ate quietly with the boys. The continuous echoing noise of their forks assured me dinner was acceptable.

"This is good," Father said to the boys. "Do you like your beans, Marcos?"

"Yes, Dad, they're real good," Marcos answered enthusiastically. I glanced at Veronica, giving her a Mona Lisa smile.

"It's true, the food is good," said Veronica.

"I'm glad you like it, Veronica. I can teach you how to cook. What's your favorite?"

"My favorite is your white rice with red beans and pork."

"Wow, that's good. I'm glad you all like my cooking. I thought you just ate it out of hunger." We laughed.

When I walked back into the house, Father smiled. His eyes looked like calm ocean water. My heart palpitated with joy for a second; smiling with Father made my face feel beautiful, as I reflected his contented grin. I felt his warmth and love. Then he looked away, and his eyes turned gray, like a rainy afternoon. How could I ever forget that look? Once again, I didn't dare ask how he felt or if he thought we would be okay. Questioning adults had always been one of Mother's biggest no-nos.

Our chaotic environment calmed down slightly, and I began to adjust to the new reality. Mother had been our general, and I no longer had to keep to her strict chore schedule. Back when she was home, whenever I boarded the bus at school in the afternoon, I'd fall into the suspense of *Mother will be waiting*. But she was no longer waiting, so my tension faded. School continued to be my refuge. It was the only place I felt safe. Oh, bittersweet days!

§ § §

Dinnertime wasn't always fun. Veronica and I didn't share the dining table with Father and the boys because we felt better eating outside.

"Hey, Stupid, come here! Bring more rice and beans," Father yelled at me once.

"I have a name, in case you forgot," I said, as I entered the house.

All four boys, plus Father, stared at me with dropped jaws. I put more rice and beans on the table, then walked outside to sit with Veronica. There was silence inside and out; I saw Veronica's jaw had dropped as well.

"Be careful, Dori," she whispered, "Dad can hurt you."

"I don't care, Veronica, just eat," I told her.

Father never called me "Stupid" again.

9. "Take Care of Them"

Four days after Mother left, I woke up at six and yelled out the usual, "Everyone get up, time to go to school!" and was surprised to hear Father say, "Oh, it's okay. They can stay home—they don't have to go to school today."

"Yes, they do," I dared answer.

I waited for the kids to get up, but there was silence.

"Guys, you'd better get up and get ready, or else you're going to get in trouble with Mother!" I shouted, but I was met with silence once again.

I made coffee, but that old trick didn't work. So I came up with the perfect new trick to get them out of bed: TV! They loved television.

Just as I was about to turn on the TV, I heard the door to my parents' room squeak open. I turned around and saw Father coming out with a small bag in his right hand. He wore his white Guayabera, and his face was cleanly shaven. He looked at me, his expression serious, and said, "Take care of them."

"Yes, Father," I answered automatically.

I watched in complete shock as Father strolled toward the front door. I heard the kids jumping out of bed, the spring mattresses making squeaky noises as they got up. The herd of kids rushed out to the living room, and they too watched, motionless and speechless, as Father opened the front door and quietly headed out.

He hadn't had his morning coffee. Skipping coffee was really unlike him. Coffee was something he never left the house without.

"Dad, where are you going?" shouted Marcos.

"Be good. Doris will take care of you," Father murmured over his shoulder.

He opened the trunk of his car and placed in it his single piece of luggage. Then, without saying another word, he left us, not looking back.

Franco's shoulders drooped, and he looked at the ground. Alejandro stared at the car in disbelief, while Marcos, Veronica, Jonas, and I sobbed.

After his car disappeared, we went back inside. Silence filled the house once again, and we could still smell his Old Spice in the air. We stared at each other.

"I didn't hear him get up and get ready. I didn't hear anything," I finally said to my siblings.

We didn't go to school, just like the day Mother left. We spent the entire day staring blankly out the door, out the windows, hoping Father would come back. But he didn't. Later, still numbed by disbelief, I went into my parents' room to see if he was gone for real. I noticed how he'd taken all his best clothes.

I had been anxious about our well-being ever since Mother left, so Father leaving us now was no laughing matter. I told the other kids, "Let's not tell anyone we're alone, okay? It's the only way we may be able to stay together."

The kids were too upset and teary to listen.

"Guys, this is our house!" I told them. "This is the reason why we shouldn't tell anyone, because if we do, we might get separated! What if we never see each other again?"

Franco paced, walking almost in circles, while the others wept. My heart ached to see the kids sobbing yet again. We didn't know why Dad had left us so early in the morning, before anyone could get ready for school. I remember just sitting outside with the kids and losing track of time; then, later on, I made lunch.

Alejandro kept giving us hope. "Watch, he'll come back." His words seemed like a promise, so we kept watch, hoping Father's leaving was an illusion.

"I'm numb," said Franco eventually, laughing nervously.

Marcos loved talking to people, and it worried me he might tell someone. Veronica seemed horrified, which scared me even more. The rest of the kids were teary. Evening arrived quickly. The golden Puerto Rican sun settled down for the night, and our hearts settled into anguish.

"Okay, take your showers and go to bed," I finally ordered. "Veronica, Jonas, Marcos—kids, don't cry. Try to sleep. We have school tomorrow."

The following morning, I yelled out the usual, "Kids, time to get up and get ready for school!" I was touched to see them get up in the morning without making a fuss, but it had been a hard night for everyone, and we were all extremely sad. It was an awful, silent morning. The air of abandonment pervading the house was most unwelcome.

Usually, we were happy kids; usually, we amused ourselves making fun of each other, calling each other Caveman or Ape or Joyicentro, Micaela, Girly, Tarzan; even Father didn't mind being called King Kong. He'd play baseball with the kids sometimes. The kids looked forward to hanging out with him; he was their role model, and now this.

That morning, though, although it was adorned by a stunning blue morning sunrise, there were no jokes or giggles or funny name-calling. We shared vulnerability and uncertainty; we didn't know what would happen to us. We left the house together in silence. I wanted to believe it was a dream. Upon reaching the main road, I walked Jonas and Marcos to their bus stop.

"Hey, look at me," I told the boys. "Do *not* tell anyone

we're alone now. We're going to stay together, and I'm going to take care of you."

They nodded. I was proud of them. Josefina Leon Zayas High School was the farthest away of all our schools, so as usual, my bus arrived first. As I climbed aboard, I tried to contain my tears, but it was a struggle. When my friend and fellow athlete Mary said, "Doris, sit here," her voice seemed to come from far away. I felt like a magnet being pulled toward my siblings. I turned to look at Jonas and Marcos once more. I then glanced at Veronica and Alejandro and saw the shared look of vulnerability on their faces, which must have been on mine. Franco stared straight ahead but seemed defeated.

I watched them until my bus was so far away I couldn't see them any longer. I sat in silence, without answering Mary's "good morning."

My body was a mere shell, my heart left behind with my siblings.

"Doris, are you okay?" asked Mary.

"My brothers, Veronica . . ."

"What is it?"

Mary stared at me, no doubt wondering why I appeared paralyzed. My extremities were cold. The voices and laughter of other kids, and Mary calling my name, brought me back. I gave Mary a quick glance and said, "My siblings . . . oh, it's nothing."

I hugged my backpack; and every time the image of Father leaving popped up, it made me weak. Luckily, Mary didn't ask any more questions. She lived in a hectic home herself, and it was the best thing we had in common. Mary was a happy girl, though.

I thought again about Marcos, who was an absolute chatterbox; he'd talk to anyone, old or young. I kept wondering, *What if he can't help himself from telling people Mother left, and now Father has left us?* The way he held a devastated look on his face, and the silence, was unlike him; anyone could tell he was not okay. I felt awful about having to press him not to tell anyone. I thought about the kids sobbing, about this huge secret, and about my own fears.

Mary kept talking and sharing stories, even though I wasn't listening.

The entire day, I felt out of place. I feared for my siblings. What if something happened? What if Marcos couldn't stop himself from divulging the truth about Father leaving? What if I got home and found someone waiting to take us away? What if something happened to one of my siblings? What would I do?

Although it was a regular, hot summer day, I felt cold and extremely nervous. I jumped every time someone called my name. Other kids' voices and the classroom lectures echoed in my head without making any impression. Thank goodness for gym class; the physical activity of running set me free, making me feel strong.

Weeks later, Mother's letters began to appear. They seemed harmless. She was staying at Tato's house at 50 Vermont Street, in Brooklyn, New York. Mother wrote things like, "I'm trying my best to find a place large enough for us, hopefully soon."

When she was at home, aside from her normal grueling treatment, she'd taught us values, work ethics, and religion. Her letters revealed a different side of her. Her reminders and guidance made me feel invincible.

"I trust you'll all attend school and behave and go to church. We shall be together as soon as I find a new place."

Through our letters, we could sense each other at a distance. I sensed that she sensed in me a broken spirit, and I could feel that she was worried but couldn't do much for us. I didn't let her sense that I was horrified, that I feared someone might break into the house, that we were all alone. I didn't let her sense that I didn't miss her—for once my limbs were healing—and I could take care of the kids, or that I was relieved to be freed from her wrath.

Several days after Dad left, we were relieved to see Victor appear. He was our second eldest sibling and lived in La Carmelita in Ponce. Like most of the boys, he resembled Mother. He stood six foot two inches tall and had black, shiny hair and a fine, long nose. He also had Mother's onyx-black eyes. His cinnamon skin was dark, toasted from the sun. He worked twenty miles away from our house, and he'd drop by on days when he wasn't too rushed or tired.

"Hey, guys, where's Dad?"

"He left us," Marcos replied flatly.

"What did you just say? Are you serious?"

"Yes, it's true. Dad left us a few days ago," I answered.

"What . . . ? But it's impossible. Did he say anything?"

"He told me to take care of them."

Victor's face turned pale. He seemed as disconcerted as we had been when Dad left. "It's true," I insisted. "His room is empty. Go and see for yourself."

Victor walked toward my parents' room, stamping his boots as if they were full of cement. He took a quick look around and muttered, "*Ave María Santísima*. Dear Mother of God." He stared at us, scratching his head. "This is impossible. I don't understand this . . . it's just impossible. I knew about *Mother* leaving, but I wasn't ready for any more surprises." He frowned.

"Can we go stay with you?" I asked.

Victor's shoulders sagged, and it was almost unbearable to see him experience the absence of Mother, Dad, and our three little siblings. Once again, we were all lined up;

113

staring at him, just like we'd stared at Mother, then Father. We were all in agony, trembling. Marcos and Jonas began sobbing again; my body felt frozen.

We deserved some good news, I thought. The kids' faces, as they hoped for Victor's rescue, looked like souls awaiting their turn for heaven. I wondered again how a seven- or eight-year-old would be able to resist the temptation to tell his schoolteacher or his friends, *Mommy and Daddy left us, and we are all alone.*

Hopeless, we continued to stare at Victor. He walked in circles and pulled his hair backward, and finally said, "Listen, I'm sorry, guys. You know my house is small—you are too many, and I can't take you." His "you are too many" pierced my heart. My knees felt like they couldn't hold my body up much longer. Containing my tears, I kept staring at him, hoping he would change his mind.

"We can sleep on the floor!" Alejandro volunteered. Victor remained silent, while my heart pleaded, *Please don't leave us.* I couldn't keep from trembling. We were all afraid; Victor was our last hope.

"Guys, I can't," Victor said, smiling nervously, sweat rolling down his face.

"I can't take you, but I'll stop by as much as I can and check on you, I promise. I have to leave now." Before leaving, he repeated, "Remember, I promise, I'll stop by tomorrow, and as many days as I can."

I embraced Marcos, and we watched hopelessly as Victor left. Silence and sadness filled the house when he was gone, paired yet again with a cold air of abandonment. Things were more uncertain than ever, and it hurt me to hear our brother say flat out that we were "too many."

That evening I went to bed with a heavy heart, my limbs cold and numb.

Victor visited us as much as he could, just as he promised. Acting as our parents, he and his wife, Mora, claimed financial assistance for us. Victor made an arrangement with a small neighborhood store, Juana's, to provide us with food. The store didn't have much; it only sold essential canned grocery items and stale bread. He'd sign the monthly assistance check, and we'd go to the store and pick out our groceries for the month. I had asked him for stamps so I could continue writing to Mother. "Dori, don't tell Mother about Dad leaving, and don't waste the stamps."

"Victor, that's not fair. Mother deserves the truth!" I said firmly.

"What are you *saying,* Dori?" Victor yelled. "Mother is thousands of miles away. She'll be upset, and there's nothing she can do. Just tell her everything is fine—don't you dare tell her about Father, is that clear?"

I answered with a vague "okay" but planned to tell her, regardless.

When Victor visited, he'd tell us, "You guys get along, and boys, I don't want to hear you've been fighting or hitting the girls, you hear me? Doris, how's Mother doing, did she write?"

"Yes, she said they're doing well and Raquel was sick but she's better now," I said.

"Raquel is sick? Huh, sounds strange," Victor reflected. "Well, hopefully she's better and it's nothing serious—and Mother may have plans for you guys to move soon."

I didn't wait long, though, to tell Mother the truth, against Victor's wishes: Father was gone. I didn't tell Victor I had written to Mother, *Father left us just days after you did. He told me to take care of the kids and didn't come back.*

Trying to run things for the entire household was like

reciting a litany. Just getting home from school every day was overwhelming. I had to make sure the kids changed out of their school uniforms before they went off to play—barefoot, of course. I taught them to hang up their socks so they wouldn't need to go crazy in the mornings looking for them. I'd make supper; then the dusty cement floors needed to be swept; the dishes had piled up; the shutters needed to be closed. It was laborious, and I got no help.

"Hey, kids, you know what Victor told you!" I'd yell at them. "He warned you about not misbehaving. I'll tell Mother you don't do anything, you lazy bums."

I'd threaten the kids, but whenever Veronica said no, it was no. She didn't care for my threats to tell Mother. Between the threats and the dirty looks and the fighting, I realized we were never going to make it.

I wrote to Mother and complained that the boys didn't listen and how they'd broken the TV playing their rough games. Mother's replies were enlightening—she wrote, "I trust you. Be strong and don't let them govern you. Tell them I said to behave."

Mother's suggestion about their behavior worked a little, but the household demands still overwhelmed me. Desperate, I wrote to Naomi and poured out all my agonies and sorrows.

"Mother moved to look for a new place for us to live, but Father left us, and I don't know what's going to happen!"

Naomi showed up a week later with Diego. "Can we go home with you?" I asked.

"Are you kids going to school?" Diego asked.

"Yes, we are, but we can go to school in Arecibo," Franco suggested.

Diego held his silence for a moment, looking away, clenching his fists; then he admitted, "I'm truly sorry, but there are too many of you; we don't have the space."

116

I felt weak. Once again, we stared in cowed disbelief: just like we stared at Mother, then Father, then Victor. It was hard to believe this was real. I didn't have the strength to watch someone leave us yet again. Diego stalked through the house and vented to my sister, "How could anyone do this? This is craziness! Listen, kids, I can't take all six of you, but I can take two. You're still too many, but at least the burden will be less for Doris. I'll take Veronica and Alejandro for a few months, and I'll enroll them in school in Arecibo, all right?"

It had to be. I packed a sack of clothes for each one. "Doris, you're a good girl," Diego told me. "Keep writing, and let us know how things are going."

Unable to speak, I just nodded. Now, we all loved Diego, and aside from Mama Blas and Tato, we had never felt so loved by anyone. Still, it was chilling to see Alejandro and Veronica climb into Diego's truck, while pleading with our eyes, *Please don't leave us—Lord, please make him change his mind!*

An echo of the previous three times our loved ones had driven away, four of us stayed outside until we couldn't see or hear Diego's truck anymore. The cruel air of abandonment settled over us yet again as the night approached, as we all trembled, and Marcos and Jonas sobbed.

"Guys, I'll take care of you. Don't worry, I promise," I said. I made them such a promise under an unforgettable red Puerto Rican sunset—a red sunset that made us all dream and hope and pray to Jesus for a miracle.

"You know what, guys? We're going to make it!" affirmed Franco, the great optimist.

"Really?" asked Marcos.

"Sure we are—you'll see. We'll have new shoes and live in a new house even. Someday, you'll see. We're going to be okay. No one is going to separate us. Let anyone try!"

Franco's tone became angry, and he snapped, "I'll be right back."

He took off in the direction of the mango tree. Seconds later, he returned with Mama Blas's old machete.

"Let anyone *try* to come onto our property and take you away, just let anyone try! I'll take the machete to them!" he declared. Then he sat on a boulder in front of the house and spent a long time sharpening the machete, until its blade shone like white gold against the red sun. He paused to wipe sweat from his forehead, and then said, "There, guys. Let's see what happens to anyone who tries to remove any of you from our home."

Franco kept the sharpened, shiny machete handy every afternoon. The boys became his little babies; he kept them under control. Just like Father, Franco refused to let them cry and calmed them down when they wanted to.

We loved and cared for each other. We shared our dreams of a perfect home, and being okay, and staying together.

As the only girl still at home, I was too ashamed to tell anyone about the things I needed. Victor's wife never asked me. In particular, I was ashamed to tell Victor that I needed feminine hygiene pads, so I'd pick through the garbage at school to find them. Sometimes I'd spend an entire weekend with the same pad if I didn't find one to change to. The pain and my body odor were unbearable, but I was young and naive and resigned myself to enduring our scarcity for the sake of my brothers, for the sake of staying together—even if it cost me my life.

The toughest thing to endure was arriving home from school tired and hungry. In my mind, I could still hear the faint yelling and threats from Mom, Father calling us names, and Mama Blas's careful steps as she counted her prayers. They were gone, but the house preserved their presence somehow. In the meantime, termites and bats took over the place.

Our uninvited guests were disgusting. On several nights, we were awakened by flapping noises. When I turned on the lights, we'd have bats flying over our heads. It was the most disgusting thing I've ever seen. They were pitch black and reminded us of the Dracula movies. The more we tried to chase them out of the house with the broom, the more screeching noises they made. Then what little furniture we had, began to be consumed by termites, and life was just . . . interesting. In the end, all we could do was laugh—laugh at the fact the house was falling apart, and laugh at how we kept the radio on to mask our parents' absence. Good thing the neighborhood knew we were a big family, which often enough caused my parents not to accompany us to church or school events. It was important for us to stay together, following our upbringing, working hard together, going to school every day and walking to church Sunday after Sunday. It was our salvation and the key to avoiding suspicion.

10. The Abandonment

Oh, unforgettable memories, how much I treasure
you!
—The author

I was in tenth grade and was saddened to learn that one of my classmates, Paolo, had been withdrawn from school by his parents. The teachers had tried to dissuade them, but it was legal, and his parents argued that he was needed for farm work. Paolo was one of my running friends. He was old-fashioned and ran in his own cut Bermuda shorts, refusing to wear the team's uniform, but he was a good soul. I loved him. He gave me some French perfume on the last day he attended school, and I saw him only once afterward. I treasured the perfume, and even Franco thought it was a nice gift.

Surprisingly, I found tenth grade easier than ninth. I had better grades and liked the new atmosphere. I still dreaded bullying and didn't know what I'd do if I were called "Freckle Face" again. But I was still popular. I met new friends—and along with them my new running rival, and former bully, Marta. She always wore nice, brand-new running clothes and shoes. I felt bad for Marta, though, as her membership on the team depended on her mother's pressure to win.

"If Doris beats you one more time, you're off the team!" Marta's mother once yelled in my presence. Until then, Marta had been laughing about my bare feet and my threadbare running uniform, saying, "Look at this Jíbara, running barefoot! Ha ha, look at her, she runs wearing a worn-out uniform!"

I'd stare at her while enduring her whipping, hurtful remarks, peering at her new clothes. I'd feel small as I looked down at my dusty feet. But poor Marta couldn't beat me. I pitied her on the day her mother escorted Marta away from the track for good. She left in shame and stopped mocking me afterward. At that moment I learned that money wasn't everything.

During the abandonment, we were grateful for everything we had . . . and grateful for nothing. Poverty was our faithful companion. We held poverty like we held babies, close to our hearts—in acceptance, with no hard feelings. It filled our space with nothing, and the air of abandonment crowned us with uncertainty. It mocked us and weighed us down, consuming our energy from the need to keep going to school and church. I'd listen to my siblings cry out things like, "These pants don't fit; I don't want to go to church!"

My heart shared their pain but didn't take no for an answer. Giving up was not an option. Asking for more was something we just couldn't do. It was a sign of weakness, and it raised suspicion.

The house decayed, and the linoleum deteriorated. The roof developed new leaks every time it rained. The little food we had was being spoiled by mice. We'd put away most of our food items in the tiny refrigerator, except for the canned goods. Breakfast didn't go beyond occasional coffee and bread. Fortunately, our schools served generous meals, which was gratifying. The boys were obedient; they adapted. On the days on which dinner consisted only of white rice and boiled green bananas, they ate without complaining. Letting them wander into the woods served its purpose; there they ate fruit and sometimes found chicken eggs. Finding eggs was like striking gold. I'd remind them to make sure they ate breakfast and lunch at school.

It was a good thing the boys loved to eat—and it was also a good thing Diego had taken Alejandro and Veronica for a while. Veronica was still a fussy eater, plus she was the most stubborn child I knew. I was happy she stayed with Diego and Naomi, then moved on to Victor. When she was with us at the house, she was often sad. Thank God for Blas's teachings about dignity and poverty.

"To be poor is to live with fewer means. You must learn how to do more with less. It's not about how little you have; your heart, morals, and character are what define you as a person. Work hard, be strong; your dignity no one can touch."

There was nothing to welcome us home from school but the joyous songs of birds—and the old, ancient house. It welcomed us like a mother, with open arms. Its location alone, nestled amid the flowers and lush vegetation, made us feel happy. The boys and I began to look forward to our afternoon chats.

"How fast did you run today, Dori?" Franco would ask.

Laughing, I'd reply, "Faster than last time. The other students practice on the weekends. I don't have such luxury."

The boys sat at the table while I cooked, talking. After

supper, I'd let them play for a little while, then make sure they took their showers before seven; we didn't have any hot water, and after seven, the water got really cold.

Luckily, they were pretty healthy; they'd rarely complain about headaches or not feeling well. If they did, I'd ask them to go to bed so they could get better.

In the mornings, we were considerate of each other, using the bathroom as fast as we could so each of us had a fair amount of time to wash up and get ready for school. We left the house together in harmony. The reminder of "don't tell anyone we are alone" was my daily prayer. We were aware of how important it was to follow Blas's teachings about work, dignity, and character.

In the evenings, while my brothers built wooden cars, I'd write about whatever inspired me. Other times, I'd reply to letters from Mother or Naomi, or I'd write to Tato.

Franco became caring and enthusiastic. He did well in school; all the boys did. My shyness didn't wane, though. The embarrassment of wearing the same old school uniform day after day, along with my broken shoes, was difficult for me sometimes. Running was the highlight of my days. It made me popular, but I avoided attention otherwise.

Living without parents under extreme poverty was especially painful on Sundays, as it was a family day. On our way home from church, we wished we had our own family to return to, but we had to keep our secret.

Diego and Naomi brought Alejandro back after a couple of months. My sister had a second baby, though, so she kept Veronica for help. Caring for Marcos, Jonas, Alejandro, and Franco was dismaying, and there were times I doubted I could go on. Being invited to special events at school took a painful toll on me. I declined the invitations, because I didn't have any good clothes to wear; I'd rather stay home than be embarrassed. I managed to remain an athlete, though, and practiced for as long as I could after the last class period.

Over a year had passed when Victor asked, "When is Mother planning to take you guys?"

"I don't know," I replied. "She said soon."

"Sure, she *keeps* saying soon. Which is craziness; pretty *soon,* people are going to start talking. Dad's friends in Ponce keep asking for him, and I don't know what to say anymore."

Victor's comments made me nervous, because he seemed so angry at Mother; so I changed the subject. "Victor, the boys need haircuts, and they're complaining about needing clothes." I hated to ask, but it was obvious the boys were looking like girls.

"We'll see what happens. I don't have money for clothes or haircuts. There isn't money for everything you need, Doris. I mean, look at how you're living. I can't believe this."

It hurt me to listen to Victor's remarks; it made me feel we were an inconvenience to him. I wished we didn't have to depend on anyone. This reminded me of Mother's venting against her sister; it made me feel that if I could, I'd take care of the boys without bothering anyone. I learned not to share too much with Victor. As long as the kids were happy and okay, it was better not to bother him.

Any time the school sent a letter about upcoming parent–teacher meetings, I wrote back a brief note about not being able to attend because of child care and work— Mother's old excuse. I repeated it over and over. It felt wrong to lie, though later, I was glad I had. The boys got to participate in field trips and learn new things, but I was still preoccupied that if the school learned the truth, we might be taken away, and I might never see my siblings again.

On Saturdays, I did the laundry by hand, which took hours. We had a square cement box, a *pileta,* with a washing board attached. It held enough water to wash an extra-large load of clothes. Oftentimes, the palms of my hands bled from all the scouring I had to do. I'd get pains around my waistline from standing so long in the same position. By the time I finished, water dripped down to my feet. Washing clothes outside made my hands cold and wrinkled. Cooking made them achy.

During summer vacation, I planned an occasional day of fun and hurried through my chores so we could go to the river. Oh, those were glorious days! We'd walk a mile downhill, passing fruit and coffee trees. The little birds would sing around us. Once at the river, the kids would jump in the water immediately. Watching them swim and play made me happy. We shared laughs as the gentle breeze filtered through the trees; the river felt like a precious sanctuary. Our days of fun were brilliant in every sense.

After swimming for a couple of hours, we'd hike up the river, which was so much fun. Some parts were steep, with large rocks that were challenging to climb. I'd let Jonas and Marcos lead so I could watch them.

"Be careful!" I'd yell.

A swirl in one of the pools intrigued us. The water moved in a big circle. We didn't like the serene movement; it was mysterious. The thickness of the vegetation made our path look a lot darker. Carrying no watches or radio, we knew when it was time to go back by the way the sun settled.

"Let's go, it's going to get dark soon," I'd say.

During our walks back home, I collected flowers and small rocks in bright reds and vibrant tones. The boys collected rocks with sharp edges and whatever seemed to be an artifact. They were fascinated by starting a fire with rocks, and they were on the hunt for perfect, sharp-edged specimens. They believed these artifacts had been left by our ancestors—and perhaps they were right. We realized if our ancestors made something, so could we; if they had no running water or electricity, then we had it easy.

Our hike back home seemed never-ending, because by then we were tired and hungry, but we had strong legs and kept moving. I'd keep saying, "Hurry up, it's getting dark."

Marcos tended to stay behind, exploring. One evening he called, "Wait, I dropped something!"

"Come *on*, Marcos, we don't have all day," I replied.

"Guys, if you don't wait for me, I'm going to scream!"

"Go ahead, Marcos, scream all you want. You'll be taken away, not us," retorted Alejandro.

He sprinted and caught up. "Wow, Marcos, you can run!" I teased. "Guys, did you see him?"

Marcos chuckled. "I like to run!"

"What an athlete! Now, keep moving, we have to get home before dusk."

Alejandro began to tease Marcos, "So, Micaela likes to run. Ha, ha!"

Marcos shouted, "I'm going to get you, girly!"

They kept bickering back and forth almost until we made it home. "Okay, admit it, you guys are apes," Jonas said. I laughed so hard my stomach hurt.

"Hey, listen, I hear a car!" said Franco suddenly.

"You lie," Marcos answered.

"I think it may be Victor waiting for us," said Franco.

The bickering stopped, and suddenly Franco began running toward home. We laughed and all began running.

With home in sight, though, we would approach as slowly and cautiously as cats on the prowl. After entering our empty house and feeling safe, I'd catch my breath and pick up the laundry, make the beds and separate regular clothes from our school uniforms to iron another time. The boys spent hours analyzing and admiring their rocks and artifacts. Then I'd cook supper, and later on, during our daily outdoor chat around six in the evening, we'd tell each other about how someday things would be better, and we'd be exemplary men and women. Our never-ending inspiration was our religion.

Soon, I no longer blamed our parents for the abandonment. We loved our parents enough to forgive. Our second mother was the Church, where week by week we were uplifted by the readings and the spiritual healing offered by the Gospel.

Once, Franco got to participate in a weekend retreat for men, and I was proud of him.

On Sundays, making our way back home from church in the early afternoon, we'd walk by various restaurants. One was a *lechonera,* specializing in pig roasts, and the smell was quite succulent. We also passed by some of my classmates' houses—such as the Maldonados, who had seven children. Once, upon hearing our footsteps, they'd lined up across their balcony, smiling and waving at us. They all looked alike, with their straight black hair, high cheekbones, and caramel skin.

Across from the Maldonados,' at the bottom of the hill, was Doña Belen's house. We'd slow down, curious, waiting to see her face peek out a window. People still accused Belén of witchcraft. A very few times, she'd come out of nowhere and never say a word but stare straight into our eyes. We'd smile at her as a sign of respect. She always wore a long black skirt with a black blouse and covered her head with a black bandana. She was petite and had abysmal eyes.

Marcos would make me laugh hysterically when he whispered, "Don't look at her, she's a witch!"

"Marcos, if she were really a witch, she'd be riding a broom—but I bet she knows what you just said. I bet she knows Mama Blas isn't home anymore, and I bet you she knows we're alone! Now she's going to follow us."

Marcos began to shake uncontrollably and hung on to my forearm, praying Hail Marys. I laughed so hard I could barely walk.

"Boo, she's going to get you, all of you!" Franco and Jonas repeated. Alejandro laughed, too, and walked ahead of us.

"Stop it!" Marcos cried. The way Marcos kept looking back, and his look of distrust, was priceless; he held his breath, eyes wide open, staring in dread. Even though he was young and innocent, he was superstitious, just like Mama Blas.

Marcos and Jonas became afraid every time we walked by Belén's house, and so we walked as fast as possible.

As we passed the different houses, we were elated by the exquisite cooking smells emanating from them. By the time we got home, we were starved. Once home, Franco kept Blas's machete handy. We had no other luxury than cooking rice and beans with corned beef, seasoned with our own oregano and garlic. Sometimes we'd kill our own chickens for the meat. I stir-fried yellow plantains and picked a couple of avocados when they were in season. The aromas were soothing enough, making us forget about the aromas from all those homes and the restaurant. We sat and ate our delightful meals in simplicity.

Sometimes we sat down together to pass Mother's most recent letter around, and then we'd talk about it. We learned after Father had left us that he'd joined Mother in Massachusetts. She had shared through her letters that her home search in Brooklyn proved unsuccessful, so Massachusetts was the final destination. Mother wrote saying how sorry she was Father had abandoned us and how she'd never forgive him. We wondered what it was like living there; and she told us about the colorful foliage during the fall and the cold winter days. In her letters, she'd say things like, "Did you receive the package I sent you? It wasn't much, but I hope you like it."

I was excited to read about a package she sent us, but weeks went by, and we never received anything. I'd assumed she'd forgotten, or maybe she couldn't afford to send it, so I didn't ask after my response. "Don't worry. We're doing okay."

Mother's replies always concluded with an "I trust you." Yet, in her writings, I could sense her extreme worry and restlessness. Reading her letters, I could almost see Mother's sad eyes and feel her pain. Some of her letters were shorter than others, as if saying, *tell me the truth*. I kept myself from telling her I needed things, remembering what Victor had said: "Why worry her? She's thousands of miles away, and there's nothing she can do."

I decided we just had to do our best until we were all reunited again.

I often thought about Mother, wishing on one level she was home . . . but then, on another level, glad she wasn't. I felt her leaving us behind had saved us, actually. The beatings had become too frequent when she was home; I had been distracted in school, I was constantly hiding swollen limbs, and my self-esteem had deteriorated from being a social butterfly to one who was extremely shy.

During one of our afternoon chats, the boys made fun of Father, calling him a *jíbaro* in the United States, a lowly

Puerto Rican claiming he spoke English.

"Dad has more body hair than King Kong," Jonas said.

"If he didn't have blue eyes, he'd be in captivity," said Alejandro.

"You're crazy. If Dad ever hears you . . ." I protested.

"So, what's *your* name?" said Alejandro.

"Merrrcado," said Jonas, drawing it out.

"What about a nickname?" Alejandro asked.

"Caveman!" Marcos shouted.

"And where are you from?" asked Alejandro. "I am *jíbaro* born in Ponce, but now I live in Massachusetts," he answered himself.

During the holidays, we especially missed being part of a family; we wanted someone to go to, to visit with. Aside from Victor, and occasionally Naomi and Diego, no one ever visited us. Lorena lived the farthest away and had given birth to her second child by then, and she didn't drive. Our Aunt Honora knew Mother was gone, but she never came to see how we were doing.

Some days I assisted the kids with homework, other times Franco did homework with them. On other occasions, I'd write. Writing became a pure, honest talk between the pencil and my soul. Other evenings, the boys kept busy building wooden cars and racing each other. We didn't need TV; their noise and fights were entertaining and distracting enough.

"Be careful, you guys, you are going too fast!" I'd say. "Stop, you're stirring up too much dust, it's not funny!"

Thankfully, the injuries they incurred didn't go beyond scraped limbs. We enjoyed Christmas; even though we were alone, it remained our favorite season. However, the first day of school after the holidays was our least favorite.

"Hey, Doris, look what I got for Three Kings Day," Aby once told me. "What did you get?"

"Mother only gave a little something to my younger siblings. We are too many."

To the younger boys, I'd say, "Hey, seal your ears and don't listen to the Three Kings Day stories, okay?"

I hated to see them feel left out. I could tell they waited long beyond Three Kings Day to get their gifts, always anticipating, hoping, and waiting—until our entire Christmas season was over, and they gave up the idea of getting any gifts.

In 1983, at seventeen years of age, I was a high school senior. I felt older, wiser, and more confident than I ever had before. I felt proud we were doing so well in school, despite our poverty. Clothes were always an issue, though. Jonas and Marcos in particular fought back and forth over what little we had. "I don't have any socks. Hey, you take those off, they're mine!" or "I'm not going anywhere, we don't have anything to wear!"

By eleventh grade, I'd started losing track races to another rival, Damaris. I didn't have running clothes; we were given just one uniform to participate in major events, and I couldn't wear it every time. So I cut down an old pair of heavy nylon jogging pants, and over time, the inseam began to cut into my right inner thigh. The pain led me to slow down and lose races. For weeks after, I'd limp. The injury just got worse over time. I knew I needed medical attention but wouldn't risk the boys getting taken away.

Eventually, the leg wound led me to withdraw from running practice and competitions. I got tired quickly and couldn't run as fast as I used to. My leg throbbed so badly I could barely sleep at night. I concealed my pain, though, and prayed it would heal. In the meantime, I competed in other sports: shot put, the javelin, and the discus.

My friend Mary won first place in shot put and javelin. I won first place in the discus. Soon I returned to the track:

still unhealed, scared, and agonizing. No matter how hard I tried, I couldn't do well as I'd done before. I was terribly worried about the wound not healing, and I don't know how I resisted the temptation not to go to the hospital and risk anyone finding out my parents weren't home.

Instead, I found a bottle of Mama Blas's old oil and used it on my wound. I had no idea what the mixture was, except it smelled incredibly strong. It burned so badly every time I applied it that I almost saw stars. There I was, back to silent suffering, back to my dark world of pain. But I healed eventually, miraculously.

Mother gave me strength by responding positively to my letters and concerns. Reading her letters, I could feel her energy and power coming through. The miles separating us didn't matter. She was still my mother, my influence, my blood.

I'd write to her and complain about how we felt uncomfortable about going to church in our old clothes. "As soon as we go into church, people's heads start turning, and they stare at us from head to toe and whisper. The boys dread going to church. It's so different from going to church with you. People stared then, but there was silence."

Mother wrote back, "Church is between you and God, not about how others look at what you wear. You do what you are supposed to do, and keep your chin up. You are no less, and they are no better."

Then, during my senior year, Mother wrote, saying, "Get ready to move."

I was shocked. I answered, "Mother, I want to graduate from high school, so I don't think it's a good idea for us to leave school and move now."

In her next letter, she said, "You could go to school here, but if you really want to graduate there, it's fine."

I was confused once again when she wrote, "Have you

received the packages? I wasn't too sure about your sizes, but I think they will fit."

Once again, we checked the mail every day, but nothing came in.

"Is someone taking our mail?" Alejandro asked suspiciously.

"I really don't know," I answered. We checked the mail faithfully every day, but nothing ever came except her letters.

During my senior year, one afternoon, while in class, the school principal entered my classroom.

"I'd like to see Doris Mercado Torres," he said to the teacher. My teacher looked at me; nodding, I raised my hand.

"Doris, please come with me to my office," said the principal.

Every head in the classroom turned my way. I went pale, wishing for one second my name was *not* Doris Mercado Torres. It seemed I lacked strength to rise from my desk. I thought about my siblings. Containing my tears, I thought, *Oh, my God, is this it?*

I could barely keep up with the principal as he strode confidently back to his office. My heart pounded harder than my steps. When we got there, he said, "Doris, have a seat."

There were two gentlemen in his office, wearing dark suits.

"Gentlemen, this is Doris Mercado Torres," he told them proudly.

They smiled at me, and one of them said, "Miss Mercado Torres, we're here on behalf of the University of Puerto Rico."

I just stared, wondering what was going on.

"Doris, based on your athletic performance, we're

here to award you a full scholarship to the university. Congratulations! We hope you accept and continue your education at the University of Puerto Rico."

They had the whitest teeth and smiled with such happy faces, as if they were speaking with someone important.

"Thank you," I choked out, half-smiling. "I . . . I have to discuss this with my parents."

They gave me some documents, and both men shook my hand. I was relieved this wasn't about my secret and had nothing to do about the fear that my brothers and sister would be taken away. Giving them a bigger smile, I said, "I'm very happy."

"A great future awaits you, Miss Mercado Torres! Tell your parents, and come and visit the campus. If you need transportation, just call, and it will be arranged."

I left the principal's office hugging the documents they gave me. I couldn't stop smiling. But then I thought, *Mother . . . she said we were leaving.* Should I accept the scholarship and go on with my life, or should I obey Mother?

For the final competition at the end of my senior year, I managed to participate in the 400 meter relays and discus, winning first place in both events.

§ § §

A few weeks before the school year was over, in spring 1984, both Marcos and Jonas brought home letters from school saying they had head lice—and wouldn't be allowed back in school until they were cleared of it. I didn't know what to do; we all panicked.

"Don't use the hairbrush!" I said to Jonas and Marcos.

Shortly after, Victor stopped by for a visit.

"Jonas and Marcos have head lice," I told him. "The

school sent letters, and they can't go back to school until it's cleared up!"

"Great," said Victor. "I'll go to the pharmacy and get some lice treatment. I'll come back later on, okay? Don't share the hairbrush for now."

I felt bad because he looked so tired. Victor lived a good fifteen miles away, but the same evening, he returned with his wife, Mora. Now, Mora didn't seem to care much about us and never asked me if we were okay or if I needed anything—but she gave the boys the lice treatment. Victor told me to check them again every afternoon to make sure they were clear.

"Hey, boys, remember to stay away from us—you have some disgusting beasts living on your heads!" Alejandro teased them. Victor pressed his lips together but laughed out loud. Marcos tried to laugh but cried instead.

We all used the treatment faithfully, and I told the boys not to tell anyone.

11. Graduation

By my senior year, taking care of my siblings for so long had taught me a thing or two about running a home. Reminding the kids to keep our secret was like a daily prayer, and it kept us in harmony. Our harmony compensated us with a pleasant atmosphere, and our environment, although impoverished, was filled with goodness. The hitting was a thing of the past.

Caring for the kids made me feel I wanted to save even more children. I learned that, when given a chance, children are the most amazing, adaptable creatures imaginable. They hold the meaning of life and hope and goodness in their hearts.

Day after day, we walked into an empty, dusty, aged home, and at times we felt small and meek, with little connection with the outside world—but we had each other. We might complain, "We don't have any clothes," or "I don't want to go to church with broken shoes, people are always staring," but it was our way of venting.

I didn't know what to say to my siblings when they

said these things; but in my heart, I shared their pain as I listened to their complaints.

I couldn't let any of my friends or classmates visit. I couldn't risk the possibility of news spreading about a bunch of kids living alone or let anyone know our two youngest, Jonas and Marcos, got home before me and wandered through the woods until I arrived. I had instructed them to change out of their uniforms and play in the woods quietly until I made it home. They knew that when it rained, they could wait inside the house and lock the doors. As a matter of fact, there was no such thing as house keys. Every morning I'd have one of the kids lock the front door and emerge from one of the windows.

Every afternoon after practice, I felt like a caged lion waiting for my bus. I wished I could sprint the ten-mile distance from school straight home to my brothers. Every afternoon, I wished someone we knew would drive by and give me a ride home—someone like my godparents, or any of Mother's customers—but it never happened. Miss Serra was the only person who drove by, but I couldn't ask her. She was my teacher. We kept too many secrets, but it was necessary. It was our reality.

"Don't talk to strangers. Don't come out of the woods until one of us gets home from school. If anyone sees you and asks, say Mother is on her way, but don't let anyone in the house. Most importantly, don't give anyone any explanations or excuses. You know how much Mama Blas hated excuses."

Sometimes I sprinted home once I got off the bus; sometimes I walked with other kids. I had to balance my behavior and resist the temptation to run every day. Sometimes the boys heard my voice and came out of the woods when they did, but my classmates weren't suspicious. Many kids played in the woods, especially boys.

The Armor of Love and Hope

Despite that we were poor and wore old uniforms, the boys were popular. They were friendly, yet another trait which worked in our favor; they'd always say hi to everyone and were respectful when they talked with neighbors and other kids. They knew how to have fun, too; it was rare for them to emerge from the woods empty-handed. Usually they had pockets full of fruit or sharp-edged rocks. According to the season, they might pick passion fruit, avocados, raspberries, oranges, or bananas. Other times, they simply played and explored the woods. They always had something to do; aside from longing for a family or wishing for Christmas gifts, they were happy kids.

It was our duty to extend kindness to our neighbors and reply in kind to their warm hellos. Marcos especially loved our neighbor Don Antonio Franceschini. He was in his sixties and of Italian descent. Jonas and Marcos often walked down to chat with Don Franceschini, and he shared many stories with the boys. His property extended a good forty acres; he was a widower and quite loving to all of us.

Whenever we were home, especially during weekends and summer vacation, the boys' inexhaustible noises while playing helped camouflage the emptiness of the house. I'd turn the radio on medium volume to enhance presence. We used body language to communicate as well as our voices. Upon hearing someone's steps approaching, one glance toward the direction of the person's approach was sufficient, and all the kids would be on the lookout. We wanted to stay together—we were all wounded in the heart, alike—and we had to continue the concealment, for the sake of staying together.

One day, Ms. Serra taught the class a lesson about living in poverty. "It doesn't matter how old your clothes are or how many times you've worn them. As long as they're clean and neatly pressed, your clothes are as good as mine or anyone else's."

I blushed as I looked Ms. Serra straight in the eye. I tried to read her. I was afraid she knew something; yet her words caused a huge weight to lift from my shoulders. Her lecture was a treasure that gifted me with a little self-esteem. I took her lecture home with pride, and afterward, I pressed our threadbare uniforms with a little more enthusiasm.

Graduation time approached. My friends purchased caps and gowns and had their senior pictures taken. My senior picture was taken, too, but I didn't have eleven dollars to buy the package. I wrote a letter to Naomi explaining I wanted to attend graduation but didn't have the things I needed. She showed up the next weekend with Diego, bringing me a pink dress and white shoes. She apologized for not visiting us; she'd just had a baby, after a difficult pregnancy.

I wanted to request enough money to buy my senior pictures, but I thought their gesture was generous enough and that asking for more would be rude.

Diego was kind, as always, and continued to believe in us. I showed them my scholarship papers; Diego scanned my papers quietly, then nodded and mumbled to my sister. He then said, "Doris, you are a conqueror!" He looked me in the eye and pronounced, "You've done well."

Luckily, a summer jobs program had recently been introduced at our school, and I was given a summer job between my junior and senior years, part-time. I worked during the weekends cleaning classrooms with other students; we had a blast! After our assignment was complete, I received a check for $121. I bought fabric, T-straps, and other things I needed for a prom gown I had designed. The same week, I decided to go to Aunt Honora's house and ask her if she would make my dress.

Honora was a respectable seamstress in Hacienda La Carmelita. The best part was that our beloved Mama Blas lived with Honora. I made sure the boys looked extra shiny and pressed their Sunday outfits, and out we went. The ten-mile walk from La Pica to church, then to Hacienda La Carmelita, felt like a penance. The sun was hot and fried us without mercy.

Aunt Honora gave us no more than half a smile when we arrived, but we treated her with love and respect. And we finally got to see our heroine, Blas, each of us giving her the longest, warmest hug. Oh, such a distinctive scent of sage and amber! I kissed her face over and over. For her part, she was joyous as a little baby.

"Doris, you're good! Do well, and make your mother happy," she told me. I held on to her warm hands tightly; I wished I could fit right inside her heart and stay there.

Aunt Honora took my measurements; she seemed pleased with my design and was surprised at the materials. She gave me a pickup date, and I was happy and grateful. Then Aunt Honora gave us a tasteless meal of rice and beans. Even at seventeen years of age, I could make better rice and beans—which the boys raved about, as a matter of fact. But we ate in gratitude. While we ate, though, I became tense under Aunt Honora's calculating stare.

"You know," she finally said, "there are rumors about a young girl near here who takes care of a bunch of kids all on her own. People are talking."

Honora's tone was negative. I couldn't keep my hands from shaking. I smiled at her nervously as a sign of respect, without answering. My aunt had no problem denigrating me but never bothered to ask how we were doing or if we needed anything. I was grateful she would make my prom dress, at least. I gave the boys a single pointed glance, and they got moving.

As I stood up, I said, "Mama, we have to get going." Mama didn't answer; her head was down. I called out loud, "Mama!"

Our sweet Mama Blas had fallen asleep, and I was glad she probably hadn't heard Honora's nauseating comments. As we left, Blas gave us the most loving hugs and blessings; her little round face lit up in an innocent smile. The second we walked out of Honora's presence, we felt lighter. We left content, and our discussions on the way back about our visit helped us rid ourselves of Honora's negativity.

I felt danger when I was around her. I dreaded going back, but Blas's presence made it worth it. The long walk back home made us nervous. We tried to hurry, hoping to beat dusk, but it wasn't possible. We watched as the sun turned orange, then dark gold. Soon, we were walking in near-darkness, and I was scared. We were a good three miles from home when we heard men approaching on horses.

"Let's hide," I told the others.

We slid behind big trees along the roadside and watched the five horsemen parade by. The horses' huffing and puffing made me feel like I was in a horror movie. We watched the men but didn't recognize any of their faces. Four of them wore white hats; the fifth didn't wear a hat *or* shoes. He had long, straight black hair and dark coppery skin. He rode a younger horse and, clicking his tongue, shouted, "Dale, Valentina!"

The horsemen talked loudly among themselves. Their sleeves were folded up, revealing muscular arms, and each man held onto the reins with a single hand. The marching of the horses was extremely loud and powerful and intimidating. After they passed, we emerged from the woods, listening to the hoof beats far ahead.

We continued home, paying close attention to our surroundings. The noise of the horses eventually faded. Fearfully, I asked Franco, "Where did they go?"

Laughing, he said, "Maybe they turned down a dirt road."

I was nervous; walking home this far felt like crossing the world from one end to the other. "Hey, guys," I suggested, "next time we go to Aunt Honora's house, we should leave early in the morning, so we can get back before dusk."

When the time came to return to Honora's house, we left the house early, as agreed. When we showed up at her place, Aunt Honora said, "Let's see."

I followed her back to her sewing room. She had tons of fabrics in different colors and textures and an old Singer in the middle of the room just like Mother's. My dress was hanging on a rusty nail on a white hanger on the wall. It was gorgeous.

Awkwardly, the school required all girls to wear white on their prom day. My dress was long, with a round neck, long sleeves, and a skirt consisting of three layers of ruffles, starting from the waistline. It was made of a galloon material with a layer of crepe underneath and pearl buttons on the back. Aunt Honora appeared calm and friendly as I inspected it; she laughed at my expression and asked me to try it on.

The dress fit perfectly, and she didn't charge me a cent. Taking a deep breath, I thanked her. The best gift yet was that Mama Blas got to see me in my prom dress. She thought I looked like a bride. Blas made me a promise. "Doris, you are a treasure. Do things well and, I promise, when you get married, I will buy your wedding dress."

I smiled and hugged her and carried my prom dress home in a brown paper bag, rejoicing in it, thanking God for the first time in all my school years—I was going to attend graduation and prom! When we got home, I hung the dress up, feeling overwhelmed by the smell of new clothes.

I had some money left over, but by the time I went to purchase my senior pictures, it was too late. I had missed the deadline. I was heartbroken.

Graduation day finally arrived, and I wore the new pink dress Naomi had bought. Naomi didn't attend my graduation; nor did Victor or Lorena. None of my family did. The boys had nothing to wear, so they couldn't go. I scanned the crowd, looking for any familiar faces, but there was no one. At the end of the ceremony, I was able to order one five-by-seven graduation picture and one three-by-five prom picture from the local photographer who was snapping photos. I was awarded two medals, one for relays and one for discus, and a certificate for being an athlete. Graduation was a joyful time for me.

Veronica returned home a few days after graduation. But I faced yet another challenge: parental presence was mandatory for the prom. I was consumed by the thought that I might not be able to attend. I approached the school principal during graduation with an elaborate explanation of why my parents couldn't come.

"Mother can't attend—I have many siblings she has to care for. Plus, my father works."

"Doris, one of them should bring you," he told me. "Those are the rules."

I felt embarrassed and remembered Mama Blas's lecture about excuses. She'd be extremely disappointed if she ever learned I had made one up, let alone one so vague. But what else could I do? Feeling hopeless and defeated, I said to my best friend, Mary, "I can't go to prom; my parents can't attend. Can you think of anything?"

143

Mary blurted out, "I know who wants to go, my aunt and uncle!"

Excited, yet a bit insecure, we decided to visit her aunt and uncle. I was nervous, hoping it wasn't too late. I was relieved to arrive at their house and find Mrs. Batista home. Mary introduced me and told them about my situation.

My family knew the Batistas, though not well; we walked by their house every Sunday for church. Mrs. Guillermina Batista was a robust woman who stood five foot ten and had a strong native Indian appearance. Her eyes were as expressive as her personality, which was bright, loud, and giggly. Her voice was thundery, and overall, she had a strong presence. She gave me the biggest, whitest smile I've ever seen.

"I'd be honored to go with you to your prom," she told me when I asked.

Her entire being radiated the greatest warmth and love. This was way too much for me; it was too hard to believe as I handed Mrs. Batista the prom tickets. I was happy and relieved; it felt like a dream.

I told Mr. and Mrs. Batista my parents' names, which they agreed to use; Mrs. Lina Torres and Mr. Enrique Mercado Castellar. Mrs. Batista practiced saying my mother's name. Lifting her chin up, she would say,

"My name is Lina Torres."

He would intone, "I am Enrique Mercado Castellar, but call me sir."

"My daughter's name is Doris Mercado Torres," they would chorus.

The five of us laughed out loud.

"Doris, are you *sure* your parents don't mind?" asked Mrs. Batista.

I was tempted for a moment to tell them the whole

truth, but then I said, "Oh, no, they don't mind. Mother can't go, and Father has to work."

"All right, then." Mrs. Batista smiled; I smiled back and felt guilty—but I really, really wanted to go to prom.

"I have to get back home now," I told them. Mrs. Batista hugged me before I left. I was scared to have to walk back home; by then, it was half past four in the afternoon, and it was a good five miles to our house.

"See you soon, Mrs. Batista. Bye-bye, Mary." Luckily for Mary, her house was just up the hill from Mrs. Batista's. I left quickly, thanking God for this gift. Once I passed the first curve, I sprinted for as long as I could, then jogged and power-walked for a while, and repeated the same sequence until I got home.

I kept reminiscing how Mrs. Batista had walked toward me with open arms when she met me. Aside from Mama Blas and Tato, no one had hugged me as Ms. Batista had. I felt so much love; in fact, she had almost quenched my thirst for motherly love. Her eyes had sparkled when I placed prom tickets in her hands. It all seemed like a dream.

Prom day arrived, and of course, I did my own hair and makeup. As I was about to change into my dress, I heard Victor come into the house. I stepped out of my room and smiled at him. "I'm going to prom!" I said brightly. He looked away and didn't say anything, so I went back into my room and began to dress as fast as I could, so my brother could see me in my dress before he left.

As I began buttoning the back of my dress, Victor's voice echoed in the living room. "Marcos, go tell Doris she's not going."

I was still in dream mode about being able to attend prom, so I couldn't believe what I'd just heard; my body froze. I could feel the tension in Victor's voice and Marcos's hesitation.

"Go on, move it, tell her she's not going anywhere. She's staying home."

"Victor, she's been getting ready since four," Franco said, trying to keep the peace. "Aunt Honora made her dress."

"Why don't you want her to go, Victor?" asked Veronica.

Victor didn't answer. There was dead silence for a moment, until he shouted indignantly, "Marcos, what are you waiting for? Go tell her!"

I glanced at myself in the mirror and saw my fear, but I told myself, *I'm not giving up! This is my dream!* In a split second, I grabbed my shoes and my bag and jumped out the window. I dashed down a small path behind our house, flew up into the bushes, crossed the road, then took a second path to our neighbor Mariam Reyes's house, passing coffee trees and another neighbor's house on the way. I barged into Mariam's place, gasping for air. "Victor doesn't want me to go to prom, but I really want to go!"

I don't know how my dress failed to get dirty or ripped from jumping out the window or from brushing against the bushes as I sprinted through them, but it didn't. This remains a mystery to me to this day.

"Doris, go into the girls' bedroom," Mariam said firmly. "This is *my* house, and no one is going to keep you from going!"

Trembling, I went into the girls' bedroom and stayed there. I found my friend and fellow athlete, Aby, doing her own makeup. Her chestnut brown hair was shiny and neat, and her milky skin glowed against her off-white dress. Her smile was serene and calmed me. I sat on her bed holding my bag and shoes; slowly, my heart stopped pounding, and I began to feel delighted and safe.

Doris Mercado

About ten minutes later, someone knocked at the front door, and I heard Marcos say, "My brother says Doris can't go to the prom."

Before Miriam said anything, I came out of the room.

"Yes? What is it, Marcos?"

"Victor said you can't go," he said fearfully.

I looked straight into his eyes. "Marcos, you go tell Victor I'm going," I said firmly, chin held high, my hand on my right hip.

Marcos stared at me. With his sweaty face, dirty clothes, and bare feet, poor Marcos looked like a little caveman. I looked straight into his eyes and raised my eyebrows, which meant I was serious about what I said. Marcos bowed his head, turned around, and left quietly.

Mariam looked at me, saying, "Well said. It's time to go, girls. Doris, don't you worry."

I began trembling as we headed out the door to the car. As we left Mariam's house, I was frightened of the possibility Victor would try to stop us. Luckily we made it to the main road unbothered and headed out to Jayuya. We soon arrived at the school, and I spotted Mr. and Mrs. Batista waiting for me, wearing off-white outfits and joyful expressions. They flashed proud white smiles; Mrs. Batista said, "My daughter," and extended her hand to me.

"Yes," I said, extending my hand to her.

We held hands and entered the hall. They enjoyed prom, and believe it or not, they responded to my parents' names, occasionally shaking some of my teachers' hands as they were introduced.

Some of my classmates knew my actual parents, but they didn't question me.

"Very nice to meet you, I'm glad you both made it," Mr. Gonzalez said.

"We're very glad, too; she really wanted to be here today."

"Doris is a good student, with a full scholarship to the University of Puerto Rico. She has a brilliant future ahead of her."

Mrs. Batista placed her hand on her chest. "Sir, we are so proud of her!"

The Batistas were overwhelmed to learn about my scholarship offer. "We didn't know you'd been scouted by the university," Mrs. Batista fussed. "A good education is so important. Do your parents know about this?"

I felt weak; I looked into her eyes, and her kindness made me want to tell her everything.

"Would you forgive me for something, Mrs. Batista?" I asked weakly.

"What do you mean, Doris?"

"Ma'am, I thank you for being here for me. My Mother *does* know I run . . . and she will always appreciate what you've done for me today." I was giving in—and I suddenly decided I *would* tell them, but not tonight. Not on my prom night.

"Listen, I'm proud to be here. This is a big accomplishment," Mrs. Batista said, smiling and clutching my hand.

I held on to our secret and just said, "Thank you, ma'am."

"You're welcome, Doris. Now, go on—dance with your friends."

I was happy; and for the first time in a long time, I had a carefree smile on my face. I turned around to look for Mary and Aby—and suddenly I saw Paolo, my old running friend, wearing a nicely pressed white shirt and khaki pants. "Paolo! What are you doing here?"

"Ah, is not important . . . actually, I wanted to see you, so here I am."

He appeared both happy and sad—he didn't get to graduate, but at least he was here tonight. We stayed together for the rest of the evening, reluctant to part. His almond hair was shiny, his olive skin kissed by the sun. He smelled like orange flowers and had green eyes that made me feel both settled and safe. He'd always seemed so honorable to me, and doubly so now.

Glancing at the Batistas, he asked, "Are those your parents?"

"My neighbors—my parents couldn't be here."

"Your neighbors? Well, they seem like nice people."

"They were heaven-sent. I'll always remember their willingness to help me when I needed them," I said quietly, reflecting on my desperate run to Mariam's house. She had ensured that my chance to attend prom was not spoiled.

"What an amazing deed. Do you know how many kids don't get to go to prom because their parents are tied up? You are one lucky girl," Paolo nodded decisively. He then wrapped his arms around me, and we danced to the last song of the evening, some sort of ballad. In his arms, my life felt renewed.

When it came time to depart, we said good-bye with teary eyes. His eyes agonized over our last words, and then he embraced me tightly and wouldn't let go of my hands. I was so embarrassed I didn't dare look Mrs. Batista in the eye later. I never saw Paolo again.

The Batistas' company was the most delightful thing in the world. They enjoyed the prom, and even though most of my classmates in fact knew my parents, no one questioned me about the Batistas. I thank those classmates and bless their humility.

Departing finally from the Batistas was a sad moment.

I wanted to stay with the Batistas and wished they could take care of us. The best thing was thanking them—for giving me the best gift ever. From then on, I loved them profoundly, as my own parents. Guillermina Batista's last words while hugging me were, "I'm proud of you. When I see your parents, I'm going to tell them myself what a good girl you are."

I smiled at her and hoped she'd have such opportunity.

12. Last Letter

In June 1984, a month after my graduation, we received a letter from Massachusetts. It included Mother's last letter, along with four airplane tickets— which gave me awful chills as I held them.
The letter read,

Dear Daughter,
We'll officially reunite effective September 15, 1984. I was unable to get tickets for all of you. Tell Franco and Alejandro I will send their tickets as soon as possible. I'm really sorry they'll have to wait a little longer. Tell Victor I said to take care of them until I'm able to send tickets, which will be soon. Make sure you leave the house early, because the traffic to San Juan is horrible.

I was left feeling uncertain. In one hand, I held a full scholarship offer to the university; in the other, I held Mother's order to reunite. I wished I could stay here and keep taking care of the kids, but I just didn't have the means. Our new home would be in Massachusetts, because it seemed to be the best place for all of us.

Whereas many of my classmates had already figured out their lives—college, the military, even marriage—I felt my life had come to a sudden halt. The idea of giving up the scholarship and just waiting for September 15 to leave for Massachusetts was perturbing. I had never given up on anything before.

The kids surrounded me, anxious: Marcos with a sweaty face, Franco with a half-smile of nervousness, and Alejandro with a cold stare of fear. Veronica waited as I read, suspicious, and Jonas kept quiet.

I re-read the letter a second time before I gave them the awful news, whispering, "Guys, this letter is from Mother. She says we're moving to Massachusetts—but only four of us for now, Jonas, Marcos, Veronica, and I. It says here she'll send tickets for Franco and Alejandro later."

Veronica raised her eyebrows and covered her mouth with both hands.

"No tickets for us?" shouted Franco. "You're joking, right?"

"I'm serious. Here, read the letter and count the tickets—there's only four. They're supposed to be for the four of us, so . . . I guess you're staying here by yourselves."

Franco's face went pale, and so did Alejandro's. Franco scanned the letter, his face filled with pain; then he forced a nervous grin and said, "Uhum."

The smile dropped off his face almost immediately. I took the letter from his hands and repeated to Alejandro, who also stared, frozen, "It says you guys will move next."

"Next? When?" asked Veronica.

"I don't know. It doesn't say anything else, except they were only able to buy four tickets, and they'll send two more tickets soon," I answered.

Marcos began hiccuping. "Why are Franco and Titus not going? They're going to be here alone. Well, I'm staying! I'm not going anywhere!" He took off running toward the horse's back on the other side of the farm, his feet thumping noisily against the soil. The other boys went after him, calling his name, leaving Veronica and I behind.

I felt nauseated as I reflected on the fact we'd first seen Mother leave, then Father, then Victor, then Naomi and Diego. This time, four of us were leaving Franco and Alejandro behind. It seemed brutal and harsh. Looking away from Veronica, hands shaking, I cried, "How long are we supposed to live like a rubber band? We get stretched in all directions by everyone! We try so hard to do what's right and stay together and feel better—and for what?"

Veronica covered her mouth once again in reaction to my remark. "Dori, don't say that," she muttered. "What a bad thing to say."

"I don't care, Veronica!" I said relentlessly. "Just look at Marcos. Just picture such a day when the four of us have to leave Franco and Alejandro behind! I wish I could get a job and take care of them myself!"

A million thoughts rushed through my head; I wished there was something I could do to keep them all here, but the reality of our living conditions was harsh enough as it was. This command from Mother to come to Massachusetts, splitting us apart, didn't feel right. Deep down, I doubted. Deep down, I feared her order, her offer for a better life, feeling unconvinced—it was too good to be true.

I loved our schools and liked to believe our teachers were truly our foster parents. Day by day, they instilled civilized values in us with so much care and kindness. It was a blessing to get our education in little, under-populated Jayuya. Would we get the same education away in the States? Would the kids be all right? Would it work?

A while later, the boys resurfaced from the woods. Marcos had begun to deal with the idea of our departure, of our leaving the motherland, but they all insisted they didn't want to move. I didn't blame them; I shared their uncertainty. Mother had included a telephone number with her letter, so I decided I'd to go to Ponce the next morning so I could call her.

Franco agreed to stay with the kids, so the next day I took the hideous envelope with me and headed to town. I approached the first phone booth I saw, which was located near a bakery. The operator was kind and helped me place a collect call. "Hello," my father answered.

"Dad, this is Doris."

"Doris?" His voice was raspy and aged. "Are you okay?"

His inquiry was shameful and didn't deserve an answer. He spoke as if nothing had happened—as if leaving us amounted to nothing. I hated the thought of living with him again already. But I said, "Yes, Father, I'm okay. How are the kids?"

"Oh, they're doing well. Raquel was sick, but she's better." His voice grew a little fainter. "Hey, kids, Doris is on the phone," he announced.

I heard little kid voices in the background.

"They can't wait to see you guys. Doris, did you receive the tickets?"

"Yes, I did, Father, and it's why I'm calling—to speak with Mother about it."

"It's good you received them. Just tell Franco and Alejandro to hang in there, we'll send tickets for them as soon as we can. The kids say hi—they're eating breakfast. Well, your Mother is here. Take care of yourself and take care of the kids."

I sighed and didn't answer him. I felt like hanging up and ripping up the entire envelope, along with the plane tickets. Then I thought about the kids and our poverty, which made me feel we had little choice but to accede to Mother's wishes. I wished I could stay personally, as my scholarship covered both room and board.

"My daughter," Mother said. "How are you? Are the kids okay?" Like Father's, her voice sounded old and battered.

"I'm okay. Everyone is okay," I told her. I was relieved to hear her voice, but my Lord, the connection sounded like we were three worlds away!

"I think you're going to like it here," she said. "It's

Massachusetts, but they call it New England. It's beautiful. Make sure you tell Franco and Alejandro about my plan to send their tickets soon, probably by October. I'm glad the time has come for us to be together again."

Her response sounded like a long echo. Mother's admiration for New England and reunion sounded grand, but I couldn't shake off my doubt.

"I'm doing well here, and we are . . . okay." I thought about the scholarship and the harshness of the four of us leaving behind our two brothers.

Mother sensed my hesitation. "Are you really okay? What's the matter?"

"Mother, do you remember how I ran in school? Well, the University of Puerto Rico awarded me a full scholarship. All I have to do is accept it, and I'll get my college education here. It will cost nothing."

Mother paused for a moment before she said, "There are many schools here you can attend."

"I understand, Mother, but the scholarship here is free. As for living there—first of all, I don't know good English. I'd have to learn it first. I may as well get my education on the island."

"Doris, we have our own home now!" Mother said firmly. "You have to come with the kids. I'll have your father look into schooling. There are programs to help you learn the language. Make sure you tell Victor the date and time, yes?"

The thought of sending the kids along and staying behind, accepting the scholarship to the university, crossed my mind again. For a split second, I thought about what might happen if I *did* stay behind, about how my life might turn out better as a result. But then I envisioned the scandal I'd create with my family if I stayed, if I didn't obey Mother's wishes. I said, "Mother, would you tell the kids I said hello, and I hope Raquel feels better?"

"Sure, I'll tell them. You'll see them soon, Doris."

"Okay, Mother."

I hung up, wondering if Mother even understood what a scholarship was. I felt doomed, and shaken. Uncertain or not, I had to go to Massachusetts. I wondered how we might make it if we stayed on the island, and how we'd survive—but the kids needed Mother.

As I headed back home, I felt a deep uncertainty settle over me as I slowly let go of the opportunity of a lifetime. Worse, I hated to bring bad news to the kids. When I made it home, the kids didn't go crazy asking questions; they just stared in silence as I walked down the hill, shoulders down.

"What's the look on your face?" Franco asked finally. "Did somebody die?"

Asking if someone had died was a phrase we used on the island when we suspected bad news. I looked at them with teary eyes and replied, "Mother said we have to go, because there are other schools there. I tried to tell her about the scholarship, but she didn't say anything about it. She said we had to leave as she'd found a place for all of us and there are programs to learn English and she'll send tickets for you and Alejandro as soon as possible. I guess we're leaving."

"What about Dad? Did he say anything?" Franco demanded.

"Not much. He sounded so tired and different," I said.

The kids kept staring at me in astonishment. "Leave home for *what*? We live here, so we should stay here!" said Veronica, as she looked away. I'd always thought she possessed some extra sense, beyond the normal five. The way her eyes stared out in the distance gave me goose bumps.

"I think its best we tell Victor when he visits," Alejandro suggested.

"I agree. Maybe we can get him to delay the tickets. In six months, I could be a correctional officer—I'd be working," Franco declared.

"Wow, I wish *I* had a job," I said. "I'd stay if I did. But we can't live like this much longer. The house needs work. Those disgusting termites—I don't know how to get rid of them."

"I like it here. I don't want us to leave," said Marcos, barely containing his tears.

Jonas listened in fear, wiping at his own tears, and wailed, "People are going to notice we're alone. You watch!"

"Jonas, be quiet! Keep your voice down. This is no time to give up, do you hear me?" I whispered urgently, as I looked toward the main road to make sure no one was going by, listening to our conversation.

"Marcos, go turn on the radio, we're talking way too loudly," I directed.

"Okay," said Marcos, as he stomped off to turn on the radio.

"Jonas, we could get in big trouble. Don't you dare say anything," Veronica threatened.

"Guys, I'll be right back," I announced. "I'm going to make coffee." They loved having coffee, especially during our usual chats as we sat outdoors.

Once the coffee was ready, we continued our conversation. "I don't want to go anywhere," Marcos said sadly.

Franco said, "Look, seriously. I was offered a job at the local jail. The jail is so close I don't even need a car—I could walk to work. If I needed a car, I'd borrow one. I could save money and fix the house. Plus, guess what? The sheriff's name is Torres-Mercado. Well, he knows our name is Mercado-Torres—isn't this something? I wonder if we're related. I just happened to make friends with his kids, and they're cool. They want to meet you guys. I told him we'll stop by their house one day after church."

"Wow, I'd like to meet them," I said enthusiastically. "I wish we didn't have to leave! Maybe I could get a job close by as well."

"We should stay here!" Jonas cried.

Veronica nodded in agreement, saying, "I don't like this one bit."

"Hey, Franco," Marcos said, "what if people move into the house after we leave? Can you imagine if someone breaks in?"

"Let's make a sign that reads, *Travelers welcome, stay at your own risk*," Alejandro suggested, laughing hysterically. The rest of us laughed too.

"It's actually spooky. The bats would chase people out. Can you imagine the running and screaming?" Franco said.

All the boys laughed, but Veronica frowned.

"Imagine a stranger reporting the bats flapping over their heads. Imagine Dad's owl staring straight into a stranger's eyes! Imagine the sound of the wind blowing through the coffee trees and the mango trees. Imagine the termites making crackling noises through the furniture," Franco said, while all us kids listened, pale and motionless.

"How disgusting, I've got goose bumps," I said.

"I bet no one would want to live with the bats, mice, or yucky termites," Veronica said.

"Those bats have been here for a while," said Alejandro, shrugging. "They look like little demons, little vampires even. You know, guys, we've watched too many Dracula movies for too long. Maybe the bats were the ones eating the sugar. We can try dealing with the bats, but not the termites—those are way too disgusting. The roof needs some patching, too."

Laughing, Franco said, "Yes, it's about time our lifestyle got an upgrade from the Stone Age. If we're to stay, the house does need fixing! It's a good thing the structure is cement, strong enough to endure hurricanes—it's still pretty solid. But we can't keep walking on dusty, bare floors, either."

"I don't know, though. Mother might hear if we don't obey," Veronica said.

"I hope no one can live in this place," said Jonas in gloom.

"Jonas, it's evil to curse!" I scolded.

"Yes, I hope no one can ever live in this house, *ever*. I hope whoever comes here gets hunted by *el cuco,* the devil witches, and ghosts," Marcos said.

I looked at Marcos with raised eyebrows and finally gave up, letting them vent.

"Why in the world do you think we're still here after all this time?" Veronica demanded. "This is where we belong. I'm warning you, guys, it's bad luck to leave!"

"See, we should just stay!" Alejandro cried.

"I'd stay with Naomi if I could. I liked going to school in Arecibo. I made new friends there," said Veronica.

"We'll get in serious trouble with Mother if we stay," I told her. "Victor may not let us, anyway. I don't know what to tell you. We're supposed to leave in three more months."

At my words, the air immediately began to feel heavy. We became tense, reflecting on the fact that we wouldn't be living together in the house for much longer. We felt we didn't have much choice, and we were all drained by the thought.

I went in to cook supper, but I was so distracted by

the dread of departure that I soon scalded my left forearm with boiling water.

"Jonas! Go get me a piece of aloe vera, hurry!" I yelled.

The pain was unbearable. I kept my arm under cool, running water; then, when Jonas returned, I sliced up the piece of aloe vera and tied it around my forearm—and went back to cooking. What choice did I have?

"That's not good," Veronica said, glancing at my wound. I looked at her, and her dark eyes stared deep into mine. She scared me sometimes.

"Veronica, I need help cooking," I told her.

"I don't like to cook."

"Listen, you need to help," I scolded. "You never help. Stop being so stubborn—we're all in this together."

Veronica frowned and didn't bother answering me or helping me cook. By the time we had eaten supper, I'd lost track of time, and I'd forgotten to remind the kids to take their showers. It was almost seven in the evening by the time I remembered.

"The water is cold!" Marcos cried.

"Can we just take showers in the morning?" Jonas inquired.

"No, guys, you have to shower now, so hurry up before the water gets colder!" I called as I sat on my bed, flipping through the plane tickets in the special delivery envelope. Finally, I removed the intrusive envelope from my room and placed it in a far corner of the living room, on top of the old TV stand.

Then I went through my scholarship papers and graduation awards. Although we were poor and Massachusetts offered a better life, it was hard to feel excited about leaving. We were all doing well in school, we laughed and dreamed together, and we loved this place.

Our harmony and happiness set us free; I felt whole when I was with the kids.

§ § §

One evening, a few days after receiving Mother's letter, Marcus called out, "Watch it, guys, a car is coming!"

It was always scary to hear cars approaching, especially when it was getting dark. We'd always rush for cover. I dashed from the living room and hid behind the kitchen door with Veronica. Franco flew into the house and grabbed the machete, holding it with crossed arms behind his back. He stood behind the main door, yelling, "Who is it, guys?"

"I can't tell yet," answered Marcos.

Jonas sprinted toward the mango tree and climbed up partway. "Hey, guys, it's the Americans!" he soon announced.

Franco laid down the machete, and we all emerged, relieved and smiling, to welcome our old friends, the Americans. They often visited their friends three houses further down; at a place we called the House of the Steps. They were a young couple who liked to go scuba diving in our river.

The House of the Steps was my all-time favorite house. It sat secluded from the road, sporting wide brick steps that led down from the road, forming a big Z. The house was larger than ours. It also had a large patio that was surrounded by grapefruit and lime trees and a cool fire pit. It was in much better shape than our house.

We left the safety of the house and waved at the Americans. Marcos shouted, *Hola muchachos!* Hi guys!"

Smiling, they stopped and handed Marcos a small bag; then, waving at the rest of us, the car moved slowly away. "What did they give you, Marcos?" Alejandro inquired.

"Hey, guys, it's chocolate!" Marcos said, chuckling. It had been an eternity since we ate chocolate, and so we soon gobbled it down.

"Listen, kids, brush your teeth—it's time to go to bed," I said, as I turned around and walked into the house with Veronica.

"Maybe we should go to the river tomorrow. Most likely they'll be there scuba diving," Franco suggested.

"Guys, there's another car coming," Alejandro announced suddenly.

"You lie," said Marcos.

"I can see the car lights. Come see."

"Maybe it's more Americans," I said.

We all looked for cover, and Franco grabbed the machete again. I closed the kitchen door and waited behind it with Veronica. "Who is it?" Franco shouted.

"It's Victor!" came Alejandro's excited reply.

We all emerged as Victor's car approached. When he got out, he looked around at us and said, "Hey, you guys seem energized. What's up?"

"The Americans stopped by and gave us a bag of chocolate," Marcos said cheerfully.

Victor chuckled. "So they're visiting again? They are nice."

Franco said bluntly, "Victor, a couple of days ago, we received a special delivery letter from Mother with four plane tickets, dated for September 15."

"What?"

I went into the house and got the letter.

"Here it is, Victor. It's true. I don't want to leave. If I could, I'd stay—but I don't want to be a burden on anyone."

Victor hurriedly opened the special delivery envelope, took out the tickets, and read the date out loud. "Wow, so four of you are leaving on September 15."

162

I said, "Victor, Mother said for you to take Franco and Alejandro, and she'll send their tickets as soon as possible."

Victor didn't reply; he just read the letter silently. He held it as if it weighed a ton. His eyes scanned line after line, carefully. Then he lifted his head and looked off into the distance, his eyes watering.

"What about the house, Victor?" asked Marcos.

"I'll seal all the windows and doors," he said quietly. "Nothing will happen to it. Wow, guys . . . September is just around the corner."

"Can we delay their departure?" Franco asked. "I don't want them leaving yet."

"Delay? I don't think so. Mother wouldn't be happy. Plus, I don't think it's possible."

It was starting to get dark, so we all went inside the house. I made coffee, and Victor sat down with us at the dining table. "I'm proud of all of you," he told us solemnly. "You're all special, with your teamwork and love and respect for one another. I hope you treasure this time. Never forget it. Always look back and remember that although you didn't have much, your happiness was your greatest gift.

"You *should* be proud of yourselves," he continued. "I must ask you, however, no good-byes. You must promise me you will never tell me good-bye."

His voice was so deep it almost rumbled through the house. There was silence, until the *coquí* frogs began their melodious singing. Nighttime approached. Oh, how I hated the nighttime now . . .

We sat motionless, clutching our beat-up coffee cups, the special delivery package sitting in the center of the table. We stared at it, and it seemed to stare right back at us. Victor's eyes grew darker and teary again. He got up, wiped his eyes, and put his hands on his hips. While looking away, he announced, "I've dreaded this day—but I'm glad it finally came, because you can't keep living like this. Once you're gone, I don't think I'll have the stomach to stop by here again. Just the thought gives me goose bumps. I'm really sorry I couldn't be of greater help. I'm sorry I will not be seeing you for a while—but do your best. Remember, this is where your heart will always be. This is home, guys. The circumstances are unfortunate; but you all deserve a better life."

We'd never had Victor talk to us like a father before. While he talked, I wished I could get a job so I could stay and care for the kids in Jayuya, where we all belonged.

"You can come and visit, Victor," said Marcos, almost playfully.

"I wish I could," said Victor.

I was touched by Marco's innocent invitation. I could tell he'd grow up to have a most generous, caring heart.

"Listen, Doris, I have to take Veronica—we need help with the baby," Victor said. "I'll bring her back soon."

"Oh, okay," I said, as I thought, *Oh jeez, here we go again.*

I helped Veronica pack a sack of clothes, and it wasn't long before Victor asked, "Veronica, are you ready?"

Veronica didn't answer. She just hung her head in sadness; it was obvious she didn't want to leave us. "Yes, she's ready," I said for her.

"Doris, be careful—and don't tell anyone you guys are alone," warned Victor.

We turned on the lights, both indoors and out, then watched as Victor got in his car. Veronica followed, but with slow steps. We watched the car disappear into the fog and darkness.

I missed Veronica immediately and felt abandoned again. I wanted to experience what it was like *not* to fear

164

nightfall and the horror that came with it. I wanted to know how it felt to go to bed without fearing for my siblings, without constantly listening for vehicles approaching or footsteps over the sounds of the wind. I wondered what it was like not to hear the kids sobbing with fear at night. I wondered what it might be like to close my eyes and just fall asleep, feeling safe for once. Would this ever happen?

I then pictured Veronica feeling secure in the company of my brother and his wife, happily playing with the baby. I pictured her waking up without sharing our tension, without having to constantly look out for people who might reveal our parentless state, without turning up the radio to camouflage the absence of our parents. Every evening, we were like little birds heading for the safety of our cage, and I'd bundle us in.

"Guys, it's getting dark, hurry, help me close the shutters."

Then I'd wait for the kids to get in bed. Once everyone was in bed and wrapped into his threadbare blankets, I'd turn off all the lights. Franco slept in my parents' bedroom. Jonas, Alejandro, and Marcos slept in Mama Blas's bedroom, and I slept in the small room by the kitchen.

Once the lights were off, anytime we heard steps approaching, we'd keep still, listening, until the steps disappeared into the night and we felt safe again. We'd wrap ourselves tight in our worn little blankets and pray, trembling and waiting for the night to pass. It seemed poor Marcos got spooked by any little noise.

"Did you hear something, guys? Let's pray—I think someone is out there. Maybe it's a witch!"

Most of the time, Franco and Alejandro would laugh out loud at his fearful imaginings. Often, I intervened with, "Quiet, guys! Marcos, I think it's Dad's owl singing. Go to sleep, it's all right."

But sometimes Marcos was too scared to fall asleep and would start sobbing. We'd all get up to comfort him. On a few occasions, we'd even open the front door so that he could see there was nothing outside.

"There's nothing out there, you monkey! Would you like to go see?" Alejandro said in a playful tone.

Marcos would look around fearfully, and little by little he'd relax.

"You see? Anyways, let's just stay up for a little while," I'd suggest, so Marcos felt better.

The four of us would stare at the stars for a long time, listening to the melodious singing of the frogs and the other little animals. On full moon nights, this was comforting. The moon glowed pure silver, like a faint, distant lamp. The trees looked beautiful as the wind swayed them gently, and the mist made the leaves shine. Every now and then, we'd see shooting stars. Then we'd make wishes under the moon's silvery light.

The night breeze smelled like crisp new wood and herbs and flowers. It always seemed so peaceful; and after Marcos felt better and we had admired one more silent night, we'd go back into the house quietly, and I would turn off the lights. Sometimes we'd fall asleep quickly; other times, we'd call out to each other in conversation, and our voices would ring through the house. Because of the open floor plan, our voices would echo crystal clear; sometimes we told jokes and made each other laugh. The kids were talkative anyway; and we were used to chatting at night until we all got sleepy, whereupon we'd say a final good night and fall asleep.

On one particular evening, after we were all in bed and the lights were out, Franco called out, "Hey, guys, when I went by my friend's house today, they were playing this crazy movie called *The Exorcist*."

"What?" I asked, wondering what it was about.

"Believe it or not, I ran home. It was pretty darn scary," said Franco, chuckling.

Everyone began laughing. "What a chicken," Alejandro called.

"Guys, its late—remember, we have school tomorrow," I told them.

Franco's tone lowered until he almost whispered, "In the movie, this girl kept yelling, '¡Échale agua bendita a tu madre!' 'Throw holy water at your Mother!' She looked disgusting, and her skin slashed open every time the priest threw holy water at her."

"Be quiet, Franco!" I shouted. Then I trembled.

"Jesus, Mary, and Joseph," Alejandro said, but began laughing hysterically, out of nervousness.

Marcos cried, "Stop it, Franco!" and began reciting Hail Marys.

Jonas said, afraid, "I'm scared, Jesus, Mary, and Joseph."

I was horrified at the thought myself, so I jumped out of bed and turned on all the lights for a few minutes. Jonas, Franco, and Alejandro got out of bed as well, though Franco remained in my parents' room. He called, "Sorry, guys, I'll never mention that crazy movie again. Don't worry—it's just a movie."

We remained tense and scared. I hated nighttime! Eventually, I said, "Guys, go back to bed, I'm turning off the lights."

"Wait! Don't turn off the lights yet!" Marcos yelled.

"Hurry up, Marcos, we have to get up early in the morning," I said.

Trying to ease the boy's fear, Franco called out, "Hey, guys, I feel like a king . . . I can't even tell you how comfortable Mom and Dad's bed is!" He laughed, and the kids joined him; and eventually, we all fell asleep.

13. Revelation

Not long after, I visited my friend Aby Reyes, Mariam's daughter, who was already in cosmetology school.

"College is different, Doris!" she told me enthusiastically. "No more school uniforms! You have to act professionally and be organized and take good notes. I have so much reading to do, but I enjoy it. You have to have good pronunciation, too."

I was happy for her, but I felt odd that I wasn't going to school as well. Aby looked like a young adult, dressed up as she was in casual business attire. She had *ojos brujos,* gypsy eyes; an even, clean, fair complexion; a long, fine nose; and chocolate brown hair. She kept her hair short, almost giving her a boyish look. Her hands were small and sort of wrinkled. She was a French manicure fan.

I smiled and nodded.

"Well, it's going to get dark pretty soon, so I have to go home. Take care, Aby—and good luck with everything."

"Thanks, Doris. Stop by on Sunday, so we can do our nails."

"Sure, I'd love that."

I walked home, feeling sad. I wanted to go to school so much.

I'd hung on to our secret for as long as I could; but then I figured, because we'd soon be leaving, I'd share the news with Aby. Her family had always been caring and kind to us. So one day in August 1984, when Aby was visiting our house, I told her, "Listen, Aby. We're leaving Puerto Rico on September 15."

"Oh my God, Doris, are you serious? All of you kids? There's so many of you! My parents want to move to

Pennsylvania, but I don't want to go. I don't want to quit school now. I don't want to go anywhere," said Aby.

"I'm sorry Aby . . . I have to tell you something. I've been living here alone with the kids since tenth grade. My parents are living in Massachusetts."

Aby stood up and yelled, "*What?*"

"There's no reason to be alarmed," I told her quickly. "Please don't tell anyone. I assure you we're okay. I mean, you've seen us going to school and church all this time, haven't you?"

"Yes, but Doris, but, how have you managed, even as an athlete?" she sputtered. "I didn't realize you guys were living alone! I haven't heard anyone talking. You know how rumors spread in this small town. Everyone knows everyone's business."

I grinned, my jaw locked like a pit bull's, speaking through my teeth, "Aby, people can know your business only if you *tell* them. In our house, we learned our business is our business. We don't share; we don't explain—end of story. What is most important is the fact we're well, and we're doing what we're supposed to do. As long as the kids are safe and happy, the only pleading I do is in church, to the Lord. If I need to talk with someone, I write to Mother, or Tato or Naomi, or take a long hike and see Mama Blas. She is our voice and ultimate confidant."

Aby stared at me with clouded eyes, seeming somewhat intimidated. She said, "Jeez, Dori, relax. Oh my God, I can't believe it. You even went to graduation and prom!" She stared at me fearfully.

I felt somewhat uncomfortable and regretted revealing our secret to her.

"Aby, I don't want people to think they can come onto our property and take the kids away," I explained. "Franco is our watchman. He keeps a machete handy. If the moment ever comes to protect the kids, I'm not standing in his way. I hope you understand," I said.

"Oh, I understand. Handsome Franco is cool—he's always happy. Everyone likes him," she said cheerily, her eyes clearing; but I remained still and serious.

Suddenly Aby said, "Doris, I'll be right back!" Then she took off running out of the house, and I knew exactly what she was going to do: she was going to go tell her mother. I went to the door to wait.

Moments later, Mariam came running down our hill, wearing a long nightgown in broad daylight, rollers dangling from her hair as she ran toward me, extending her arms. "Doris!" she called out. "Doris, are you okay? Is it true Doña Lina and Quique aren't here?"

I sighed. "Yes, it's true. Please, don't tell anyone about this. We're okay, I assure you."

I had to allay her concern, so I gave Mariam a summary of how I'd done things. "I get up in the morning," I explained. "We leave the house together. I cook every day. I do the laundry on Saturday mornings. We go to the river on Saturday afternoons when the weather is good. Then church on Sundays. The kids are always playing outside. I run, read, write. We love listening to music. We have fun."

Mariam stared right into my eyes while I told her this, breathing hard. I was scared and figured Franco might be mad at me for telling Aby about our secret. As if I'd summoned him, Franco appeared out of nowhere with the kids, glaring at Mariam like a bobcat, moving slowly, machete in hand. He glanced at me, trying to sense whether I was okay.

"Hey, guys," I said.

The younger boys peered at me and at Mariam as well, but made no move to come indoors.

Franco appeared to trust Mariam, so he let his guard

down, laying the machete on the ground.

"Good afternoon. How are you, ma'am?" he said to Mariam.

Mariam seemed nervous. "Hello, Franco. *Muy bien, gracias,* very well, thank you." She looked at me. "Well, you kids are brave, aren't you? Doris, would it be okay if I came to pick you up every day around six?"

"Sure, after I cook for everyone and make sure they've taken their showers," I said, wondering why.

"Very well, then, I'll see you tomorrow around six. Don't worry, I won't tell anyone—but if you need anything, just come to my house. Be careful, kids."

We felt better when she left, though we all appreciated Mariam's concern. As it turned out, Franco wasn't mad at me, but Marcos and Jonas were. "You fresh, why did you tell her?" demanded Marcos.

I pressed my lips together, containing a laugh. "I'm really sorry, but you know they're a good family, and they care about us. We can trust them."

Marcos just frowned in response.

After that, Mariam came by every day around six. "Doris, come on!" she'd yell from the main road. Franco stayed outside with the boys while they played, and every evening, I'd spend an hour at Mariam's house. It had new cream-colored linoleum and more furniture than ours. I'd help Aby with her cosmetology homework and let her practice French manicure on me. Sometimes she practiced styling my hair. I was happy and felt safe at Aby's house. Her father, Ivan, even fixed my broken shoes, sewing them together with a thick needle until they were as good as new.

I really wished, now, that we didn't have to leave our house. I grieved over the upcoming departure from my friends. The boys laughed at me whenever I came back home with a new hairdo.

"Take your hair down, you look weird," Alejandro would shout. At other times, Franco would say, laughing, "*Ea diante,* Oh darn, what kind of beauty school is Aby going to?"

I'd tease them right back. "I'll also learn how to cut hair—especially cavemen's hair."

Franco kept laughing. Aby liked him, but he didn't like her, calling her *pati flaca,* skinny legs.

During Victor's next visit, I told him, "Mariam Reyes knows we're alone."

"What are you saying?" he responded defensively. "Who told her?"

"Her daughter, Aby, used to go to school with me, and I told her," I said. I didn't dare tell him it didn't matter anymore if anyone knew, since we were leaving anyway.

Victor snorted like a bull. "What did you tell her?"

"I told her we're okay."

Victor remained serious. His black eyes almost reminded me of Mother's threatening ones.

"They're good people, Victor," I added.

Victor's face relaxed, and he looked away in reflection. "Yes, they are. Just be careful, and don't tell anyone else you're alone. We need to avoid concern." He looked at me. "Well, Veronica is doing well—she's a great help. The baby likes her. I'll bring her back soon," he said.

I didn't answer but felt as if I hadn't seen my sister for an eternity.

§ § §

I thought about the Batistas and their deed of escorting me to the prom. I decided to visit them; I had to see them one last time before we left so I could share our truth.

"Hi, Doris, how are you?" said Mrs. Batista when she

found me at her door. Once again she hugged me, pressing my forehead against her cheek. Responding to her warmth, I looked at her and wished *she* was my mother. She smiled at me like sunshine; I felt she could read me and had taken me into her heart.

Her embrace felt good and true and sincere, her love as strong as a rock. My heart rejoiced. I felt so safe with the Batistas.

I smiled at both of them nervously.

"I have to tell you something," I confessed. "The reason why I asked you to go to prom as my parents was because I'm actually living alone with my siblings—but nobody knew."

Hands clasped under her chin, Mrs. Batista said, "Doris, what do you mean? Where's Lina?"

I inhaled and lifted my chin. It was now time to share with Ms. Batista about my truth, "Mother left us three years ago. Father left a few days later. They're living in Massachusetts, but we're joining them soon."

Covering her mouth, she sighed, "*Jesús, Dios Piadoso,* Jesus, and merciful God."

I immediately felt awful and blurted, "Don't worry— we're okay. Thank you for making my dream come true. I really wanted to go to prom. Mother taught me how to do things around the house from a very young age, and she taught me how to cook when I turned nine. She took the three youngest ones, and I'm caring for four boys and one girl, Veronica. My brother Victor took her temporarily to help with his new baby. But we're all doing fine."

Mrs. Batista's eyes grew dim, and both the Batistas seemed overwhelmed.

"Please don't tell anyone," I said. "We've been told we are too many. My brother Victor said it, and then Naomi and her husband said it. I decided it was best we didn't tell anyone so we could stay together. I don't mean to scare you—but I assure you, we *are* okay."

As Mrs. Batista stared at me in astonishment, I smiled serenely and tried to assure her again that we were fine. She looked at her husband; the woman was pale, speechless. I kept smiling and tried to get her to understand my reasons for not telling her before.

"Mariam Reyes knows. I see her every day. She takes me to her house after supper. Please don't tell anyone," I begged.

I understood it was risky sharing our secret, but it felt good to tell the Reyes family, then the Batistas. I loved both families.

While waiting for her approval, I started thinking about the kids, knowing they were home alone with Franco. Suddenly, I felt I needed to get back to them.

"I'm really sorry I didn't tell you before, I just wanted to go to the prom," I said, as I prepared to leave. Suddenly, I became worried, and struggled to contain my tears.

"Doris, are you sure you're okay? Are the kids okay?" Mrs. Batista whispered with teary eyes, both hands on her chest.

"Yes, we're fine," I assured her.

I could tell Mrs. Batista was battling conflicting emotions; after all, she knew Mother and Father and Blas. I felt guilty, then, for putting the Batistas in an awkward position by revealing our secret and involving them in the deception.

"I'm proud of you," she said finally. "I never would have known. What about the university? Does Lina know about the scholarship offer?"

"Yes, ma'am, I called my mother and told her about it—but she said we still had to leave. You see, some of my family knows we've been alone, but they said we were too many and couldn't help much. Others didn't bother visiting us at all. I thought it was best to care for the kids on my own. We don't have much, but we go to school and church, and they're happy."

I had begun to feel more at ease but remained nervous. I loved and respected Mrs. Batista—and the more I talked, the more concern I saw in her eyes. I didn't want her involved. I didn't want anyone involved. After a hundred assurances that we were okay, she finally let me go, and I felt she believed me and would respect my wishes. However, I was still scared and insecure about what she might say or do.

I walked home feeling different and sad—and exposed. I thought about the Batistas' happy faces at the prom. I didn't want to make them sad, but I'd thought the best way to preserve their happy memory was by telling them the truth. I was happy these two guardian angels had come into my life. I knew I'd be gone soon, and I'd rather have them remember me in a way that they could share our mystery— or whatever they wanted to call it, a miracle even, because we managed to stay in the little house and to hang in there without giving in.

We had become experts at surviving, experts at keeping secrets. We were extremely poor, but we had our home. The kids never went to bed hungry; there was always something to eat. They were healthy, with lustrous hair and skin and white teeth, probably from eating fruit and vegetables daily. In fact, another of our dear neighbors, Don Aníbal, used to give the kids papayas and baby bananas, among other fruits from his farm. Don Aníbal's family were very fond of Mama Blas; when she'd lived at home, they'd often come to her for herbal remedies.

Every once in a while, I'd ask myself, *Am I doing the right thing by keeping our secret? Could they have better lives if I didn't? What if something happened to them? What would I do? What would I say to Mother?* I'd then dismiss my insecurities and accept that the Lord had been merciful so far, and one day we'd be just fine.

As time wound down toward September 15, we prepared to leave. There wasn't much in the way of clothing or shoes to pack, so we decided to fill some boxes with avocados and other fruits. Alejandro and Jonas climbed the mango tree and picked, while Marcos did the catching. Marcos was the smallest boy, but his body was all muscle. His hands and arms were thick, and his legs and feet were toned. Franco walked around cutting down grass and clearing up their walking path. He never let his guard down when watching over us.

"Hey, Franco, be careful handling the machete!" I'd remind him.

Later, Jonas and Alejandro raced each other up the avocado tree. "Hey, Popeye, are you ready?" Alejandro asked Marcos.

"Stop calling me names, you ape!" replied Marcos.

They started dropping the fruit, and Franco and Marcos ran back and forth catching avocados. Marcos looked like a star athlete running in all different directions catching avocados.

When he was done, Franco said, "Good job, man, you didn't drop a single one!"

Marcos looked up at his big brothers, proud. He laughed, revealing dimples in both cheeks, chuckling. Myself, I had no choice but to laugh. I envisioned our future for about two seconds and prayed we would never be apart.

My brothers picked exactly forty-seven avocados. When they brought the sacks into the house, I said, "Oh my God, this is too much!"

"Let's share them with Victor," Alejandro suggested.

"Why would Victor want them? He has more avocado trees than *we* do," Franco pointed out.

"It's a good thing we love avocados. Now we have to pack them so they don't go to waste. You guys are completely crazy," I said.

They were proud and kept laughing as we packed four boxes with vegetables and fruits, including the forty-seven avocados.

Our last visit to the river, our sanctuary, was almost unbearable. We went swimming, but silently, burdened with sadness. I could feel our absence already. I tried to forever record in my memory the melodious sounds of the water cascading through the rocks and the birds singing, along with the breathtaking sight of the sun's golden rays piercing through the trees, illuminating the water and the plants. Ferns trembled in the breeze as fans, bromeliads, and vines glowed against the trees. It was a world within a world, a living cell that concealed and protected us. In my heart, I wept. *I don't want to leave you, Motherland.*

This time, during the hike up the river, none of us collected rocks or artifacts. We couldn't believe it was our last day at our sanctuary. We were leaving behind our adored homeland and the precious little home that had provided refuge all this time. We were happy, in a way, because we were going to reunite with the rest of our family; yet my heart remained uncertain, and I couldn't imagine leaving.

It was a privilege to grow up in Jayuya, Puerto Rico, and share such peaceful and humble surroundings.

14. Precious

September 15, 1984, arrived; two months before my eighteenth birthday. On this day, I woke up nervous, my chest tight. Cold sweat dripped down my face. Everything looked gray and dull; the sun didn't seem as bright as usual, and the wind was quiet and still.

Victor arrived early, walking into the house with heavy steps, saying nothing. The boys got out of their beds quietly; on this day, there was no wrestling to use the bathroom, no morning jokes, no teasing.

As I did every morning, I made coffee, and Victor drank it with us. But this was no ordinary day—this was the day we abandoned the house that had provided us with maternal refuge.

We got ready early, and Franco and Alejandro brought our boxes out. The reality that the four of us would soon be separating from the two boys was nauseating.

Before leaving my room, I went through my awards and the scholarship papers. My room had a built-in shelf that was piled high with pages of my writings and school notebooks. I took five medals and certificates I had won, a Miraculous Medal prayer book, an old rosary Mama Blas had given me, and my graduation cap and gown and prom dress. I lay the scholarship papers on my bed. I looked around at my room one last time. The cement walls looked gray and rough. My simple little bed looked decayed and lumpy—and my scholarship papers were lying on it. I was abandoning them too.

We didn't take anything from the house or throw it away; we just left it all in place. The big paintings of the Madonna of Perpetual Help and the Last Supper remained;

so did the dining table and a few pieces of dishware and dinnerware, all bent and disfigured from so much use. Mother's old Singer remained parked in a corner, as did some of her old sewing accessories and her extra-large scissors, which had worked so perfectly in her strong right hand.

We stepped out of the house in silence. This was no doubt the most horrific day of my life. As we left, I placed my hand on the main door, Marcos by my side, and said silently to the house, *Precious, thank you for your shelter and protection. My home sweet home, I leave with you my soul, the echoes of our laughter and tears, our secrets, and our agonies. They're yours to keep. You'll always be in my heart.*

I could feel Marcos trembling by my right side, and Jonas hiccuping by Marco's side, and Veronica, pale as a ghost, by my left side. Alejandro walked back and forth in little bounces, his hands clasped together before him as if in prayer. Franco sat outside by the mango tree, in the spot where Father used to sit, head down, clutching the machete. He seemed to be in great anguish, but I thought it best to let him be.

It was a numbing experience to imagine that in a matter of two or three hours, we would leave each other.

Once we were out, Victor began to seal the windows with plywood. The hammering was unbearable. Sealing the main door, as he soon proceeded to do, was a burial of our secrets, the abandonment, and all our agonizing moments. Christmas holidays and the other days when we felt most forgotten were forever hidden, untouched, and forever preserved. My heart remained in the house— willingly locked in it, where it belonged.

Once Victor was done sealing all the windows and the front door with the plywood, he walked away, wiping sweat and tears from his face. While I stood there surrounded by the kids, a sudden chopping noise and the sound of trees falling caught our attention. In a matter of minutes, Franco had chopped down coffee trees, banana trees, and part of the mango tree. Alejandro sprinted toward Franco, and they both walked away for a few minutes.

"You stay here, guys," I said to the rest of the kids, but we all understood Franco was hurting and needed his moment.

Victor headed their way, walking with heavy steps. After some whispering and a few high-pitched, agonized tones, the three emerged from the woods with long faces. Franco walked in the middle, holding the machete, with Alejandro and Victor on either side. Suddenly, Franco turned around and threw the machete in the direction of the mango tree, and it lanced straight into the ground.

"Marcos, Jonas, don't stare—you too, Veronica, and don't ask questions," I warned them.

Victor then asked Alejandro to put his toolbox in the trunk.

"Okay, guys, when you get in the car, I don't want any of you to look back—it's all I ask. I trust you all to do me this favor," pleaded Victor.

We all nodded in agreement. We boarded the car, stiff with anguish; and the second Victor started the engine, a current of tension ran through each one of us, and we all jumped.

"Please, guys don't look back," Victor pleaded again.

We kept our promise to Victor and never did look back. As the car left our neighborhood, none of us said a word. I stared at the houses as we passed; inhaling the aroma of freshly picked coffee, and admired the mountain views for the last time. Cold sweat dripped down my face; I felt weak and wanted to throw up. Victor could read us; he knew we were all suffering. To break the monotony, he turned on the radio.

The ride to the airport seemed too short.

When we got out of the car and Victor opened the trunk, he laughed out loud, saying, "Wait until Mother sees all these boxes! She's not going to believe this!" Victor kept laughing, holding his stomach until he couldn't laugh anymore. His laughter soothed our tension a little, and we laughed with him.

"Who did this?" Victor asked.

"I did," Franco said modestly. He had sealed the boxes with masking tape.

"Well, Doris, say your prayers so these don't rip open," Victor said, chuckling, while adding, "I don't even want to picture avocados and oranges rolling all over the place. Dear Mother of God."

"I'm not ashamed; I could not care less if people stare. Those are *our* avocados and oranges," I said boldly, and we all laughed.

We checked in, and our four boxes went out of sight on a conveyor belt that led into a wall, and then it was our turn to part with Victor and the boys. We lined up, and he stood in front of us with teary eyes. We all held each other's eyes for a moment.

"It's better to say 'see you soon,'" Victor said confidently.

"Thank you for what you did for us," I told him. "You are our second father."

He gasped for air as I hugged him tightly. I then glanced at Franco and Alejandro, who would be going with Victor. I wished it was all a dream—but it was harsh and real. None of us said good-bye to the two boys; it would have been too painful. We shared warm smiles and chuckled. Both boys kept laughing out of nervousness; Alejandro stood in one place with his hands in his pockets, while Franco paced, almost in circles, wiping away tears.

"Victor, can we have your blessing?" Marcos asked innocently.

"Yes, can you bless me too?" asked Veronica.

The rest of us just stared at Victor, nervous; I couldn't talk.

"Oh—I never thought I'd be blessing a sibling, but I'm honored." Looking into our eyes one after the other, Victor intoned, "May the Lord guide and protect each one of you always." Then he chuckled. "Oh, no, guys, now I feel old!"

We laughed, but his eyes filled with tears again, and suddenly he couldn't talk. He nodded and squeezed both hands into his pockets. Then the four of us who were being exiled walked slowly toward the gate. We kept looking back at our brothers, until we lost sight of them; and then we faced forward toward our future.

I felt cold. Later, as we boarded the plane, I said to Marcos, who was clutching me tightly, "Let go! You're going to dislocate my arm."

"Jonas, you're stepping on my feet!" Veronica cried.

"Look at the wings, guys," Jonas said in amazement, staring with big, bright eyes.

"Hey, guys, Dad is going to be waiting, you know," Veronica reminded us.

I nodded to my sister. "Veronica, you sit with Jonas and I'll sit with Marcos."

When we got to our seats, Marcos wrestled with the seatbelt, and soon we were all giggling at his antics. Once we were in place, we looked out the plane's windows to see if we could spot Franco, Alejandro, and Victor one more time—but we couldn't.

During takeoff, things didn't feel right to me. I felt I was leaving against my will, in mere obedience to my parents.

The kids giggled nearly nonstop for most of the flight. Eventually, Jonas started talking with another family, and Marcos looked around eagerly, giving away friendly smiles. He then turned to me and said, "I'm thirsty."

"You can ask the stewardess for something," I answered. "Go ahead."

"Hey, Miss, I'd like some water please!" he shouted to the flight attendant. The woman looked at him in amazement, probably wondering at how thick his voice was. Faces turned toward us. I put my index finger over his lips, reminding Marcos to keep it down. Soon, Marcos was given the water he'd asked for, and he shouted a cheerful "Thank you!" which made his voice radiate throughout the airplane. He couldn't stop laughing.

Unfortunately, the pilot soon announced that we were in for some turbulence. The second we hit the disturbed air, some of the overhead compartments popped open, things fell out on top of people—and Jonas began screaming. We overheard some women crying out loud Ave Maria prayers. The more we stared, the more they prayed. An older couple held hands while praying very loudly, and I wondered, *What if we die today? Is this a sign? Is it bad luck to leave, as Veronica warned us? What could possibly await us? Where are we really heading?*

Marcos clutched his seat so tightly that he pulled out some kind of life vest. I felt vulnerable as I stared at my siblings, not knowing what to do. I was helpless; I'd done all in my power to keep them safe for years, and now there was nothing I could do, after all we'd endured! I'd never felt a greater fear of dying.

The turbulence passed eventually, but Jonas didn't stop crying for a long time, and he remained tense for the remainder of the flight. I could sense the great distance from our home already. I wished I could turn back. I wished

I could call out for Franco; even after just a few hours, life felt awfully strange without him and Alejandro.

I wondered what our lives would be like from this point on.

15. From Paradise to Hell

Eventually, we landed at John F. Kennedy Airport and left the plane feeling shaken. When we gathered our luggage, we found our boxes were beaten up, but they hadn't burst open; we thought it was hilarious. Each of us carried a box; we looked like we'd come on behalf of the Three Kings, except we were four.

Our radiant complexions lit up the concourse. At the time, Jonas had golden skin and light brown hair, highlighted by the sun. He appeared tall for his age. Marcos had reddish-brown hair and a peaches-and-cream complexion highlighted by a few freckles. He wasn't so tall and stomped along while walking. His look was comical; he had an extremely friendly demeanor and was like an open book. It was amazing he never told a soul about our living alone. Complexion-wise, both Jonas and Marcos resembled Father. Veronica had long, black, silken hair, warm cinnamon skin, and a petite frame; she resembled Mother the most.

Shortly, we spotted Father; he looked old, round, and short. He wore a baseball cap; blond curls covered his ears on either side. At first he gave us a Mona Lisa smile, but suddenly smiled again, broadly, and said, "Come on, let's go!"

The boys ran toward him, hugging him at the same time. His ocean-water eyes reminded me of our good old days, when we went to Plaza Las Delicias in Ponce and had lots of fun. He kept smiling and helped us carry the boxes.

As we left the airport, the others seemed happy and relaxed in Father's presence. I felt cold; then, one by one, the kids also complained about being cold. We felt strange without our brothers. "What about Franco and Alejandro?" I asked Father at one point.

"Oh, don't worry. We just couldn't get tickets for everyone at once. They're coming soon, maybe in a couple of months," Father said optimistically.

"Look!" Marcos shouted.

We had never seen escalators before. We stared at anything and everything. Upon walking out of the airport, we had a new surprise, the family vehicle: a Ford Pinto. It didn't look like much, but under Father's use and abuse, the little car sure was all it could be.

Once I climbed into the Ford Pinto, I started feeling homesick in earnest.

Father headed to Tato's apartment in Brooklyn for a quick visit. It was late at night by then; New York looked colossal, and I couldn't believe people lived in such tall buildings. Father listened to Gordon Lightfoot songs while driving. Tato's apartment at 50 Vermont Street was quiet and dark. I didn't feel safe entering the building, and didn't understand how she could live so high from the ground and only a few feet from her neighbors.

Tato had cooked for us; she made the best red beans I'd ever had in my life. After greeting us, Tato gave me an eighteen karat gold bracelet with dangling white and pink pearls.

"This is a gift for you. It's one of a kind, so don't lose it." Grandma Tato's eyes glowed like diamonds mixed with emeralds. I'd never been given a gift of this sort before, and I was so happy.

The kids giggled incessantly during our visit; it was the first time in three years we'd done anything out of our routine. New York felt right; I could sense many fellow Puerto Ricans lived there, and for some odd reason, my heart accepted New York as a possible place to live.

It was almost midnight when the time came to head to Massachusetts. We were tired, and the drive seemed never-ending. Eventually, though, Dad drove us into a complex of brick buildings. Our new "home" was in the heart of it. The complex was dirty and smelled like decomposing garbage. There was loud music echoing among the buildings, and groups of people hung out on every corner, even this late.

This renewed my uncertainty about leaving Puerto Rico.

"More buildings," I muttered. I had expected to find my family living in a regular house, surrounded by trees and flowers and mountain views.

When I opened the front door and set foot on the floor of my new home for the first time, I was overwhelmed by a sense of wrongness. I opened my mouth, and words came from deep within me so that it felt like I was vomiting them out. "Cursed be this hour, for there is nothing for me here!"

Everyone stopped and looked at me.

"Where did you learn to speak in such a manner, and why do you curse?" Father asked with a frown.

I wasn't accustomed to cursing; it just came out spontaneously. My father was upset, especially because I didn't answer him. But I had no answer. My heart could envision nothing here for me. The boys stared at me with big eyes; they'd never seen me curse. Veronica stared at me, too, and I nodded firmly, as if to say, *this doesn't feel right*.

And it didn't. There was trash on the ground. It smelled bad. I thought about our old home, where we could breathe clean air and wake up to glorious mornings.

When we finally walked in, tears ran down my face as I saw Mother. She looked aged, more so than Father, and she walked more slowly than she had before. Mother's black hair was long, well below her shoulders. Her face seemed swollen. I was glad to see her, but I felt like a wounded bird. I needed rest. I wanted her love, and I was glad to return her children to her safely.

All the kids rushed to hug her.

"Oh, look at you, all grown up, my God!" She hugged them, and they kept hanging on to her like little ducklings. Veronica sobbed.

Our younger siblings were so different now. I didn't expect them to look so grown up. They sounded different, too; and I could see I would have to get to know them again. Uma wore pajamas and held a plush unicorn. Raquel looked a lot like Alejandro, but with darker skin. She said hi to us, and we laughed. I thought Sergio was pretty tall for his age, and his face was different.

Mother hugged me and grabbed me by my shoulders.

"I can't begin to tell you how proud I am," she said.

I sobbed while hugging her. I *wanted* to make her proud.

After all the commotion had settled down, Mother showed me the apartment. I couldn't seem to let go of the tension I'd felt when getting out of the car and stepping through the door the first time. My chest was tight; my stomach felt like a big knot. I was scared. The apartment seemed cluttered, but there were three bedrooms upstairs. I thought, *we left our little house in the high country to live in a box like pigeons.*

The little kids made me laugh every time they spoke English and danced happily to English songs. When Uma showed me some break-dance moves, I laughed out loud. Later she took me to her room and showed me their bunk beds and a little radio. Everyone seemed happy, and I looked forward to a rest from too much work. But when we finally went to bed, I didn't feel well. I missed the house terribly and felt as if I'd just lost the greatest love of my life. My heart was broken. Falling asleep was tough; the air was too still. Suddenly I felt heartbreak, a horrid agonizing pain from very deep that was almost too painful to bear. My whole being missed my little home, and there I was, ripped from my very own soil.

Upon waking up the following day, I was appalled; the neighborhood was dirty and gray and didn't have a single tree to break the monotony. We couldn't step outside and drink coffee as usual. Life was different. I didn't feel free at all.

"Mother, this place is disgusting," I said.

"Your father says they are trying to make it better. The police make daily rounds, to maintain order."

"Jeez, the police? My God, Mother, this doesn't sound good!"

"Well, *I* didn't want to move here. Your father was the one who signed the lease."

"This environment is no good for the kids," I said honestly. I felt ill once again, thinking maybe Franco and Alejandro shouldn't live in this place at all.

Mother listened, but kept quiet.

The kids got up early as well. As the boys ate breakfast, Dad planned a day of fun.

"Today, guys, I'm going to take you to see the dinosaur footprints by the Connecticut River," he said excitedly.

The boys chuckled in response.

"There are different kinds of dinosaur footprints, you'll see," Dad said.

There was a lot of energy at the table, and too much food: hard-boiled eggs, hot dogs, sausages, French bread, coffee, and orange juice.

"Guys, hurry up and get ready so we can get going! We'll see other places, too," Father promised.

Marco's face lit up for a second, but then he said, "I don't have anything to wear."

"What do you mean?" Mother asked quickly.

"We don't have any clothes," he answered.

Confused, Mother asked, "What do you mean, you don't have clothes? Where are your clothes, Marcos?"

"We left everything behind—we didn't have much anyway," Marcos answered.

Turning to me, Mother inquired, "Doris, did you bring their clothing?"

"We came with what we had," I said.

"Doris made us go to school in the same old clothes every day," Jonas said.

"I wasn't going to let them miss school just because they had old uniforms," I answered.

"We had no clothes. None of us did," said Veronica.

"We had to go to church in the same old clothes. People stared at us," added Marcos, his tone loud and upset.

"Thank God we *went* to school and church. Thank God none of you flunked, and thank God it's over. Veronica, why are you complaining? You got to stay with Naomi, then Victor. You had it easier than any of us," I scolded. I still felt relieved, though, and looked forward to better days. "It doesn't matter anymore," I sighed.

Mother seemed upset. Her face turned red, and she began to breathe heavily. I recognized those signs from the old days.

"Are you listening to this?" she demanded of Father. He listened but didn't seem bothered. She looked into the kids' faces and said, "How come you didn't bring anything to wear?"

"We didn't pack clothes because there wasn't anything good to pack, except the avocados and fruit," I said truthfully.

I couldn't understand why Mother didn't seem to understand that we didn't have much to bring. Mother stared at the kids, as if seeking an answer, but they said nothing more. She then turned to me and said fiercely, "How dare you bring them here looking like orphans? Why didn't you bring their clothes?"

I was surprised by Mother's anger. "Mother, their clothes were paper thin, and we managed with whatever little we had," I answered fearfully.

"How irresponsible, look at them—you didn't take care of them at all! They look like they just came out of an orphanage. Look at you, all prepped up! You'll have a high price to pay for this, you irresponsible pig!" Mother shouted.

Her insults were hurtful; my heart ached, and my legs couldn't hold my weight. I didn't understand; I was scared and didn't know what to say. Mother clenched her fist and scowled at me. "How dare you!"

Chills went down my spine, and I began to cry. Her accusations felt like a death sentence. I thought our arrival was reason enough for celebrating, despite the lack of clothing and shoes. So my joy and pride were short-lived; suddenly, I was back to the stench of accusations and living in fear. In a low tone, I told her, "Mother, the dress I wore yesterday was one Diego and Naomi bought for me, and I worked a summer job and bought my cap and gown, and the things I needed for prom. Otherwise I couldn't have attended. We had nothing—but what matters is we've made it."

Mother stared at me silently, face stern and fist clenched; she didn't seem the least bit interested in how I'd managed to attend graduation. Father didn't say one word.

Then Mother nodded and threatened, yet again, "You

will pay for this. Watch, you'll see. How *dare* you."

Confused and trembling, I looked around at everyone—at the kids with their long faces and my quiet Father. I couldn't understand why no one defended me. In a split second, I realized after all I'd done, there was no way I could take one more insult. I turned around, facing Mother and Father, and roared, looking them both in the eye, "No, Mother, how dare the both of *you* for leaving us behind to live like animals, as if we didn't need anything. We had no uniforms, we went to school with broken-down shoes, and we were the worst-dressed kids in church. I had to dig through trash cans for feminine pads—we had nothing. It's clear there's no appreciation here. I'd leave this place if I could! I want to go back home!"

My face was redder than Mother's. My siblings stared at us, quiet and scared, but their innocence was great—just like old times. Mother continued to breathe heavily, fists clenched, black eyes as dark as night. I felt deceived, disappointed, and exhausted, and I didn't want to live with them anymore.

"I want to go home," I repeated.

"Did you hear what she just said?" Mother said to Father.

I could see the peace and harmony I'd shared with my siblings was over. I had felt safer in our old house, even on those long, fearful nights. How could I endure this? How could I get out? I had no energy left—not even enough to stand on my own two feet. I realized then I'd brought the children I'd protected so carefully straight into hell.

"You're not going anywhere, do you hear me?" Mother shouted. "Don't you dare say those words again; do you think I'm playing? You'll not be permitted to go anywhere by yourself, are you clear?"

"It's clear I've gone from paradise to hell," I affirmed.

"Outrageous! Did you hear her?" Father said to Mother.

"Damned be the hour I set foot in this place," I said. "Is *this* what you brought me here for, to destroy me?" I demanded, accusing both my parents. Neither one knew what to say. Father wouldn't even look me in the eye. I turned and left the room, as Mother emitted a menacing *hmmm*.

Several days later, when I least expected it, Mother grabbed the broomstick and began hitting me in the head and upper back with it. I covered my head with my arms, and she continued beating my arms and upper back until the broomstick made a final cracking sound and broke in two. By then, I had several bumps on my head and severe bruising on my arms and upper back.

I felt completely deceived and betrayed. Too quickly, Mother had forgotten about what really mattered; too quickly, she'd gone back to the beatings.

The day after the first beating, I got out of bed feeling very upset, resenting the kids for complaining and not even trying to defend me—especially Veronica. Only Jonas appeared to be sincerely on my side and sympathetic to me.

Later, when everyone gathered in the living room, and Mother listened to the kids' adventures and complaints, I felt sick to my stomach.

"Don Aníbal gave us fruit and Don Franceschini took us to his house a lot of times in the afternoon," Marcos said.

"Doris didn't clean the house too much—she never swept underneath the beds," Veronica said.

Mother listened attentively. "She didn't clean?"

"No, Mother, she didn't clean the house," Veronica said.

"Look who's talking—the master of stubbornness, who

would never help with anything! The same one who got to stay with Naomi and Diego, then twice with Victor!"

"You shut up," Mother told me.

"Once the child protector, demoted to an outlaw," I challenged. I didn't care how heavy my limbs felt or that my arms throbbed.

"Wasn't the broomstick enough? You want more?"

I looked Mother in the eye, hating her comment, and said, "What they're saying isn't true. If *I* didn't take care of them, then who did, the Indians? Why don't you ask them? Veronica was lazy and stubborn—she wouldn't help with anything. Now she has the nerve to say *I* didn't do much, and you believe her! Suddenly, I'm on your most wanted list. I wonder, then, who it was who graduated from high school? Who was awarded a scholarship to the university? Who wrote you a hundred letters and kept you updated for three years? Apparently, Doris was someone else. All I've gotten is your insults, you breaking the broomstick on my back, your rejection. You've never asked a single one of them if they helped, or how we made it."

I took a deep breath and said, "You may as well kill me. I'm not staying here."

Mother paused for a second but remained hostile, breathing heavily.

"You fresh—!" said Marcos.

"Shut up, Marcos," I snapped.

My disappointment changed me and finalized my relationship with my mother. The bond we had once shared through our letters was forever gone. I was constantly tense and never felt safe around her.

As time passed, I turned inward, choosing to keep things to myself. I didn't want to know my mother anymore and didn't want her to know me. I began to write in a new notebook Father had given me. I thought about my friends in high school, about Naomi and Diego, and then about Victor. I reflected on Victor's last words and decided to write to him. I confided to him that we had moved directly from paradise to hell and told him what had happened.

Victor called our house several days later. Mother seemed happy to receive his phone call at first, and they discussed Franco's and Alejandro's impending arrival. Then her tone changed when Victor asked her about me.

"Doris? Yes, she's fine," she said, adding cheer to her voice. Then she paused. "Oh, you want to talk with her? Sergio, get Doris, Victor is on the phone."

When I came downstairs, Mother mumbled an *hmmm* before giving me the phone. I reached for it, ignoring her hostility. I didn't need to stir up her wrath; I had to remain strong and attempt to lie low, so that I could reach for help where I could.

"Hello?" I answered.

"Doris, Victor here. Listen, I know Mother is probably listening. I received your letter. I'm really sorry; try to hang in there. I understand you don't want to live there anymore, but life out there is dangerous. I'll write to you— just check the mail and watch out for my letter. *Ay Dios mío*. Dear Lord. Thank you for sharing with me, Doris. You have my confidence. I won't share this with anyone. I promise I'll write to you, and you can tell me anything."

I tried with all my strength not to burst out crying. I felt better but wished I could tell Franco and Alejandro not to bother coming, for they'd be walking right into the pit of hell.

"Listen, put Marcos on the phone," Victor continued. "I'm going to set him straight."

I handed Marcos the receiver and went upstairs.

"Hi, Victor," Marcos shouted in excitement—but suddenly his excitement turned into silence. He then started to repeat, "Yes. Yes, I will."

I then heard Marcos give Mother the receiver before he stomped away into his room and whispered with Jonas. After Mother hung up with Victor, she yelled, "Hey, Marcos, and you, Doris, what did Victor say?"

Mother's tone was extremely malicious.

"Uma, just tell her I said 'nothing,'" I whispered to my little sister.

"Mother, Doris said 'nothing'!" Uma yelled.

"*Hmmm,* nothing. Marcos, what did Victor say?"

I could hear the boys mumbling, but Marcos repeated the same thing as I, "Oh, nothing," and stayed in his room with Jonas.

"Nothing," Mother parroted, while waiting to see if Marcos said anything else—but he didn't.

I felt better for having spoken with Victor, because I now had someone who believed in me, someone in whom I could confide. I continued writing to Victor and apologized for disappointing him, sharing with him that I had to leave soon to save myself. I could tell Mother was trying to get close to me on her good days, but I didn't trust her, so I held back.

§ § §

"I want to go to school!" I shouted at Father one day. So he took me to a place that looked like an abandoned building, and I started an English as a second language program. I was introduced as the new Puerto Rican girl, the youngest one in the program. Unfortunately, as I introduced myself, my slashed arms were exposed to the class's gaze.

"What are those marks on your arms, Doris?" asked my new teacher.

"Looks painful—did you burn yourself?"

"Yes, ironing," I said, and felt bad for lying, but I wasn't going to tell the truth in front of a whole class of strangers. I wasn't going to say, "Oh, I get beaten up at home."

I was touched, though, and overwhelmed by the new American teacher, who modestly got me some first aid ointment. I thanked her—and I wanted to tell her everything. But at least her kindness and sympathy made me feel better, almost making me forget about my swollen limbs. It helped me forgive Mother.

By some strange miracle, it finally got through to Mother that something about our situation back home didn't add up.

I thought I'd have a heart attack any time she brought up the topic of our clothing and talked with the kids about it. I wished I could just walk out and ask someone for help. How could I endure?

The kids and my parents gathered and listened to some of our stories, such as the picking of the avocados, the visits to the river, and my secret of having them play in the woods until Franco or I arrived home from school.

"Oh, my God," Mother said modestly.

"Hey, kids, you're all hypocrites!" I yelled out.

The tone of their conversation changed, and I heard Mother get up in response to my comment. I didn't care. I was in my bedroom, and she soon pushed the door wide open with a clenched fist—I was surprised there was no broomstick in her hand. I'd been sitting on the edge of my bed, my face in my hands, pleading to the Lord for a miracle. When I looked up, my red eyes won the stare-down. She didn't take a step further. Making the *hmmm* sound, she turned around, closed my door, and walked silently away.

After asking the kids about the missing packages on

several separate occasions, suddenly, one day, I heard Mother say to the whole group, "You mean to say you never received *anything?*"

I couldn't bear to hear the topic brought up yet again. The kids were puzzled, though. "No, Mommy, we never received anything," Marcos said.

She then asked Jonas and Veronica, "Are you sure? I sent you packages on many different occasions."

Jonas and Veronica confirmed once again that we never received anything. Mother then confronted my father in front of everyone.

"Did you send them the packages?" Her tone was menacing.

Everyone stared at Father, but he didn't answer. He wrinkled his lips, barely mumbling something.

"Answer me! Did you send them the packages?" Mother shouted.

I was sweating, and my knees shook. I feared she was going to jump him. Then I was afraid of what might happen if he denied not sending them. I couldn't even imagine what she'd do to me. Father frowned, mumbling, then just turned and walked outside.

Mother then turned to us.

"I gave him packages with good clothes to send to you at least every three months," she said.

"We received letters, but never packages," said Jonas.

"We never did, Mom. Dori had Alejandro check the mail every day," Marcos said.

Obviously, Father had *not* sent the packages. He never revealed what he'd done with the contents. Every now and then, Mother threatened him on the subject, but he never once admitted he'd failed to send them as she'd ordered. I was extremely disappointed, embarrassed, and repulsed by his actions.

"The entire time, we lived beyond poverty, yet we kept our chins up, and showed everyone happy faces, so no one suspected," I told Mother.

"I sent at least fourteen packages with new clothes and shoes, including toys," Mother said.

We all stared at her. I was completely drained.

"Too late now," I said sarcastically.

I almost added *I already paid the price,* but hesitated. Things were bad enough. No matter what happened now, I was terminally disappointed in my parents, and my heart was set on leaving, regardless. Ever since our reunification, I'd had trouble sleeping, I was always nervous, and I felt staying would end in my destruction. I enormously resented Mother. My limbs were back to their state of constant healing, and I'd give her hateful looks every time she went out shopping and came back with a new broomstick to replace the last one she'd broken on me. I felt like telling her, *you may as well buy a dozen at a time!*

"I promise you guys, I'll never forgive him for this one," Mother said, obviously feeling deceived herself.

It didn't matter anyway; she never recognized anything I'd done. She never treated me with love, never apologized for her insults or for demolishing my limbs over and over with the damn broomsticks. I couldn't understand what had happened to the mother who'd written me countless letters, believing in me and offering advice for all my concerns and aches. I had believed in her then, and she had believed in me—or so I thought. It hurt me to see she had turned on me so quickly.

She watched me every day, like a hawk.

"She can watch all she wants, I *will* leave this place," I promised Veronica.

"Don't keep repeating those words," Veronica pleaded. "She'll hurt you."

Doris Mercado

"Don't you realize the reason why I need to leave? I have no idea where I'm going, but one thing I know for sure is I wasn't born tarnished—and I'm going to save myself no matter what."

16. Reunification

A few months after our arrival, our parents sent two airline tickets to Puerto Rico for Franco and Alejandro. The idea of reuniting the whole family felt healing to me; it gave me hope, and I felt whole once I had accepted it would happen.

Both boys arrived looking aged and tired. Franco couldn't stop smiling, but mysteriously; and it turned out he felt just like I did.

"Listen, I feel trouble—I don't have a good feeling about this," he said to me later, privately.

I'd never seen him so afraid and uncertain in my whole life. Franco was always personable, happy, and bubbly.

He was right, though. Trouble just welcomed us into its arms. Even though the family was together now, I became more and more anxious, wondering, *What is going to happen to us? Is coming here really the end?*

Alejandro was perplexed at the new neighborhood, and I was worried about my brothers. They were now young men and were quickly noticed by the slum dwellers around us. There was constant fighting and drinking in our neighborhood, and the police often came around to check on "suspected drug deals."

We turned heads any time we went out together, probably because we were so many. I hoped the troublemakers wouldn't break into our place while we were gone, and fortunately, they never did. Jonas's bike was stolen once, but it never went beyond that.

Soon after he arrived, I pulled Franco aside and complained about the rest of the kids. "They're misbehaving, saying I didn't take care of them or didn't do cleaning, and Mom is after me now. She keeps hitting me with the broomstick. Look at my arms. I can't even brush my hair. I'm running away—you'll see. I'm leaving, no matter what."

"What?" said Franco, and he immediately called Jonas and Marcos into the room. He grabbed them by their ears and yelled at them. They ran crying to Mother. He also yelled at Veronica, but I told him to let her be, she was sorry and was trying to help me now. Mother knew better and eyed me, and Franco noticed her fist.

"But what's happening here? She took care of them! She took care of all of us!" Franco protested to Mother, staring at her red face and clenched fist.

By then, Alejandro had learned about the packages of clothing that had never turned up. He then yelled at the kids, "Not cool, guys—you should know better! Remember, I kept checking the mail and we never received *anything,* so why are you acting like its Doris's fault? Not cool!" he scolded.

Infuriated, Mother yelled at me, "What gave you the right to complain to them?"

"You think I'm going to hold back the truth? I've told them everything!" I challenged back.

Franco looked at Mother, concerned, and tried peacemaking. "Well, we didn't have much, but it wasn't Doris's fault. I mean, look at them. They're not skinny or sick. We did the best we could."

Mother eyed me, nodding. I didn't care. Marcos and Jonas were teary-eyed, and Veronica went into her room.

Franco and Alejandro arrived in the same predicament as the rest of us, of course: in deteriorated clothing and shoes. They almost looked like two old men. Angry and embarrassed, Mother planned a shopping trip to a local mall; eleven of us squeezed into the tiny Ford Pinto and headed out. When we got there, the boys experienced a major adrenaline rush. Marcos and Jonas pointed and laughed and were astonished at all the clothes and shoes on display. It was the first time they'd been in a place like that.

Nothing interested me at all. I just wanted to go home. I walked like a zombie; all I felt was Uma's little hand holding on to mine. Her love, right then, made me believe I still had a little hope.

We swarmed the men's department at one store, and the boys ran back and forth trying on new clothes and shoes, making a huge mess in the fitting room. Not many people approached the area while we were there, but security did.

"Everything okay here?" a tall, muscular man asked.

"Everything is okay, sir, we are just trying to shop for four boys," Father said, laughing. "They recently arrived from Puerto Rico."

I didn't care for the security guard's look of distrust. I just turned and walked away.

I was disgusted at Father as he went on in a friendly demeanor, shouting out, "There's nine here, but altogether, thirteen!" Father's eyes were cheery, but I looked at him in disdain. Neither he nor Mother had ever apologized for condemning me about the lousy missing packages. Fortunately, Marcos interrupted Father's loud conversation with the guard. "Hey, Dad, can I buy these?"

"You dumbo, those pants are too big!" said Alejandro.

"Shut up, I like them," Marcos shot back.

I went to the racks and quickly looked for the right size. "Here, try these on," I said.

Marcos grabbed them and went to try them on. When he got back, he said, "Dori, they fit perfectly!" He looked up at me and chuckled.

In many ways, I thought of myself almost as the kids'

true mother. I missed the closeness we'd had back home and knew that soon, I wouldn't be there for them. But I had to save myself.

"Hey, boys, look at Micaela in his new pants," Alejandro said, whistling.

"Stop it, or I'm going to scream!" Marcos shouted. He didn't mind being called by other names but hated being called "Micaela." Alejandro and Jonas laughed as if someone had tickled them. Once Franco heard their laughing, he laughed as well, and so did Father.

"You all need to stop," I told them. "We're going to get in trouble. Marcos, stop shouting—we're not in the mountains anymore."

I turned and walked away, as a huge wave of sadness washed over me. I wanted to cry; I wanted to scream, *what just happened?* But the touch of Uma's hand kept me grounded, so I kept walking along with her as I tried to tame my pain and anger. Though I cried on and off as we walked, my little sister was happy and innocent, unaware of my anguish. I sent my thoughts out toward my precious little home, so far away in the mountains of Puerto Rico. Although I was surrounded by all my siblings now, I barely accepted our new surroundings as just a temporary home, no more.

The boys' shouting and laughter echoed through the entire store. "Hey, Jonas," Alejandro called. "Khaki shirt, khaki pants—you look like an explorer! Would you like a pair of boots and a hat too?"

"He's Jacques Cousteau, the great ocean explorer," said Franco, chuckling.

He made me laugh, which made me feel whole—it almost healed my broken heart.

"You guys know Jacques Cousteau? I love watching his program," Father said.

"Yes, there's Jack Cousteau, right there," said Franco, pointing at Jonas. Father laughed out loud.

"Shut up, you girlies, I like them, can I leave them on, Mother?" asked Jonas.

Mother laughed and covered her mouth, but Dad laughed hysterically. "No, we have to pay for them first!"

With a half-smile of contentment, Jonas went off to change his clothes.

"I want to go to the science store, Dad," said Sergio.

"Boys, we have to get going. Jonas, you need shoes, hurry up!" said Father.

Jonas came back with brown hiking boots; I laughed, but he was puzzled by my laughter. "You like these?" he asked.

"They're cool," I answered.

Examining the soles, he said, "Look, Dori, they're perfect for walking on rocks."

"Since when do you know anything about boot soles? Wow, they're waterproof too, Jonas, good pick," I said, pressing my lips together, trying not to laugh. It was a relief to realize I'd brought back some smart kids—I was happy.

But even as all this action occurred, even as Mother stacked a cart full of things the kids were in desperate need of, my heart began detaching from my family. I began envisioning my life apart from them. I had to go. I didn't want to hurt anymore.

Franco made the kids laugh by trying on a pair of sunglasses.

"Hey, Dad, look at Franco, he looks like Hector Lavoe!" Franco laughed as well.

"Whoa, guys check out Alejandro, he looks like a doctor," Franco said.

I decided this was one of the best times the kids had experienced in a long while, just trying on new clothes.

"Keep it quiet or we're going to get kicked out of the store," Veronica scolded.

"Veronica, go find a hairbrush," Alejandro teased.

"Grab a pair of scissors, too, you look like a hairball," said Marcos.

"You're stupid, both of you!" said Veronica.

We finally finished our clothes shopping spree several hundred dollars later. Then we went to the art and science store, and Sergio bought some dinosaur toys. He took a while about it, and I got tired of waiting.

"Are we ever going to leave this store?" I vented. I didn't choose anything for myself; I didn't want anything.

Veronica came up to me and said quietly, "Dori, I'm scared. I don't feel good. I'm so lost."

I felt awful for her, but said sincerely, "It's not fair what you guys did, all the complaining. I took care of all of you—you know I did. Mother's after me now. I'm going to leave soon, for good. I'm getting away from all of this. If I don't, I'm afraid I won't survive. Do you have any idea how much force it takes to break a broomstick on someone's head?"

Veronica looked at me in anguish.

"What are you two whispering about?" Mother demanded suddenly.

Veronica and I froze. "Nothing," Veronica answered after a long moment.

I could feel Mother's fiery eyes on me. I didn't answer at all. Those happy days back home all seemed like a dream now.

"It seems like I left my lungs behind, along with everything else; I can't even breathe," I vented to Veronica, and I didn't care if Mother heard me.

She signaled for me to keep quiet. Mother then moved away, letting out a hateful *hmmm,* which made me feel like I was in trouble again. Uma came back to me.

"Dori, would you like to see my favorite doll?"

"Sure," I said.

"See, it's a Cabbage Patch," Uma said, laughing, handing me the doll.

I laughed. I'd never seen a Cabbage Patch doll before. They reminded me of our babies: bright happy eyes, chunky bodies, and comical dimpled smiles. I adored them.

Living in the slum introduced me to absolute misery, but writing about my feelings kept me attuned to myself. Writing kept me from drowning in the great dark suction that wanted to swallow me whole. I hated every second of my life, now I'd transitioned from the high country, with its pure air and humble surroundings, to a filthy slum. I had never woken up or gone to sleep as tense or scared as I did then. Every single day, I feared for my life.

Although I knew I had to leave to save myself, I didn't know where I could possibly go, and I just couldn't tear myself away from the kids, especially from the younger ones, who were absolutely in love with me.

Soon I would be twenty years old. After two long years of living in the slum, my self-esteem had almost hit rock bottom. I felt inferior because of Mother's insults, threats, and physical attacks, which continued up until age twenty-one. I got to leave the apartment occasionally, to go to work or do a little shopping, but my outings were monitored. My limbs got accustomed to throbbing, as they were repeatedly damaged and had to start the healing process over and over again.

I couldn't envision any future for myself. Would I be okay? Would I make it? How?

I missed going home to the old house. In this new

place, I arrived at a box where I didn't feel safe or loved and wasn't called "Dori" but rather "Stupid." Rather of enjoying luscious trees and clean air, I had to pick my way around the garbage and used syringes littering the ground. Instead of birds singing, boom boxes played graphic tunes and constant fighting broke out. I knew I'd have to be really strong if I was going survive; I had to set a firm focus on my dreams to make it through. No matter what life handed me, I'd have to hang on and never let go.

At night, I began to write in a new notebook I titled "Once Child Protector, Demoted to Outlaw." I knew it was daring to do so and was aware that if Mother got a hold of these writings, she would break *all* my bones. But writing down my feelings helped me forgive Mother and the kids. I'd write wistfully of my life in high school, my friends, our happy days, and our trips to the river.

I wanted to know what had happened to us, and why.

Despite growing up with Mama Blas, who was a devoted Roman Catholic, a woman who recited ancient prayers daily, I doubted the existence of hell. I felt I was right in its pit. I felt I was offending the Lord, but I still wrote questioning the existence of hell. If it truly existed, I was in it.

I didn't know whether I was being purified for something better. What else would I have to endure? I wanted answers. I wrote letters to the Lord asking why I was going through all this, once even giving Him a deadline for a reply. I brought the kids safely; did I deserve this? Why must I endure this, and for what? Would I *ever* know peace?

After venting and reflecting, I decided to continue fighting against anything or anyone who stood in my way. I believed if we had made it this far, then we could achieve much more. I was ready for a battle—a battle of goodness.

I'd keep fighting, doing what was right and fair and honest and just—to save myself.

Father was one of my chief opponents in this daily battle. He truly scared me, the way he was always whispering to the boys, who were no longer boys, but men.

"She's stupid."

They listened to Father and repeated, "Dori, you're stupid."

Shaking my head, I'd say, "I brought you here as polite and disciplined kids. Now look at how quickly you've forgotten it all."

Despite my brave words, I was afraid of them; they grew fast, and they were all bigger than Veronica and me. We never talked now like we used to. Our coffee chats had been replaced by hanging around with Father. Whenever Mother left the house early to do errands or take the younger kids to medical appointments, Father returned to his old habits, telling us, "You guys can stay home. You don't need to go to school."

"Yes, they do!" I'd shout back. I'd glare at them and say, "You are *all* going to school. Go and get dressed right this instant. When we were alone on the island, we were a team; how could you forget those days?"

Whenever the boys couldn't find clean clothes, Mother would demand, "Where are those two pigs?" meaning Veronica and I. It didn't matter how often we'd tell her their laundry was done and it was they who left their dirty clothes everywhere; she didn't care. She'd say it was our responsibility to search for their dirty laundry and wash it.

As Veronica and I took these insults from Mother, the boys laughed, rejoicing at "the disgusting ones." Mother seemed pleased by their bullying, which scared me even more. I warned yet again that I'd leave if she kept mistreating me, but the beatings remained severe. Once,

I spent two days in bed after a beating, unable to move. Veronica never left my sight. Mother's glare in response to my inability to move out of bed was macabre.

She then told the boys, including Franco, to keep an eye on me. They spied on every move I made, but I didn't show them any fear. Still, I was to hear even Franco say, "Sorry, but I can't let you run away."

Veronica was my only hope.

"Veronica, I *will* leave no matter what, and I'll never return to this inferno," I told her once.

She frowned, then turned around and handed me the phone. "Dial 911 right now."

I contemplated the phone.

"Pick it up, Dori. Just dial, now," she insisted.

"No. I can't do it, Veronica. I don't dare to—she'll get in trouble. There are too many kids, and there will be worse consequences if I tell than if I don't. I can't do it."

"Who *cares?* Look at you! This has to stop. Only you can do it, Dori. Go on, just take the phone and dial," she pleaded.

"I can't do it. She'll go to jail," I said.

"Stop feeling sorry for her! She's not sorry for you!"

I didn't have the heart to make the call.

Later on, I wrapped up my first year in the English as a second language program and was placed in an employment and training program at the University of Massachusetts. By then, Father's verbal abuse had become an enormous burden for all of us. I fought back by believing in myself: I had to believe that I was good, that I was someone special. There were constant fights in the house, sometimes between the boys and sometimes between our parents, not to mention the standard insults and threats to Veronica and me.

I had to get out, but I had no money to purchase a

ticket back to Puerto Rico. How would I ever get back to where I belonged? The bottom line was that I didn't want to become an inconvenience for anyone. Trying to adjust seemed impossible, but I decided I'd rather bear my own cross than beg for help.

I often wished I was as innocent as my youngest siblings. They seemed so unaware of the harsh world around them; playing, drawing, and listening to music kept them too busy to notice the hostilities. Uma called to me constantly to show me her drawings, and Sergio did, too. They were so young, yet their drawings were impressive. One Valentine's Day, Uma created her own Valentine's card dedicated to me, which I cherished and preserved.

Arnaldo, one of our neighbors, began to hang out with the boys and my father. He spoke Spanish and seemed nice. I talked to him sometimes; he noticed my bruised arms, but I offered no explanation.

"You guys are noisy," he'd tell me. "I can hear your arguments. I can hear everything."

I was embarrassed.

We chatted every afternoon after I got home from school. I dated him briefly, but when he'd talk about marriage and settling down, I'd smirk. I wanted a career, not marriage. Arnaldo offered to help me, but I didn't want help; I wanted to get out on my own. He noticed the days when I didn't come out and talk with him.

One day, he asked, "What are those red marks on your arm?" But having heard everything that was going on in our household, the truth was that he already knew.

"Your mother isn't going to change," he warned me. "Maybe I should say something to your father?"

"I don't want anyone feeling sorry for me," I told him.

"No, but your father is cool," he said.

"Sure he is," I said sarcastically. "And so are my brothers

and my mother."

He didn't get it. "Okay, I'll stop by your place sometime this evening." I had no idea what Arnaldo meant, so I just shrugged.

Later on, my father yelled, "Doris, come here!"

"Yes, Father," I said, when I had reported in. Arnaldo was sitting with my father in the living room. He smiled but appeared trembling like a little puppy.

"Go and see your mother," Father said. "She wants to tell you something."

I went into the bedroom, where Mother waited.

"Yes, Mother," I said, shaken by a cold chill.

"Arnaldo is asking for your hand in marriage," she told me solemnly. "Your answer must come from your heart."

I was perplexed at what she'd just said. She didn't seem angry.

"Now, let's go to the living room," she said, and I allowed her to escort me to where Father and Arnaldo were waiting. Mother sat down on the couch next to Father; I remained standing. My father had his hands clasped together close to his lips, as if in deep thought.

"Doris, Arnaldo is asking your hand in marriage. Do you accept?" Father asked.

I looked at Arnaldo, and he displayed a perfect white-toothed smile. Then I looked into Dad's serious aquamarine eyes.

"No, I don't, Father. I don't want to get married."

I was desperate, hurting, and afraid of living at home, but the last thing on my mind was marriage. The last thing I wanted was to be rescued by a man.

There was silence for a few seconds. Arnaldo seemed confused and tried to smile, while blushing.

"Very well, you've heard her answer. I want you to leave now, Arnaldo," Father commanded.

Arnaldo stood, but froze for a moment in embarrassment. Then he excused himself and hurried out.

"Doris, you can go now," Father said.

Mother remained silent. I was afraid she'd hit me again with the broomstick, as if it were my fault Arnaldo had asked to marry me. My parents talked for a while, though nothing seemed to come of it. But the following day, she accused me, "You were dating him behind my back, weren't you?"

"We only talked," I answered.

"Sure," she sneered. "If you want to get married, go ahead."

Father laughed. I was completely disgusted at their remark.

"Just take me out of my misery. Go on!" I cried.

"Did you *hear* her?" Father said to Mother. Mother mumbled something to Father, but I just walked away.

I was completely surprised when Jonas approached me later and said, "Dori, stay away from Arnaldo. I don't trust him. He's just a talker. I think he's a wolf in sheep's clothing. He notices the way you're always working, and I think he's looking for an escape from this life."

I didn't know how to answer my little brother.

Father never said anything to me about Arnaldo afterward, but Mother seemed more malicious than ever.

When I left the next morning to catch the bus to my job, Arnaldo appeared out of nowhere, scowling. "Why did you let me talk with your parents? You said yes at first!"

"No, I didn't. You didn't say you were going to talk about marriage. I don't want to get married. I don't even know you well," I said.

"I'll be watching you," he announced.

I realized with complete horror that I now had a stalker. I wanted to tell someone but was afraid nobody at home would believe me. My energy was already consumed every day with trying to save myself from Mother, dealing with the bullying at home, and worrying about Veronica—and now this.

I felt I had no way out, that I was very innocent and naïve. I just wanted to know when I could rest from this hell on earth. I thought about telling Jonas about Arnaldo's threat, but he was too young to deal with it, and I didn't want my brother to get in trouble.

Arnaldo's harassment occurred on a daily basis for the first week, then on and off for several months. He was always going on about how I had embarrassed him, never once considering how he had set himself up to be embarrassed.

I told Veronica about the harassment but made her promise not to tell. Veronica, however, told him off—but that didn't make a difference. After long, draining months of this horror, I helplessly confided in Larry, the American bus driver. Larry appeared to be in his fifties; he had a noble look, wore glasses, had a reddish beard, and was tall and lean. Larry always seemed pleased to see me, and every day, he'd ask me how I was doing. He made me feel he cared. I told Larry what was happening as I got off the bus and pointed to Arnaldo's car; as usual, he was waiting for me. Larry gave him a long, contemptuous look and turned back to me.

"Doris, you have to call the police," he said.

Whenever I got off the bus, Larry waited until I crossed the street and walked into my workplace before continuing on his route. In the afternoons, he also waited until I made it to the apartment.

But Arnaldo was always there, stalking me.

Just when I thought I was at his mercy, Arnaldo made a careless mistake. One day, as I got off the bus as usual,

Mother spotted Arnaldo yelling out, "Go on, go to your mother!"

Drawing the attention of the other slum dwellers, he continued his mocking. I walked quickly to our apartment, head down, and didn't notice when Mother came out.

She flew by me, went straight to Arnaldo, and grabbed him by the neck in front of everyone in the slum, shouting, "You stay away from my daughter, or I'm going to kill you!"

Arnaldo looked like a helpless lizard hanging from Mother's claws.

The entire slum paused for a few seconds, and onlookers emerged from every corner. Mother juggled him enough for her hands to become slippery with blood.

"Don't you dare come near my daughter if you want to live—I'll be watching you," Mother declared, as she threw him to the ground. I couldn't believe Mother had said the same words he'd said to me: "I'll be watching you."

Everyone stared at Mother, but no one came close. They watched and stayed quiet as Arnaldo got up from the pavement and stumbled to his apartment. Breathing like a racehorse, Mother entered our apartment and headed straight to the sink to wash her hands.

"What is all that blood? What in the world happened?" Father yelled, panicked.

Silence fell over our apartment. Mother and Father sent everyone out of the living room and they talked, but in low voices; to me, it all sounded like mumbling. I felt a little relief but was almost certain the police would come for Mother after what she'd done. I heard Father let out a suspicious and loud *hmmm* at one point.

My parents remained in the living room for a long time, upset. I was afraid to tell them anything about the harassment. But the next day, Arnaldo harassed me yet again.

"Hey, look at what your mother did to me!" His neck looked red and carved up. "No one humiliates me like that!" he said angrily.

"This is enough, I'm going to call the police on you, Arnaldo," I told him grimly. "I'm going to have you thrown in jail. Someone told me you were a wolf in sheep's clothing, and they were right!"

I was ready to sprint if he tried to get near me—but he just looked at me, his expression scared, and took off in his car. I felt a tiny bit of relief—but still didn't feel safe.

The same day, I shared what happened with Larry, the bus driver.

"Doris, you have to do something," he insisted. "I'm afraid this guy could hurt you. Please go to the police. I can call them right now, and they'll come and talk with you."

"Yes, but what if my family finds out? I don't want trouble," I replied.

"No one will know, Doris. Save yourself, and do it *now*."

"Okay," I said, and Larry called the police right from the bus. I started trembling like a leaf as the police cruiser approached. I could barely stand up. Larry talked with them briefly, and then I finished giving them the information they needed. I felt better for having done so.

Later, the officers knocked on Arnaldo's door and gave him a warning, ordering him to stay away from me. I couldn't stop thanking Larry; and for his part, he never stopped showing concern. He believed in me.

Several months later, Arnaldo moved away; and finally, I could breathe a little.

Mother never talked to me about the incident with Arnaldo. I was grateful, though; her maternal instincts hadn't failed her on this one occasion.

17. Father's Help Attempt

Veronica turned sixteen in 1987, and before long, Mother was beating her as well. One day, when I got home from work, I was horrified to see that her entire face was disfigured; she looked like she'd come out on the losing end of a street fight. Her cheeks were black and blue, her eyes bloodshot, her lip broken—all by Mother's fist.

Veronica had been talking to Leo, a boy from the slum. I thought Leo was sweet and kind. He seemed to love school; but we were forbidden to talk to boys, much less date them. We weren't even allowed to talk *about* boys.

Barely able to speak, gritting out the words from between clenched teeth, Veronica told me, "Dori, you may put up with this, but I won't. I'm going to my school counselor in the morning. Please come with me."

Father walked in just then, and I became nervous because I thought he'd heard us talking. He looked serious, and paused.

"What in the world happened to your face!" he shouted suddenly.

I could sense his anger, but Veronica wouldn't answer, so I did.

"Who do you *think* did this?"

Father looked at me with wide eyes asking, "Your mother?"

I nodded, but Veronica still wouldn't answer. She was stubborn by nature, but at the moment she was also in pain and terrified. Father called out, "Lina, why did you hit Veronica so viciously?"

"She was talking with Leo, and Mother didn't like it," I said to Father.

Veronica finally made an effort to talk, but Dad was able to see her mouth was too swollen. He clenched his fists.

"Your mother doesn't realize the authorities could come here and take all you kids away," he said. "I've been warning her, but she doesn't listen."

We felt hopeless listening to Father. He then stepped outside, probably to clear his head, and Veronica and I continued our murmured conversation.

"Veronica, how am I going to go to your school?" I demanded. "You and Alejandro take the same school bus. Alejandro can't see me there with you. If he does, he's not going to keep quiet—he'll go running to Mother. If Mother finds out, you know we're both dead, right?"

"Well, I'm telling everything—and I'm going to tell them about *your* beatings, too. If we don't do anything, she could hurt us real bad. Don't say I didn't warn you."

I felt desperate, but I couldn't figure out how I'd get to Veronica's school the next day. The bus I took to work didn't go by her school, and Mother watched everyone board his or her bus every morning.

So I didn't accompany Veronica to school the next day, as she'd asked. But all day long, I kept thinking about her and how she'd tell the school about our beatings, wondering how the school would handle the situation.

After school, later in the evening, Veronica beckoned to me to go down to the basement with her.

"Listen, Dori, I told a social worker. It's done," she whispered.

We both heard footsteps right above us. It was Mother making her rounds in the kitchen. As I listened to her steps, my heart thumped, and I prayed she would leave the kitchen. We kept silent until we heard her move away.

"You have to be careful, Veronica," I said nervously.

"The school counselor told me someone will come here tomorrow. They want to speak with you," Veronica replied.

"Well . . . I could speak to them in private. We have to figure something out, maybe in the afternoon. But don't take the school bus with Alejandro; wait for me . . ."

Before I could say anything else, the basement door opened.

"Who's down there?" Mother yelled.

We froze. I then waved at Veronica to stay quiet and sprinted upstairs.

"I was looking for something," I said to Mother, pretending everything was fine. I closed the basement door without turning the light off. Mother looked at me shrewdly, as if listening to my silence as well as what I'd said. Then she walked out.

As Marcos and Alejandro came into the kitchen, I made a quick trip down to the basement and signaled to Veronica that it was safe to come up. She walked right by the boys, who stared fearfully at her injuries.

"What happened to you? Oh my God, look at her face!" Marcos cried, not taking his eyes off her as he waited anxiously for a response.

"Whoa, who did this to you?" Alejandro echoed. "What happened? Why are you so quiet?"

"What's wrong?" Franco asked as he stepped into the kitchen. He scowled at the sight of Veronica's face. I glanced at Franco and gestured toward Mother.

"Wow, her face is demolished. Jeez," said Franco.

"Why won't you say anything? What happened to you?" Jonas asked out loud.

Mother heard the questioning and soon appeared in the kitchen. Veronica refused to answer and went upstairs. Mother's face held a look of satisfaction as Veronica left;

it appeared the cause of her mutilation would remain a secret.

I kept my distance for the rest of the day, as Mother moved around our home like a dark shadow.

The following afternoon, when I got home, Veronica was sitting with Mother in the living room. I couldn't bear to look into Mother's menacing eyes.

"Listen," she growled. "This one reported me at school, and a social worker came here today. Did you know anything about this?"

"No, I didn't," I said, but Mother didn't seem convinced. I felt relieved someone had visited. The social worker had left the house just a few minutes before I arrived.

"A social worker?" Father asked, concerned, when he learned of the visit. He seemed to sympathize with Veronica and dispatched her from the living room when he arrived. And just when I thought Mother would reward me with the broomstick, an argument broke out between my parents.

"Look at her face!" Father said loudly.

"She deserves it. Don't you be a softie, now," Mother threatened.

"It's wrong! Are you trying to kill them? How can you hit Veronica so viciously? How can you hit Doris with the broomstick? Then you let them lie there like it's nothing. I'm not taking part in this. My hands are clean. I don't lay my hands on my kids," Father said, and walked out, lifting his hands high in the air, repeating, "My hands are clean."

By then, I was in the kitchen by Veronica's side, fixing something to eat. I tapped Veronica with my elbow as a sign to remain calm; we were both trembling. Mother remained in the living room; quiet but breathing heavily. The TV was on, and my little siblings were chattering as if nothing had happened.

Seconds later, while I was still fixing sandwiches,

someone tapped on the kitchen window. I looked up, and it was Father. He waved at me to come close. His eyes were serene and didn't seem mean. When I approached the window, Father whispered, "Tell Veronica to come out, but don't let your mother see you. Hurry!"

I nodded at Veronica so she'd be on the alert and thought, *Some of our prayers have been answered.* I pushed close to her, whispering in her ear, "Go outside, by the kitchen window. Father wants to see you."

I walked over quietly and opened the kitchen door.

"Go now, it's all right, he's not mad. I'll keep watch," I said.

Veronica stepped out, while I remained in the kitchen and made enough noise for both of us, so Mother wouldn't be tempted to come in. I was extremely nervous. I glanced out the window and saw Father and Veronica walking away from the apartment as he whispered to her urgently.

Minutes later, Veronica came back, her eyes filled with tears. I was afraid she'd burst out crying, so I announced loudly, "Hey everyone, I made sandwiches!"

I hoped I could distract Mother from noticing Veronica's emotional state. As Raquel, Uma, Sergio, Jonas, and Marcos rushed to the kitchen, I said, "Veronica, take your sandwich and go upstairs now."

Veronica passed through the mob of kids, cut through the living room, and went upstairs, unnoticed by Mother. I was relieved and turned my attention toward keeping harmony in the kitchen. When the kids were done eating, I hurried upstairs and found that Veronica had fallen asleep. Her sandwich lay on the side table, uneaten; my heart ached when I realized her mouth was too sore for her to eat.

The next morning, as we headed out to catch our buses, Father appeared out of nowhere and directed Veronica to get into his car. Somehow I felt less tense around him now. Though he continued his bullying, he sometimes waved at us as if to say, *don't mind me.* He didn't want Mother to suspect that he didn't agree with the beatings or bullying any longer.

"It's wrong. I told her it's wrong, but she won't listen," Father would say to us.

I listened without saying much but appreciated that he now refrained from calling me stupid. He seemed caring and talked with Veronica and me in low tones. He'd take us to the flea market and treated us with kindness. The three of us kept some distance at home, though, so Mother wouldn't suspect anything—so no one would suspect anything.

Dad often appeared ashamed around us, as if he had realized that all the bullying had gone too far.

After Father had gone to Veronica's school a second time, he told me, "Doris, something is going to happen. I can't tell you right now what it is. Just—beware."

I nodded and nearly broke down as he went on to say, "Listen, Doris. Since you're over eighteen years old, there's nothing they can do to protect you. Once kids turn eighteen, they're considered adults. But they *will* help Veronica, because she's considered a minor. I'm sorry. I'll do my best to stop this," he promised.

I thought, *Even if Father was to help me, I would still want out.*

Not long afterward, a social worker came to our home. "Which one is Doris?" he demanded. I stood up, and he said he wanted to speak to me privately.

Mother stood up, clenching her right fist, and pierced me with her eyes. "She's not going anywhere, so whatever you need to ask, you can do it right here, right now," Mother threatened.

When he asked about the atmosphere at home, I couldn't say anything; but my nervousness was obvious. He then asked other questions, which I barely answered.

"Sir, leave now," Mother said threateningly.

The social worker apologized for "bothering" us and left. A few days later, Veronica didn't return home from school. She never came back, and I didn't get a chance to say good-bye.

I don't know how Father managed this. I never learned exactly what the repercussions were, though I know Mother was irate that she had to appear before someone. Nothing happened to the rest of the kids, and I felt awful for Veronica. I didn't know how to react, either, and tried very hard to keep my composure. This distracted Mother somewhat, and though she accused me and threatened me, Father came forward to shield me this time.

"Don't you touch her—don't you *dare*. I did it. *I* told Veronica to tell the school about you beating them, since you don't listen. If you don't stop, they're coming here again. I told you that my hands were clean, didn't I?" he warned.

Mother remained defiant, and my parents had all kinds of fights after this. Once again, my life seemed like a nightmare. Veronica was with me one minute, and I was trying to save her—and then she vanished.

I didn't see Veronica or even know where she was for about three years.

§ § §

I began to have more difficulty interacting with people. I couldn't differentiate between good and bad intentions. I didn't trust men and saw evil in women. Overcoming my shyness became increasingly difficult. Uncertainty and insecurity filled my soul.

It wasn't long before Mother began physically attacking Father, too. He'd stopped bullying me altogether; there wasn't any more, "Hey, stupid." Instead, Mother became Father's target, and he'd call her "mosquito brain." He'd say things like, "Hey, guys, mosquito brain is here."

She'd contemplate him, giving him one of her deep breaths and a warning to consider the consequences of what he was doing. Even on the rare occasions when she was in good spirits, his sarcasm ruined her day. Then Mother began to reply to his taunts, "Maybe you should leave."

Father then proposed, "All right, who comes with me? Whoever stays here shouldn't say I'm their father. Doris, who are you going with?"

I didn't answer Father because I didn't want to be with either one of them. This annoyed him.

"Don't ever say you are my daughter!" he yelled, upset.

We were all mad at each other. Mother wanted to see my father out of the place and sent messages with the boys for him to leave. My enraged father finally grabbed a few things and left with his small bag, the same bag he'd carried when he'd left us in Puerto Rico. He sent back one last message with one of the kids, asking if he could stay for two more days to spend Thanksgiving with the boys, but Mother said no.

Father left on a cold day; Mother couldn't care less. I figured he'd come back soon, but he didn't. The house felt empty without him. After he left, my brothers and I had a big argument. "Father is upset at *you*, Dori! You didn't want to go with him!" Marcos shouted.

"I wanted to go with Father. I didn't want to stay here," said Franco.

"We could have left with him, and lived in our own place," Alejandro said.

"How come you didn't agree, Dori?" demanded Franco.

Mother interrupted with a one-time warning: "If I ever hear the word 'father' again, you'll see what happens."

"We could have left with him, Dori," whispered Franco.

"Listen, I couldn't pick a favorite! I don't want to be with either one!" I protested.

Too bad for me, Mother overheard my remark and revisited my limbs yet again with the broomstick. No one else got in trouble for our bickering, of course.

"I'll leave this place yet, you watch," I told Franco.

I felt bad, later, when I came across Father's Old Spice cologne in the bathroom. When Thanksgiving came, I had no interest in dressing up or doing anything at all.

After three painful years in the new home, at twenty-one years of age, I just couldn't take it anymore.

18. Homeless

One Sunday afternoon in the early fall of 1988, I packed a small bag, left home, and never returned. The moment I hit the road, I started to tremble. I prayed to the Lord to keep me and deliver me from evil.

After I left, I reached out to my two older sisters, calling them on the phone. Neither would provide solace. Naomi said, "Oh, I'm sorry, Doris! I can't help you. I don't want trouble with Mother."

Then I called Lorena, who told me, "You can't stay here, because Mother will be looking for you, and you know how she is."

I thanked both of my sisters for their lack of help, feeling a bizarre *it's better this way* sensation in my heart. I had no idea what to do, so I walked directly into the local police station.

"How may I help you?" asked a thin officer from behind a thick glass panel.

"I'd like to speak with a detective or someone in charge, please."

After a brief delay, a detective came out to talk to me—a tall, brown-haired young man.

"I'm Detective Schultz, how may I help you?"

"Sir, may I speak with you privately?" I asked, looking into his blue eyes.

"Sure, follow me." We walked into a quiet, deserted, cold-looking gray room. "Have a seat, Miss. How may I help you?" he inquired, sounding intrigued.

Uncovering my arms, I said quietly, "Sir, I don't feel safe in my home. I don't want to go back. Please help me."

The detective held his breath while staring at my arms. Then he looked me in the face for a long moment.

"How did this happen?" he asked finally. "Who did this?"

"My mother, sir; I came here from Puerto Rico three years ago. I was under the impression I came here for a better life, but I'm a prisoner in my home—a slave to my mother and her beatings."

While taking notes, he asked, "How old are you, Miss? Do you have any ID?"

I handed him my ID. "I'm twenty-one, sir."

"The fact you're over eighteen means you don't have to go back. No one can *make* you go back. Would you like to go to the hospital? Do you want to press charges?"

Shaking my head, barely containing my tears, I said, "I can't hurt my mother."

"Doris, there's a place where you can stay—it's safe."

I nodded, and he left the room. I felt relief at having finally found the nerve to save myself, and as I waited in the gray, cold, eerie room, my body began to weaken. Several minutes later, the detective returned with a tall, fit-looking African American woman. Her eyes looked fierce as a panther's, but I sensed kindness in her. She introduced herself as Mrs. Wentworth, and we shook hands.

"Doris, where are your clothes?" she asked.

"Well, this bag is all I have with me. I don't want to go back. What I have with me will suffice."

"All right, then, follow me."

The detective stopped me before I left the station and gave me his card. "Call me if you need anything. Good luck, and be safe."

"Thank you," I said.

I headed out of the police station with Mrs. Wentworth. As she opened the door and waited for me to exit, I looked back at Detective Shultz, who stood there with both hands in his pockets, and nodded. I didn't smile, but with my eyes, I thanked him and committed his face to memory.

It was raining as I eased into the backseat of Mrs. Wentworth's car. I sank into sadness the second the car took off; the radio played "Beat It" by Michael Jackson, and Ms. Wentworth wiggled her head to the tune.

My mind did a quick rewind of my life. It all seemed too much for a single lifetime, but taking a deep breath, I told myself I could accept what had happened and move on to something better.

Mrs. Wentworth took me to the hospital, where my wounds were treated. Late in the evening, we arrived at our true destination: what appeared to be an old mansion, in a town I must not reveal here. We walked into its quiet confines, and I was greeted by a woman named Marli.

The house was vast and had a large spiral staircase that went up to the second floor. I was perplexed as Mrs. Wentworth walked me upstairs to my room. It had a twin bed with a small desk and chair, but no TV or radio. There was a large window on one wall.

"Doris, this is your room," said Mrs. Wentworth. "We'll see you in the morning."

"Thank you," I replied. I laid my little bag of belongings

on the chair and my body on the narrow bed. I was exhausted; my body felt as heavy as a brick. After a few moments, I heard some baby noises, which eased my tension somewhat. Later, I learned that all the occupants in the mansion were women and that all of them had children, except me.

I fell asleep.

The following morning, I learned the shelter rules. "You must leave the shelter by seven in the morning and return no earlier than five and no later than nine," Mrs. Wentworth said. She looked at me regretfully.

"Doris, because you don't have children or disabilities, I regret to tell you that you don't qualify for public assistance."

"It's all right. I just want to find a job so I can get on with my life."

Mrs. Wentworth approved of my spirit and handed me a public transportation schedule and directions to the employment office. The same day, I walked to the employment office, about six blocks away from the shelter. I looked over the job list, which didn't have much to offer and never did. Soon I had learned the list by heart and was quick to spot new postings when I went by every morning. In the meantime, I started working part time as a cashier at a local supermarket.

Because of overcrowding and safety concerns, I was eventually transferred to a different shelter. My room there was also on the second floor, and to my relief, it had a mountain view. The new shelter's rules were about the same as the old ones, and again, I was reminded that I didn't qualify for any public assistance.

The woman in charge of this shelter, Ms. Maple, gave me a new bus schedule with directions to the employment office in nearby Springfield. She warned me to be careful when going to Springfield and gave me the shelter's phone number in case I needed help or got lost. While I looked for full-time work, I again obtained a part-time job at a local market. Whenever I was off the job, I'd take the bus to Springfield. Their job postings were more numerous than the ones as the first employment office, but I soon learned those listings by heart as well.

I also obtained help with updating my résumé, but months and months went by without a single call about a full-time job. I was terribly stressed and almost hopeless.

The winter days were harsh, and it took me a long time to adjust to the weather. Every morning I looked up and prayed for protection.

"Dear Mother of God, I consecrate to you my heart and my soul. Oh Mother of Goodness, keep me and protect me from all harm. Amen."

The neighborhood around the shelter wasn't much like the old slum, thank goodness. It was loud but clean, and there were fewer hangouts. Every day as I headed out at seven in the morning, I'd pray, "Lord, wherever I'm going to go today, please protect me." On my way out the door, I'd continue with an Our Father. Other times, when I simply felt broken, I'd pray, "Lord, I don't feel so well today. Please give me strength."

I soon met a new shelter volunteer, Alice. She was in her sixties and was a cheery woman, petite with a round figure. She had small, fine hands.

"Doris, would you like to go to church on Sundays?" she asked me one day.

"Yes, I'd love to." From then on, she picked me up to go to church with her every Sunday morning at nine. She was my new guardian angel. I learned she'd drive to New York on Saturdays to watch Broadway shows. I wanted to go, but "leisure" was against shelter rules.

I also discovered a local mall. After visiting the employment office and working my part-time job for the day, I'd go to the mall to walk around and smile at children and families, feeling touched by the sight of couples holding hands. I felt like I didn't belong there, though; I felt different from everyone else. I'd walk through the mall without entering a single store, tense and jumpy, on the lookout for any familiar faces. Waiting for the bus and watching people exit the mall saddened me. I wished I had my own home to go to. I noticed I was often subconsciously clenching my fists, out of nervousness, to the point where my fingernails would puncture the palms of my hands. By the time I'd feel the pain, my hands would be bleeding.

Every evening at six, I ate whatever the shelter offered, which consisted of donations received from local supermarkets—usually frozen, boxed, and canned food, always past its expiration date. I'd reflect on my life as I ate. I missed the kids. It always made me smile to remember the good days back on the island, when they waited at the dinner table while I cooked. Keeping our secret, our visits to the river, their smiles—it all seemed like a dream now, a pleasant dream with an unexplainable, nightmarish ending.

Luckily, my bathroom in the shelter had the most beautiful antique bathtub. Every day, I'd take hot baths and simply recharge my spirit. I'd also catch up on my readings, prayers, and my own writing, always in Spanish. I'd write letters to Naomi, Tato, and Victor but wouldn't mail them. I thought it was better to bear my own burdens instead of passing them on. I'd write to God, too: *Lord, I feel only your absence. Searching for you, Lord, is like searching for a lost friend in a huge crowd. I know you're here, yet I search and I search, and I can't find you.*

19. Nightmares

Just when I was beginning to regain my confidence, feeling proud of being able to stand up to all I had faced, I became plagued by horrible nightmares. Sometimes I'd dream of Mother against a dark background, her big arms trying to strangle me. Other times I dreamed I was praying the Our Father as a profane male voice slashed my skin with long fingernails. Or I'd recite the Creed, and a voice would be praying it backward so close by my right ear that I could feel skinny facial bones pressing against the side of my face. Upon waking, I'd feel my skin burning from what felt like cuts and bruises. I'd run to the mirror but could see no marks.

Naïve and clueless, I accepted the nightmares as relics of my past. I kept going, day by day, without much energy, without asking for help.

Once again, I despised the nighttime. No matter how tired I was, the nightmares came quickly. Heavy footsteps seemed to make the whole floor tremble, as the darkness wrapped around me. I was confused and often wasn't sure if it was a nightmare or an actual person making noises outside my bedroom door. When this happened, I fought back with prayer, jumped out of bed, and stayed up the rest of the night. My room was on the second floor, but I had cleared the window just in case I had to jump out.

Writing replaced nighttime rest. I wrote every single night until my hand felt too heavy to hold the pencil. I'd reflect and write things like, "The suffering of the poor is often quiet, often trying and nearly unbearable—but we don't give in, and it doesn't defeat us." Other times, I'd write until I couldn't see the lines on the paper anymore, or until my eyes watered excessively. "Lord, I used to feel your presence while caring for the kids. You kept us safe. I trust you, Lord, but it seems you've left me."

My energy was completely consumed by the end of the night, and I usually managed to stay up long enough to see the sunrise. Strangely enough, seeing the sun rise was like new hope, like a new promise, a brilliant new beginning. Was this a sign?

Then the cycle would recur. As the day wore down and the nighttime approached, I became my own watchman, pleading, *Dear God, please protect me.*

After getting into bed, I'd lie on my side for a little while to rest my debilitated bones. My feet burned and felt heavy. My body felt corpse like. My skin was thin. My hair felt too weighty for my head. I could hear my heart pumping and the blood flowing through my veins.

As I listened to my body and my breathing, my eyelids would close almost against my will as my tired body drifted away into a deep sleep—then the heavy steps would walk toward my bedroom door. I'd hear a heavy chain being dragged across the floor by some angry presence. I'd feel trapped in my sleep. The presence would drag the chain into my room; it sounded colossal. The presence would come very close to me, radiating anger. My body would feel completely frozen, unable to wake up, haunted and horrified.

Other times, I'd fight back hard enough to wake up, jump out of bed, and open my bedroom door. The hallway always seemed clear, the house completely silent. I never doubted or worried about the women in the shelter; they were always kind to me.

To avoid having the horrid nightmares again, I'd sit at my desk praying the rosary over and over. Then I'd write, asking God and the universe about the purpose of these torments. I'd write to see if I could come up with the answer. To my surprise, I actually got my answer one night. It emerged from deep within my soul, as I wrote, *Because I'm strong, but I need to be stronger.*

I'd have no energy at dawn, but I'd still walk to the bus stop and make my usual daily visit to the employment office.

The nightmares made me weak, but I didn't tell anyone. I'd keep a bright smile on my face and go on with my day, just as I had when I was caring for the kids back home. I was afraid that if I asked for help with the dreams, people might not believe me. Besides, I remembered Blas's teachings about complaining being weak. So prayer and writing became my only defenses. My notebook was my confidant. I was grateful Marli, the lady from the shelter office, gave me the notebooks and pencils I needed. I'd write to God over and over again. "Dear Lord, I trust you, please make these nightmares stop."

Writing to God made me feel better. I had faith He listened, so I wrote down all my fears, agonies, anger, and frustrations over and over. I figured these visitations must have some purpose. "If it's your will, so be it; I'll work hard, as hard as I have to, I don't care, but please don't leave me."

Writing was my way of hanging on; I constantly searched within myself through my writing, and I vented against the nightmares and the beasts that came to tear my flesh apart. The writing took me through different stages. I'd ask myself, *How do I feel today?* And write a six-page response that barely relieved me. Then I'd turn back to the reality of my haunted nights.

In the mornings, while waiting for the bus, I'd say hello to the other people and smile. This was how I met Naki, a sixteen-year-old boy who appeared friendly but lost. He tended to hang out by the bus stop. Naki had bright honey eyes, caramel hair, and an angelic smile that made me laugh. I wanted to know about him and know he'd be okay. One day I asked, "Are you in school, Naki?"

"Yes, I go to a special school."

"Great. School is important. Never quit school, Naki, no matter what," I told him.

Naki smiled with closed lips, but he appeared happy and relaxed. "I like my new school, and I want to graduate," he assured me. "I like working with computers."

"See, how great! Keep up the good work, and take care," I said, with a final "See you later!" when my bus arrived. Talking to Naki made my day.

I noticed some people seemed offended by my look of homelessness. When I'd hand people my résumé, I'd sometimes get expressions of repulsion in exchange, as if I looked like a walking plague—as if my résumé were dirty. Even though I was neat and clean, my clothes were too big, and they made me look old. They were out of style, too, and my hair hung untamed to a point below my waist; my untamed hair made me look like someone from a different age. I wore no makeup.

I realized my generous smile couldn't compensate for all of this, and it hurt, but I kept trying. I knew this was temporary; underneath the oversized coat and the untamed hair, there was a good-hearted soul determined for a chance to shine.

My heart was torn apart every time I saw other young girls carrying books and going into the library to study. I tried going to the library, but good-looking boys stared at me too much. Although I loved the library, I was so embarrassed about my looks that I never went back. I'd walk by just to admire the building, but it almost seemed like a forbidden place to me.

Doris Mercado

I was more or less out of touch with my family, but I eventually learned some of my other siblings had moved out of the slum. Franco had started a contracting business. Jonas began working at the University of Massachusetts; Marcos went to a school for home remodeling and moved to Florida. Alejandro pursued a religious life, and Veronica got married.

Eventually they found themselves and became again the humble and disciplined people, for whom I had once cared— my siblings, Mother's children, my children.

During my homeless years, I visited Veronica. By then, she had had a baby girl named Jari. It was a long bus ride, but I was extremely fortunate, privileged even, because the shelter had allowed me this one-time sleepover with my sister in Vermont. I was happy to see Veronica in her own home with her own family. It was an emotional visit, but I felt lost, small, and simply broken. The one saving grace was that little Jari smiled at me as if I were the best thing she had ever seen.

It seemed like ages since I'd been in a real home. Veronica's home scent reminded me of some of Mama Blas's favorite scent mixtures, mint and lemon. My sister's house was cozy. She was a packrat, which made me laugh. I could barely walk around the place; there were multiple layers of rugs on the floor, many plants, a fish tank with two guinea pigs, a smaller fish tank with a turtle, and a cage with several lovebirds.

Veronica seemed fine, but despite having her own home, there was a deep sadness in her eyes. We talked about Jari and about how Veronica preferred to live apart from our family. My looks were sufficient for me not to go into detail about my life, except to say that I was still looking for a job and that I wasn't in school.

I couldn't sleep on this particular night. Morning

arrived quickly, and soon it was time for me to leave. "Doris, take care," Veronica said with concern.

I looked at her. "Don't worry about me, Veronica. I must go on."

Hitting the road, and walking back to the bus stop, felt harsh and painful. "I must go on," I repeated, trying to fortify my strength.

20. Light

One day in late December 1990, I left the homeless shelter at seven in the morning, as usual. I was twenty-four and felt I had lost half of my life; I was going into my sixth straight year of turmoil. Three years of abandonment, then from paradise to hell. But I had to go on; every day, with the faith of a child, I'd look up and murmur, *"Acompáñame, Señor.* Lord, please stay with me." Then I'd walk out of the shelter toward the bus stop, hugging my notebook to me. It was my sole companion and keeper of my most intimate dreams, hopes, agonies, and conversations with the Lord.

This particular day was cloudy and rainy. I had no winter boots—just flat shoes with no socks. I struggled in the cold as I walked to the bus stop, but I had to endure, so I sat and waited for a bus to Springfield with the patience of a saint. Waiting at the bus stop always made me nervous, as I kept on the lookout for any familiar faces. The stop was always so dirty and noisy, with people constantly hanging around.

"Lord, please keep me from harm," I'd whisper, just as Mama Blas used to whisper her prayers.

Naki appeared at the bus stop.

"Hey, Dori, I forgot to ask, you speak Spanish? Are you a Puertorra?" Naki reminded me of the kids; they also called me Dori.

"Yes, Naki, I speak Spanish," I affirmed, "and I don't like the 'Puertorra' part. It sounds harsh. I'm a Boricua, born and raised on the island, one hundred percent Puerto Rican . . . thank you very much."

"You know, I was born here in Massachusetts, but my mother is a Puertorra," he said.

"A Boricua, Naki," I said, laughing. "¡*Qué chévere!* Very nice."

Naki looked into my eyes, no longer smiling. "Why you so scared, Dori?"

I was touched by his concern. "I'm not scared, Naki. I'm just . . . dying."

"But you're young!" Naki said, staring at me in disbelief.

"Naki, I'm a tree ripped from my soil. I was about to bloom, but now I can't. This is not the right soil. Plus, I'm freezing," I said, laughing at him.

"Wow. Where'd you learn this, Dori?"

"Listen, Naki, school is important. Faith and hope are important, too."

"Yes, I go to a special program at Nari School. I used to have problems learning, but I like the new school better. The doctor told my Mom I have ADD. Hey, Dori, I have my own family, they protect me—but you cool."

There was something about him now which made me a little nervous. "I'm glad, Naki. Family is very important," I said, standing up, keeping my eye out for the Springfield bus.

"I can see you, Dori," he insisted. "You cool."

I looked at the child, mystified, not understanding what he was saying. "Naki, what do you mean you can 'see me'? It sounds inappropriate."

He laughed. "I can almost see little angels floating over your head. It means you're good. It's a compliment."

I was touched. "I've never heard anything like that before. Thank you so much, Naki."

Still laughing, he said, "You cool, Dori."

I nodded my thanks, but before I could continue our conversation, a bunch of young guys approached, distracting Naki.

"Hey guys," Naki said in excitement, shaking hands

240

in succession with at least six people. The way they shook hands, with different grips, interlocking and touching fingers—I'd never seen anything like it. I smiled at them with closed lips while keeping my distance, hugging my notebook, minding my own business. A bus approached, but it wasn't my bus.

After the handshakes were over and there were a few quiet whispers, Naki said to me, "Dori, this is my family." Every single one of them looked at me. "We watch out for each other," he boasted. "If anything happens, they're here for me."

I didn't like Naki's tone—and then I realized I was standing next to a street gang. *Dear Lord,* I thought. I had to think of something, really fast. I couldn't believe these harmless-looking young men were an actual gang. I glanced into their eyes and listened and nodded as a sign of respect, without showing fear.

"She cool, her name is Dori, she's sad," said Naki, as his friends stared silently at me. I was horrified, and glanced at Naki, giving him an *I don't want to get hurt* look. I then walked away a little, pretending I was looking out for my bus. Naki's friends moved about, acting like human radars, paying attention to anything that moved while communicating silently with gestures. When they finally moved away, I was relieved but shaken. I said in a low tone, "Naki, listen to me: don't join a gang, there's much to life . . ."

He looked at me. "They my family, they protect me, Dori. One of them is my cousin, he cool."

"The Lord is the only true protector in your life—but you must protect your own path," I said, almost scolding.

Naki listened in silence, his honey eyes reminding me of Marcos's. I wanted to hug him. I wanted to protect him; he looked lonely and lost.

"Listen, little one, stay away from gangs," I told him. "They only bring problems. And remember, be good," I insisted as Naki looked at me, motionless. My bus finally approached.

"I'm real sorry, Naki, I think my bus has arrived. Take good care, little one, and remember—stay in school, and do well," I said.

Naki smiled warmly.

"I'll be good, Dori. Peace," he said, flipping me a peace sign with his fingers. As I walked away, he called, "Dori, I can see you!"

I smiled at him and boarded the bus. I hoped with all my heart that Naki lived in a safe home and that he'd be all right. I almost felt I shared a special bond with him, because he reminded me so much of the boys. I could see some of Marcos's innocence and Jonas's purity in him.

The bus headed to Springfield, through a day which continued to be dark, rainy, and somewhat windy. By the time I reached my destination, Main Street, the rain had turned to freezing rain. The bus driver gave me an umbrella; I thanked him, and he smiled compassionately. He had almond-shaped Spanish eyes, a thick mustache, black hair, and a round face, and he wasn't very tall. This stranger's kindness made me feel alive again. I got off the bus and hurried through the freezing rain to the employment office.

My hands and feet were frozen by the time I got there, and I felt weak already. I figured I had a harsh day ahead of me, but dreaming of the better days gave me strength. I went straight to the job list, which was posted just inside the office. I knew the list by heart by now—but I stopped abruptly when I saw a new entry: "Medical Secretary." Excited, I waited my turn to speak to one of the employment assistants. "I'm interested in the new posting. Medical Secretary."

The assistant had dirty blond hair and soft-looking hands, as if they had never been exposed to the elements. His fingernails were clean and clear. He maintained a studious look while bringing up the job opening on his computer. After typing for a moment, he said, "They listed their phone number here, so let me call to make sure the position is still available."

I was praying with all my strength that the opening *was* still available. While waiting, I clenched my fists so hard my fingers hurt, muttering, "Please, Lord, let this work."

The assistant mumbled on the phone for a short while; then, covering the receiver with one of those soft hands, he said to me, "Doris, the position is still available. Would you be available for an interview today?"

I raised my eyebrows while replying, "Today, sure I am!"

The word *interview* seemed as foreign as my accent. I couldn't believe it: I was about to go on an interview for a full-time job on the same day I'd asked about it, for the first time in three years.

It was nine in the morning. "Doris, Mrs. Tauber says she can see you at eleven," the attendant told me.

I was happy, but I had no idea what I'd do until eleven. So I asked, "How about now?"

The assistant looked at me with narrowed eyes while repeating my inquiry to Mrs. Tauber over the phone. My day brightened as he said, "Doris, how long will it take you to get there?" He covered the phone receiver, and whispered, "It's not far from here."

I had no idea where I was going, so out of desperation, I guessed, "Thirty minutes?"

"Thirty minutes," he repeated.

I tried not to laugh as I realized how lucky I was to get my first job interview in years, not only on the same day it was offered but at my own requested time.

After he got off the phone, the attendant told me, "You're going to 91 School Street. Do you know where it is?"

"No, but I can find it."

He said, "If you keep going down Main Street, the second light is State Street. Take a left, and the third light up is School Street. Take a right, and you'll see it on the left. You can't miss it. Ask for Salma Tauber."

"Thank you so much!" I said gratefully, as I wrote down the name and address in my beat-up notebook. "Thank you," I said again, and he sent me off with good wishes as I headed out. "State Street, on the left," I kept repeating to myself, while power walking down Main. It already felt like a long distance to me, because it was still raining and I couldn't go any faster than I already was. My heart thumped, and I was freezing. I wore no gloves, my hands were wrinkled from the wet, and my feet were cold and numb. It was windy, and the rain slashed at my face every time I looked up to check the street signs.

I finally reached State Street and turned left. I noted that there weren't many people around, except a few walking in small groups or waiting at the bus stops. They all wore heavy coats and other winter clothing; I wore what the shelter had obtained from donations, in this case, merely a thin rain jacket, unsuitable for winter temperatures—or rain, for that matter. Just when I felt I lacked the strength to go on and had lost track of time—had thirty minutes come and gone?—I spotted School Street. As the attendant at the employment agency had told me, it was in fact the third light up State. I turned right.

I walked as fast as I could against the wind and rain—which was now turning to snow—and finally found the medical office at 91 School Street. I stood for a minute in the lobby to catch my breath, close my broken umbrella, and shake the snow and rain from my face, hair, and jacket. I combed my long hair with my hands and squeezed water out of it. I felt as cold as a corpse but thought I was presentable enough.

"This is it," I said to myself as I walked into the office.

The waiting room was neat, and color-coordinated in cranberry and cream hues. A lady sat behind a glass window with a solemn posture, reminding me of people at church.

"Good morning," I told her. "I'm here to see Salma Tauber, please."

"Good morning. May I ask your name?"

"Doris Mercado."

"Oh, yes, Miss Mercado, she's expecting you." She blinked. "Miss, is it that bad outside? You're drenched. I'm glad I'm not out there."

"The wind makes it unbearable," I assured her, just as an older lady walked toward me.

"Doris?" she asked.

I smiled. "Yes."

"I'm Mrs. Tauber."

"Nice to meet you, thank you for seeing me early."

She nodded and gave me a firm handshake. Mrs. Tauber was short and had the same hairstyle as my beloved Mama Blas: white hair pulled back into a bun. I kept smiling, no longer thinking about how cold I was, hoping she wouldn't ask me too many uncomfortable questions.

"Have you done this kind of work before, Doris?"

"No ma'am, but I love to work. I'd be glad to work for you. If you give me a chance to prove myself, I'll try. If it doesn't work out, you can let me go."

Mrs. Tauber seemed to approve of my sincerity, though I was a bit embarrassed, and worried she might have noticed my desperation. After escorting me into her office and waving me to a chair, she said in a kindly manner, "Your accent . . . will you be able to communicate with people in person and over the telephone?"

"Yes, I have no problem with that. I like helping people— plus I'm planning to go to school in the near future."

The truth was that I understood what people said to me in English, but I sometimes had trouble expressing myself; sometimes the words just wouldn't come, especially when I got nervous.

Mrs. Tauber then gave me a briefing about the position. Confidently, maintaining a straight posture, eye contact, and a bright smile, I said, "Booking appointments, answering calls, and processing insurance information—I can do that."

Mrs. Tauber leaned back in her large, high chair and focused on my résumé, seeming to think hard as she read. My chair was pretty comfortable, but I couldn't help but stare obsessively at the large, dark, wooden desk, which was stacked with piles of paper and decorated with framed photographs, all facing her. I dreamed about someday owning a large desk like Mrs. Tauber's, preferably a carved one.

I noticed her hands were wrinkled and small. She wore a little watch, which seemed tight on her wrist. I then shot a quick glance at the icicles accumulating on a magnolia tree outside her window.

I resigned myself to waiting: hands clasped together, tense, knees shaking. I dropped my shoulders and looked straight at her. My heart was ready to accept her decision, whatever it might be. Mrs. Tauber looked back at me steadily, again reminding me of Mama Blas in the way her brilliant white hair was pulled back. The simplicity of my looks, combined with my pale complexion, damp clothing, and wet hair, made me feel small by comparison. I held my breath and hoped she wouldn't ask whether I had a car.

"When can you start?" she asked, in a high but firm tone.

I couldn't believe it. Between smiles, I said, "I can start tomorrow!"

I couldn't stop smiling.

Her serious expression gave way to a small laugh. "I'll pay you eight dollars an hour, forty hours per week—and after six months you'll get benefits."

"That will do, ma'am." I felt ridiculous saying I could start tomorrow; but I felt even worse sitting at an interview without any makeup on, freezing cold and hungry as a lion.

"My business manager is out," she continued, "but I can give you a start date of January 7. This way, you'll get to enjoy the holidays with your family."

I stopped smiling. *What a heart,* I thought, *Family.* I wondered if I had been away too long. By then, family consisted of a series of good but long-gone memories, with the river visits and our coffee chats being my favorite ones. Then the reality of my homelessness passed through my mind in a quick flash. I felt a sudden connection with Mrs. Tauber; her maternal demeanor was comforting. I felt accepted. I had been given the chance I'd been longing for.

"I can start then," I told her. "Not a problem."

"Your work schedule would be 8:30 to 5:00, with an hour for lunch. Is that okay?" The way she paid attention to my responses made me a little nervous; having *any* chance was fair enough for me.

"Absolutely, ma'am, I can't wait to start."

She walked me through the office, introducing me to the staff. At the exit, she said, "Very well, we'll see you on January 7."

She walked me out and we shook hands once again. I

couldn't leave without giving her a generous smile, which she returned. Then I picked up my drenched coat and the umbrella and walked out of the office.

I paused in the lobby. "Jesus!" I breathed, and trembled as I rewrapped myself in the damp old jacket.

"Thank you, Lord, thank you!"

I headed back to Main Street. I thought about catching the bus and going to the local mall, then pictured myself catching the bus early in the mornings to go to work and, yes, moving out of the shelter soon. The freezing rain continued to fall as I walked, and my head began hurting. I couldn't believe I had found a job and reflected back on how my day had begun, smiling happily. My heart beat with joy, keeping me warm.

Amid a gray day, there was light.

I crossed State Street onto Main Street and continued on to the bus stop. I could barely see where I was going. My hands shook as I kept lifting up the umbrella enough to see the concrete ahead of me, while trying to keep it low enough that the rain didn't hit me in the face. Between the howl of the wind and the rush of the rain pounding the umbrella, I could barely hear anything at all. I thought I heard my name shouted, but I shrugged it off; this agony of feeling extremely cold, plus the noise of the rain and wind and traffic, kept me busy in my struggle to keep going. I looked straight ahead, hoping I'd get there soon; I tried to hurry, but my frozen feet couldn't walk any faster.

"Doris!"

I kept walking, trying to look straight ahead, watching for the bus stop. Then I glanced to the right—and there, rolling along beside me in his beige car, was my father. My heart nearly stopped, and I began to sob, knowing I couldn't run away from him. The car continued moving slowly along the street, at my pace, the driver's side window rolled down.

"Doris, are you okay?" Father called. "What are you doing here?"

I was horrified, hoping someone would walk by so I could ask for help.

"Doris, where are you *going?*" he called out again.

"I'm looking for a job, and I'm not going back! Leave me alone!" I yelled back, feeling helpless. I thought, *Dear Lord, not now.* My heart filled with dread as I looked to see who else rode in the car with him; but there was no one. I glared at him, my lips tight, ready to tell him off—but I sensed defeat in him. He looked different, now, almost harmless. I wondered what had happened to him.

"Come with me, I have my own apartment!" he said to me. His plea slowed my feet. "Come on, come with me! The weather is too bad for you to be out here like this," he said. I kept glaring at him as my heart thumped, and the memories flooded back. I thought twice about giving in, something I never would have done before. Why *should* I go with him? He'd called me stupid for years, never taught me anything, and abandoned us not once but twice.

Nodding my head sharply, I continued to walk away from him.

"Come on, Doris, it's going to be all right!" my father yelled. Suddenly, I felt a bizarre *Go ahead* in my heart, which made me stop. I turned back to my father, looked closely, and saw truth in his eyes, which made me trust him. He pulled up beside me, and I slowly walked around and got into the passenger's seat of my father's car.

The second I did, I thought, *What did I just do?* My heart started palpitating fiercely. *What have I done?* I felt horribly vulnerable, awash in fear, and vowed to jump out of the car if he drove in the wrong direction.

I couldn't talk. I was filled with a million emotions. I'd never imagined being in this sort of situation—homeless, with no education or guidance from anyone, and away from our little home—it all crashed in on me at once. Suddenly, I felt like throwing up. I placed my left arm on my stomach, holding my notebook against me, and put my right hand on the passenger door, while trying to pay attention to where Father was heading.

Then I glanced at my father—and saw peace in him for the first time in years. He was so different that it was almost spooky. He looked at me; his expression filled with empathy, and asked quietly, "Where have you been?"

Paying attention strictly to where he was driving, I said in a low tone, "A homeless shelter." From the corner of my eye, I noticed how his shoulders sagged, how his hands pressed hard on the steering wheel.

"We can go there and get your clothes if you want," he said in a gentle voice.

"No, thank you. It's not necessary. I don't have many clothes, plus I'm not supposed to reveal the location of the shelter."

He paused again and seemed to blush. I could sense he was battling difficult feelings of his own. "Let's get something to eat," he said, and he turned the car toward a Spanish restaurant in Springfield. I was embarrassed to enter the restaurant as I was: drenched, in flat shoes without socks, wearing a thin jacket older than I was. I felt like I was trespassing—like a wild animal that had never been around people. Dad walked close by my side, and I dreaded looking into other people's eyes. I was relieved, though, to once again hear conversations in Spanish.

Father loved to eat, so he ordered an elaborate meal for us both. I hadn't eaten a warm, fresh Spanish meal in a long time. We stayed in the restaurant long enough for my hands to unwrinkle and for my feet to feel life again. Otherwise, I didn't know how to feel quite yet; I remained nervous and watchful. My hair hung over my left shoulder, my left arm resting on the table, right arm on my lap.

We'd hoped to wait out the weather, but it didn't improve, so we decided to get going anyway. When we arrived at the parking lot for his complex, I walked slowly after I got out of his car, my extremities cold and stiff. When we arrived at his apartment, I paused at the door, pressing my lips tightly together and holding my stomach. I could smell Dad's Old Spice, reminding me of our old home, our happy days. On the door, I saw, he'd posted a sign, handwritten in blue ink in capital letters: *Catholic*. It was almost comical.

"Oh, I hung it there to keep solicitors away," he explained. "*Se pasan jodiendo demasiado*. They bother me too much."

I walked in hesitantly, with little steps, and saw that the place was all white, wide windows, no curtains. My father went off to put some things away in the kitchen. He then showed me around, saying, "Doris, you can have the bedroom—I don't use it. I sleep out here on the couch."

I listened in silence, unaccustomed to his kindness and his gentle voice; it seemed unlike him. The apartment had three rooms, all painted white. It looked clear and clean and peaceful. There were no decorations; just a large-screen TV and a dining table with three odd chairs. A crucifix hung over the kitchen sink. The dining table was piled up with coffee cans, notebooks, Spanish and English newspapers, a magnifying glass, pens, and pencils. It was clear he preferred to keep his writing paraphernalia close at hand.

In the living room, he had a reclining chair to which he had added his own unique touches. A lamp hung over its right side; two clipboards served as arm rests, and an antique table next to it was piled with several legal pads, a rosary, a thick Bible, and other books. There were some drawings of Jesus on the cross and some writings, which caught my eye: "Mechanics never die; they get new parts. One who denies his roots denies his mother, and is not a Jíbaro."

He had neat handwriting. I had always admired that about him.

On a separate legal pad he had written down his date of birth, "3/15/35," and "PONCE." He noticed me reading and said, "Oh, I'm applying for vanity car plates. It would be neat if they approved 'PONCE,'" he chuckled. I didn't smile in return, but I listened. He had so much love and passion for our native city; his eyes were bright as two little lamps.

On this particular day late in December 1990, exactly one week before Christmas, I had left the shelter with no clothes except for what I was wearing. Otherwise, I had a praying stamp of Saint Lazarus and a Holy Medal book, which I carried in my pocket, plus my notebook. "Dad, may I use the phone?" I asked. "I need to call the shelter. I have to let them know I'm not coming back."

"Sure, go ahead—the phone is against the wall, next to the kitchen sink," he said enthusiastically. Father walked away from the kitchen so I could have some privacy.

"Hello?" an anonymous voice answered on the other end, after I'd dialed the shelter number.

"May I speak with Mrs. Maple, please?"

"This is Mrs. Maple, how may I help you?"

"Mrs. Maple, this is Doris."

"Hi, Doris, are you all right?"

"Yes, I'm okay—thank you, ma'am. I'm calling to inform you I will not be returning to the shelter. I bumped into my father today, and I'll be staying with him."

"Your father?" Mrs. Maple asked, with obvious concern.

"Yes, ma'am, he has his own apartment," I replied.

"Okay, I understand," she said, reluctantly. "I hope this works for you, Doris. Are you coming back for your belongings?"

"No, ma'am. I'm not . . . I don't have much . . . there's a small jacket, but I'm sure another girl may need it."

"That's kind of you, Doris."

"Mrs. Maple . . . I found a job today."

"Doris, very good, what kind of job, is it full- or part-time?"

"Full-time. I'm going to work as a medical secretary. I'm really happy."

"Doris, I'm glad for you—I hope it all goes well! Good luck, and take care. If staying with your father doesn't work, you call me—do you understand?"

I swallowed hard. "Yes, ma'am, thank you. May I say something?"

"Sure, Doris, go ahead."

"Mrs. Maple, thank you for letting me stay at the shelter these past few years. I hope I can repay the shelter one day. I wrote about my life while I was at the shelter. Thank you for the papers and notebooks and pencils you gave me. I hope to share my story with others, and inspire them; but I will never forget you." I managed not to tell her about the nightmares. I had never shared them with Mrs. Maple or anyone else.

"Oh, you're welcome, Doris. Good luck. Just remember: you can talk about the shelter, but you can't mention the name or the location. I hope all goes well with your new job, and you keep in touch. Let us know how you're doing."

"Thank you, ma'am, I will. Good-bye," I said with a knot in my throat. I couldn't say anything more. I felt cold and scared when I hung up with Mrs. Maple, as if I had closed one chapter in my life and was moving on to the next.

Life at the homeless shelter ended with Father's apartment.

21. Father

Over means a new beginning.
—Father

Father's apartment seemed peaceful beyond comprehension. It didn't have much furniture—even the bedroom contained only a twin bed—but Father's presence was big enough to fill it. He was different; he walked more slowly and spoke gently, showing a side of himself I'd never before seen. I trusted my father now.

After talking to Ms. Maple, I went into my new room, hung up my damp clothing, and wrapped my bare body in two blankets. I lay down, feeling vulnerable; my bones seemed fragile. I stared at the ceiling, feeling as if I'd run a hundred-mile marathon. A vague light filtered in through the bare window. Without thinking about my nightmares, I closed my eyes and drifted into a deep sleep. Miraculously, I don't recall any nightmares hunting me that night.

In the morning, I was awakened by the smell of coffee. The room was sunny now, but I felt afraid, and as vulnerable as a newborn. I glanced at the black knit pants and knit sweater hanging across me; they looked dry, so I unwrapped my body, dressed quickly, and came out of the room. I walked slowly, looking for Dad, my clashing emotions still overwhelming me. He was in the kitchen, sitting on a chair in front of the sink, washing dishes; it was comical to see. "I made you coffee," he said affectionately.

While sipping my coffee, I observed serenity in him I'd never seen before. Whistling as he always did in the mornings, he looked like a little boy playing with the lather in the sink. I sat on one of the odd chairs while looking around at the things lying on his table. There were pens of all colors and piles of notebooks.

"Help yourself, I have a lot of them, I get them cheap at the dollar and cent store," he told me. "We can go there this week, if you want. There are so many supplies, even small tools. I love it."

I nodded and glanced at some of the notes he'd written. One in particular, written in green ink, made me blush: *Over means a new beginning.*

I was too embarrassed to ask him about it and thought maybe I shouldn't read his notes anyway. I knew that, just like me, he dealt with his emotions by writing. I felt protected and enlightened by his company and optimism and looked forward to a new beginning for both of us. Knowing my father for once, sharing in his peace, and the bizarre coincidence of crossing paths with him on one of the rarest days in my life—it was a gray day I'd never forget, a gray day that turned out well, one highlighted by me finding a full-time job after searching literally for years. Running into Father just moments later was a miracle indeed.

While I had planned to move forward by working until I could afford my own place, catching the bus to work every day, the Lord obviously had other plans. As it turned out, my father played a major role in this stage in my life. His affection and genuine care marked a new day; and although he seemed ashamed by the past, I had forgiven him completely.

I didn't feel comfortable asking my father how he felt living by himself, or even talking about what had happened with our lives. Like I had, I was sure he'd gone through a lot. Talking about our past was the last thing I had in mind; I had no interest whatsoever in mentioning anything about it, except to say that I missed the kids and wondered how everyone was doing. The present mattered more than the past.

Dad's cologne reminded me of the days when we were a family, when there was always a new baby, a new crawler, a new child learning how to ride a bike—our days of complete chaos, as it all deteriorated. My wonderful days with the kids, and our trips to the river, were gone. I decided I'd preserve these memories in a new notebook, full of memories that made me feel good, memories of our dreaming together. Now, it was Father and I.

"Doris, do you remember this lady we met when you guys first came here? Remember Doña Porfi?" he asked, soon after I had arrived. "She can help you get clothes. They help people."

"The fortune-teller—yes, I remember her," I said skeptically. I didn't want to be seen by anyone, not while I still looked homeless, like I needed a hundred hours of sleep. It was too soon. But Father insisted they cared, so I gave in and decided it would be okay to go to Porfi's house. As it turned out, Doña Porfi owned a white ranch-style house near Springfield College. She had two daughters, Lilly and Katy. She was short, round, and fair-skinned, with jet-black hair and mysterious black eyes. Her hands shook constantly.

When we walked into Doña Porfi's house, my nose was assaulted by a rich mélange of strong scents: candles, incense, sandalwood, patchouli, and cigar. I didn't exactly like the atmosphere. The living room appeared to be a waiting area, with metal chairs aligned classroom style. A large table held over thirty religious statues, candles in all different colors, beads, cards, coins, and small bottles with dark liquids, among other things. The incessant ringing of the phone, the constant knocking on the door, and all the people coming in and out of the house gave me the creeps. Father shouted a hello to everyone, and of course, Doña Porfi heard his voice and excused herself from a consultation.

"Don Quique, how are you!" she said, while staring at me. She invited us into the consultation room with much urgency.

"Doña Porfi, this is Doris," said Father.

She grasped my hands, held them in her own. "How are you doing, my dear?"

"Fine, thank you," I said, looking at her with an expression that demanded, *Do you really want to know?* Her warm hands squeezed mine in response to my thought. We walked into a dark little room, which made my skin crawl, and my senses went on high alert. There was a little table there with two chairs, a floor lamp, and a broom sitting upside down behind the door.

"Have a seat, Doris," Doña Porfi said to me, while staring deep into my eyes; her look was almost hypnotizing. Father stood next to me, arms crossed behind his back. I wondered why we had to go into the consultation room, but I guessed it would be the only way Father would have a chance to ask Doña Porfi for help; it would be more private there. Porfi and I sat across from each other. Holding a cigar in her right hand, she took a puff, blowing the smoke in my face. I coughed. Her eyes glowed through the smoke, boring into my own. She glanced at my father.

"You have something good here. Is she the one who came from the island with the kids?" Her voice was loud, filled with power. She seemed pretty sure of herself.

I didn't understand what this had to do with our visit.

"Yes, she's the one," Dad said, his eyes glowing like diamonds. I found his fascination with fortune-telling and superstition to be worrisome. Doña Porfi took one more puff from the cigar, blowing the smoke my way a second time.

"Doris, your father loves you, and he's proud of you. It is not going to be easy, but everything is going to be all right—and I see you graduating from college. I see a sort of spiritual calling for you, Doris."

I couldn't smile; I was ultra-tense. But I felt glad to hear my father loved me and cared and everything would be okay. As vulnerable and broken as I was, I stared right back at Porfi, hating the intrusion of fortune-telling. I thought it was evil. I didn't want my life to be fogged by divination but rather clarified by the grace of the Lord. I couldn't help but think about my insecurity about Veronica and the boys upon leaving the island.

I fought the temptation and got up, saying, "Please stop." I glanced at my father and, feeling disappointed, I told him I didn't want to hear more. He bowed his head and looked ashamed, whereupon Doña Porfi embraced me and told me it was all right.

That was all I could stand. I broke down for the first time in the six years since I had left Puerto Rico.

"They never treated us with love," I revealed to Doña Porfi. She listened, and embraced me with warmth and care as I cried.

Later, after I composed myself, I looked up and saw that Father's eyes were watering. Doña Porfi said firmly, "There is a reason for everything. You found each other. It is a new beginning, for both of you." I believed she had truly touched the truth. All my old emotions showered me, the same feelings I fought in my notebook: the agony of feeling betrayed, lost, alone, and scared in this world, feeling the Lord was absent and little more than a memory as I continued my search for him.

I had never stopped praying; and suddenly, I realized

the Lord was in fact there with me the whole time, because he kept me from harm.

I was drained by then, and we decided to get going. Once we had left Doña Porfi's consultation room, I told my father privately, "Dad, I can't keep talking about the past. And I don't want to be involved in this *brujería,* this witchcraft."

"Nah, don't worry," he reassured me.

"I'm serious—I don't like this divination. It's negative and evil."

Dad curled his lips, the way he did when Mother talked to him. Doña Porfi had someone serve us coffee; after we were finished, she escorted us out the door. As we left, she told me, "Doris, you come back, and call me whenever you want. If there's anything I can help with, you call me."

I thanked her, and one of her girls handed me a bag of clothing. I was grateful, but after Father and I left her house, we never discussed the visit again.

January 7 arrived, and I began my job. Father drove me to work every day. The first week was especially painful; two of the other girls with whom I worked appeared to be ashamed to have me there, as they soon noticed that I didn't own much clothing. My wardrobe didn't seem to change from a black blouse and black skirt to black pants, and vice versa. They dressed nicely and wore makeup.

I endured it for the first two weeks, then vented to Father, "When I arrive in the mornings, they laugh at me! The way they look me up and down and grin makes me want to hide. During lunch, I sit down at the table, and they leave. They treat me like I have leprosy."

Dad seemed serene, but laughed, contemptuous of them. "She who laughs last, laughs best. Don't worry—their shame will be their curse. We have an old saying for when others look down on you as if they were better: *Las palmas son más altas y los puercos comen de ellas.* Palm trees are taller, and pigs eat from them."

"Oh my God, Dad! I never heard that before. It sounds awful."

"Don't worry. Let them treat you like you're different, because you are indeed. Those who judge in such a manner will never make a good friend."

"I'm there to work, Dad. I'm not there to make friends."

"Good, that's the attitude! Work hard, and don't worry about anything or anyone else. What matters is doing well and following your goals."

"Thank you Dad," I said, almost believing I was in a dream. I had never heard him talk like that before. I felt blessed to know this different side of my father. I then went on to ask, "So—how long have you been here?"

"A little over a year now," Dad replied, tears in his eyes. "Your mother wouldn't let me go back to see the kids after that day I left three years ago, so I went to New York and stayed with my family there for a while. Later I came back and got this apartment. I like it here."

"What about the day you found me—how did you know it was me?"

He looked at me blankly, nodding. "It's the blood that calls. That day, I got up early as usual and headed out to do some errands. Then I thought about stopping by Mariano's shop for a shave and a haircut, but changed my mind. It was an odd feeling. I couldn't tell what it was—but I felt that day was different. The one person who taught me how to really listen to my instincts was Doña Blas. A strange feeling came over me as I was driving, a strange urge to turn back. So I did—and I saw a person under an umbrella, and thought that person must be cold. The way the person walked made me curious. I slowed down, then I noticed the long hair—and something told me it was you. I don't know why, but I just knew. After we drove away, I felt peace, and realized I wasn't meant to get a haircut that day. You are the first one I've run into after all these years. I haven't seen the rest of the kids."

I was breathless and felt bad for him. Although he had been a rascal and a bully, I guess he was just like that, and I loved him just the way he was.

"Well, I've endured many days like that one," I told him. "I must admit, though, that day was different. Even walking to the bus stop that morning felt different. It was definitely a day of uncertainty for me."

I understood, then, that being with Dad had a purpose. It felt right. *We* felt right. He looked happy when I got home from work; I could see it in his eyes. Sometimes he displayed a drawing or some of his writings with pride; other times he surprised me with dinner. We were like two pillars supporting each other; I'd leave him alone on days he seemed a little quiet, and he'd always make me laugh when I seemed quiet.

Receiving my first paycheck was overwhelming; it had been a long time since I'd held money in my hands, and it seemed like too much. "Here, Father," I said, handing him sixty dollars.

"What is this for?" He frowned.

"To help," I said.

"What about the clothes you need? Take that money and buy work clothes! See who's going to laugh at you now." Father had a habit of rubbing his hands and looking away every time he envisioned something, and he did that now.

So I bought clothes, and Dad took me again to Doña Porfi's house. Aside from her fortune-telling business, she was quite a humanitarian. She had connections all over Springfield. Among other things, Porfi talked with me about saving money. "How much you have is how much you're worth. You save your money and take care of yourself, because you're going to need it down the road."

I reflected on Porfi's advice, but I already knew it would be a tough road—as if I cared. I wasn't even afraid; it was what I wanted, and I was ready. "You know, Doris, I have an idea. I have a friend who can fix your hair really nice," suggested Porfi.

"Okay," I agreed.

So Porfi called her friend. "Mica? How are you, dear? Listen, I'm sending a relative, would you take care of her for me? Great, her name is Doris." It was hilarious the way Porfi talked: always loud, ghetto and careless, with some words in English, some in Spanish. In response to my laughing—"Doris, I don't know English and I'm forgetting my Spanish"—we both laughed out loud. It felt good to laugh. Later on, I admitted to myself in one of my writings that Porfi also had a purpose in my life.

I then headed out with her daughter Lilly to Las Dominicanas, a busy hair salon at the south end of Springfield. The air was smoky from several hairdryers going at once. They had a boom box that played salsa and bachata heavy and hard. Lilly explained that all the stylists were from the Dominican Republic, that they were "nice girls." She introduced me to Mica, the owner.

Mica nodded and smiled at me. She had chocolate skin and honey eyes and a tall, slender figure. She had me follow her immediately, sat me down, and began trimming my below-the-waist hair before adding highlights.

"Doris, you have beautiful hair," she murmured, "and a nice complexion, too."

"Thank you." I smiled. My hair was thick, and I liked the fact that Mica knew what she was doing. She handled my hair effortlessly and quite speedily.

It wasn't long before she announced, "All done, Doris. Listen, stop by and see me every four weeks, and I'll keep your hair in top shape. Please say hello to Doña Porfi for me."

"Thank you, I will. Ms. Mica, how much do I owe you?"

"Nothing, dear, Doña Porfi is like family to me, so don't worry about it," Mica said gently. I felt strange leaving without paying. "Don't you worry about it," she repeated.

"All right, Doris, time to go," Lilly told me.

When we returned to Doña Porfi's house, the old fortune-teller placed both hands on either side of her face and crowed, "How beautiful! You look like one of the girls from the Spanish soaps."

The people at Doña Porfi's were curious. Some Spanish ladies asked me if I had just arrived from Puerto Rico, and I wished I had. Doña Porfi's house was busier than a doctor's office. I pitied her clients; their faces held despair and insecurity, and they waited in the hope that she could solve their problems.

In reaction to people's stares, Father chuckled and announced, "She's my daughter." He seemed proud.

Father continued visiting Doña Porfi, but I decided not to go to her place as frequently as he did. He wasn't mad at me about it. He loved talking to people, telling stories and laughing—Father made friends easily and had his own connections all over Springfield—so Doña Porfi's house was the perfect environment for him. He would bring me dinner from Porfi's house sometimes. I appreciated the help, and although I wasn't a fan of her divinations, we developed a fond friendship.

The few times I'd see Porfi, she was kind to me. She'd made me laugh by sharing stories. "Doris, there was this lady who came here looking for a husband. One day she went for a pedicure, and they put her feet in detergent, and then she went to a dance and found a husband and left Springfield for good. Then, I helped a girl find a job in a law firm, and she married an attorney. She didn't speak much English and he didn't know Spanish, but they spoke in the language of love." We laughed out loud.

I figured she told me these stories just to make me laugh. I grinned any time she changed the subject and tried to pass on her divinations. "Doris, your strength and compassion for others is your hallmark. You are going to marry a man from another land, and I can see that you are going to settle in a different place."

"Oh, Doña Porfi, I know for *sure* that I'm settling somewhere else. I'll decide later about moving to Boston or New York—we'll see. I like doing a lot of things. I'll start little by little. I love children, and helping people; I love the church, and I like to write. Whatever it is, I'll get there. I know I will." What I kept to myself was that I also missed Mother, and I wished she knew that I had forgiven her long ago and that I wanted to be there for her regardless—as a woman, as a daughter, as someone who didn't pay an eye for an eye, but as flesh of her flesh, for carrying me for nine months and giving me life.

Later on, I began to feel strange and thought about the people at the shelter, and my life there. Suddenly, it all seemed like too much after the hectic first few months. New clothes, new hair, living with Father, his company—it was all too much. So I sent the folks at the shelter a thank-you letter and promised to keep in touch. Throughout the years, I've kept my promise. I'll never forget them and what they did for me.

§ § §

At work, the laughter turned to silence, but the sarcasm

didn't end. "Let them talk—it only means you're better than they are," Father counseled. Father dropped off my lunch at work every now and then, and that provided the other girls with another reason to make fun of me. "Oh, lunch with Daddy, she still lives at home," Milli would say to Heidi. I heard the remark and their laughter, so I stopped, turned around, and smiled at the two serpents.

The serpents tried everything they could to get me in trouble, and sometimes I had to take breaks to go into the bathroom to cry.

Sometimes, I couldn't help but cry when Father picked me up in the afternoons.

Punching the steering wheel, he'd sneer, in a rage, "Cursed be that place, cursed be it. A day will come when they need your help—and when it happens, just don't bother. Don't get absorbed in their pain. Know that however they treat you is not about *you*, it's because they're not like you, and they can't *be* like you. It's how they are, it's the poor character they have. Find another job and get out. There's evil in that place."

I was too frightened to answer Father. I wasn't used to seeing him so upset.

After a year of staying with my father, he said to me urgently one day, "Listen, Doris, I need to tell you something."

"Yes, Father?"

"You know . . . ," he began, and then paused, hands resting on his lap. "The dreams," he said, while looking straight into my eyes.

"Dreams . . . I'm listening," I said, taking a deep breath.

"No, Doris. *Your* dreams," he clarified. But despite the way he looked at me, so seriously, I couldn't recall sharing any dreams with him.

"My dreams . . ." I answered, while shaking, but I pressed

my crossed arms hard against my stomach. I had left the nightmares behind, in the past, though I had written about them in my notebook. I stared at Father, unable to speak another word.

He whispered, "Every single night you wake me up, screaming. You mention your mother, Mama Blas, and other names—a Mary. It sounds like you're fighting a battle. It's not good. I'm concerned about you."

"What? I don't remember anything like that! I used to have awful dreams while I was at the shelter, but I thought they had stopped. And Mary . . . she was my best friend since third grade. We graduated together. Dad, I'm sorry I woke you up. I can't believe it—I didn't know."

"Doris, listen—maybe we should talk with a priest. Doña Porfi says it's a spiritual battle."

"You told Doña Porfi?" I asked in dread.

"Well, you know, she's our friend. I didn't know how to go about this, so I shared it with her. It's been happening for a while, Doris. It seems the minute you go to sleep, you're in a struggle. Your screams are pretty loud and scary. A lot of times I get up, thinking that you're awake, but you aren't." Father seemed frightened.

"Dad, you're scaring me," I said, covering my mouth with both hands, trying to contain my tears. I thought I'd faint.

"Let's go. Father Santiago is waiting for us."

It saddened me, the way Father walked by my side—as if walking an ill child to the hospital. His face didn't glow as usual; his eyes were gray. He drove us in silence to his local Roman Catholic Church at the north end in Springfield.

Oh, Jesus, I was horrified. I talked with Father Santiago and poured out my life story. He asked me to close my eyes and placed his hands over my head, making silent prayers.

He then asked me to pray. "Is there a particular saint you pray to, Doris?"

"Mama Blas once told me she consecrated me to the Miraculous Medal," I answered.

"Always pray to our Lady, then, and ask her for protection," Father Santiago told me. He then called my father over and they chatted quietly, while I knelt in front of the altar.

"Lord, answer me: what is the purpose of this?" I prayed. "I trust you and thank you for protection. I'm not afraid most of the time, because I know that with your help I'll get to where I'm supposed to be. Please protect me from evil and stay with me . . . but it would be easier if I could just know the *purpose*," I pleaded.

After I finished my pleas to the Lord, I went to light one more candle before I left. I sent out my thoughts to my godparents, Mama Blas and Victor. An older woman with shiny brown eyes, wearing a black mantilla, smiled at me. I looked behind me, because I thought she was smiling at someone else. When I looked back at her, she was still smiling, and she said, "When you are happy, the Lord will give you the help you need."

I stared at her.

"I'm sorry, I don't understand."

"Because you are happy, the Lord will give you help," she repeated, smiling, looking straight into my eyes, and proceeded to kneel down for her own prayers.

I walked back toward Father; he was still chatting with Father Santiago. As I came up to them, he said, "Doris, Father Santiago is celebrating a special Mass next Sunday."

I nodded and said, "Father, can you see the little lady by the candles?"

He glanced at the woman in the mantilla. "What about her?"

"She told me something bizarre: that when you're happy, the Lord will give you the help you need."

His protruding eyes widened, and he smiled.

"Ha ha, she prophesized that the Lord will grant you things because you are not angry," Father said.

"Oh, why would I be angry? I just wonder about the purpose for all of this," I said.

Father smiled comfortingly, saying, "When you accept things as they are, the Lord will reward you sevenfold. He will reward you in many great ways, greater than you could ever imagine." He rubbed his hands together and couldn't stop smiling.

"Thank you, Father," I said, feeling hopeful. Father seemed to enjoy my conversation, and I believed he also felt peace. It was almost comical to see him smile so much right there in church. I realized having Father by my side was part of the whole purpose. He was partly the answer to my prayers, part of my conquering and new life. I felt extremely gifted sharing all these moments and the same love he rendered me when I was very young. After such a brutal crusade, here I was sharing with Father the continuation of the loving life we had once had.

Life went on, and I preserved our little memories and laughed at his demeanor, and began enjoying life; though sometimes he'd argued with people. I continued visiting church and eventually became a lay minister and mentored children.

§ § §

After waking Father up with my nightmares for more than a year, I decided to move into my own apartment; and once I did, the nightmares left me eventually—or so I assumed. I was absolutely happy and overwhelmed about moving into my own place. Father was upset that I left, but I didn't go far; I stayed within the same complex. He lived on the fifth floor, and I lived on the third.

I didn't have much to pack for my move, except new work clothes. That evening turned out to be very much like my first day in the shelter, years before: I was almost overwhelmed by the quietness and the empty, blank walls. But this was different; there was much less uncertainty. It was my own space and a sure marker of a new beginning.

I had no furniture whatsoever, so that night, I slept on the bare floor. The next day, Father gave me the little bed from his bedroom.

Father and I began taking trips to flea markets all over Massachusetts, which was hilarious. We'd find unique pieces of furniture, art, Tiffany lamps, and dishware, even jewelry. It didn't bother me in the least to mix and match furniture. We went further afield, up to Vermont, and on one trip I bought a bulky bedroom set in dark wood. The bureau had little wheels on its legs. We bought a few antique pieces, which we treasured for years; in fact, I've managed to keep a few items, which I adore even now.

I soon decided to go to college. I first began attending part-time during the evenings, but language issues continued to be a challenge. I'd call or e-mail the instructors often, because I had trouble understanding the assignment instructions. Oh, I was enthusiastic, but the language was a definitive barrier. Often I'd discuss the instructions with other students to try to better understand them. Other times, I'd stay after the end of class and ask the instructor to go over the instructions. Sometimes this helped; sometimes I'd leave even more confused.

I battled with bilingualism. I didn't want to lose my Spanish, so I'd speak to Father in Spanish, watch Spanish TV, and read Spanish newspapers. I'd take my college notes in Spanish, since I could write much faster in Spanish than in English.

Eventually, I signed up for an English tutoring program. My young tutor, Stephen, told me, "Doris, I suggest you stop writing in Spanish. You'll notice that you'll struggle less with English once you keep Spanish off your mind for a while. Read more English, and speak English with your family, and you'll see the difference. After you have a full understanding of the English language, then you can slowly return to the Spanish—that way, you'll struggle less."

This proved to be true. I began to write in English, answering my usual "How do I feel today?" diary query in my second language, and got used to writing in English. That was the key. It was hard to get away from speaking in Spanish with Father and his friends, or from watching the Spanish channels, or from reading the newspaper in Spanish; I was passionate about all of these things.

I then took literature courses and continued taking courses at my own pace, one class per semester: creative writing, medical terminology, and classes pertaining to business administration. I obtained an associate's degree in criminal justice, continued my ministry, did some human resource work, became a Spanish tutor, and kept mentoring children.

After focusing on and practicing enough English, I slowly returned to reading and writing in Spanish, and this allowed me to maintain a thorough knowledge of both languages. I ended up with 140 credits, enough to pursue a master's degree. After working with Mrs. Tauber for four years, I then moved on to a new position as a legal secretary and interpreter and got promoted to human resources.

While working in human resources, I bumped into Heidi, my coworker from Mrs. Tauber's office. Somehow she'd found out where I worked and stopped by with her résumé, believing that I would "take care of her." Nervously, she said to me, "Doris, after our jobs ended at Mrs. Tauber's, I've been looking for one—and I was hoping you'd introduce me to someone."

"I'd be delighted to," I told her. Her hazel eyes widened. "There aren't many positions available, but I know you are very kind and sensitive. Aren't you, Heidi? I can file your résumé and let you know when something comes open."

"Okay," said Heidi, and she handed me her résumé. I was delighted to introduce her résumé to the garbage can.

Shortly afterward, I bumped into Milli at lunch.

"Hey, Doris, I heard you work in human resources," she said. "Squeeze me in, will you?"

I replied, smiling widely, "Oh, so you think this is the same little girl you mocked over and over?" Glancing at my watch, I said, "Excuse me; I have to get back to work." Milli stood in the middle of the hallway, speechless, as I walked away; then I turned back just long enough to say, "Oh, by the way, go back to school so you learn how to treat people, and just so you know, there aren't any available positions at this time."

I was pleased to share my "serpent" stories with Father. He laughed loudly.

"See, they laughed at you, they gave you much grief, and now they'll surely remember you! That's the curse that goes with doing harm unto others."

He laughed again, rubbing his hands together.

22. The Meeting

I dated, but my heart just wasn't ready to settle down. After raising almost half of Mother's children, I felt I'd rather pursue a career. I also thought about my mother. As my new life went on, with me working and attending college, I couldn't continue without learning more about the woman who bore me, and how she was getting by. Sometimes I wanted to go see her, but I'd hesitate, waiting for the right moment—I didn't know how she felt or if she also wanted to see me.

By then, Naomi and Lorena had also moved to the States. After visiting with Naomi on a few occasions, she suggested a meeting with Mother, and I agreed. We arranged for it to take place at a local mall, the same mall where I used to hang out during my homeless period. I told Father about the meeting, and he urged me not to go. He wasn't happy with my wish to reconcile with Mother, but he also didn't blame me, in a way, because no matter what, she was my mother.

I decided to go anyway.

Upon arriving at the mall, I felt a mixed sensation of the old and the new wash over me. I tried to visualize my recent past as the vulnerable girl in the old, worn jacket, the girl with no home, no new clothes, carrying no pocketbook, just clutching her notebook. I was shaken by those memories of walking through the harsh winter days, freezing. It was strangest remembering how I had walked the mall, constantly feeling disconnected and tense.

This time, everything was different. I was renewed, well groomed, and well dressed in new clothing, having arrived in my own vehicle—but I couldn't stop thinking about how I had walked around this town in my ragged clothes and shoes, pleading with the Lord to stay with me. I moved with heavy steps toward our meeting place, my hands curled into fists until my fingernails punctured the palms of my hands, just as they had in the past. I looked in at the clothing stores I passed, just as I had back then—but this time I knew I could walk in and touch the displays and buy new clothes whenever I wanted.

A silk scarf in burgundy and black caught my eye. I stepped into the store and caressed it; then I looked up and saw my shining face reflected in a mirror next to the display. I paused, approving of the contrast of the burgundy against my hair and complexion, and smiled at the mirror-Doris, eased by a sudden feeling of harmony.

In that moment of peace, I felt as if my being was finally sprouting, as if my existence on this earth had been renewed; and in that moment, I could see that all six of us who had been abandoned—Franco, Alejandro, Vera, Marcos, Jonas, and I—had shared almost the same struggles, not just back home but here in the States as well.

I knew they would agree that the transition from the island, adapting to new surroundings, then polishing the English language and putting aside Spanish as a second language was not easy. It certainly hadn't been for me. I had to accept, though, that putting the English language first hadn't changed me; my roots would never change, and home would always be home. As Father had once said, "Puerto Rico is part of the United States. We were born American citizens. Therefore, we have the luxury of expressing our pride of being Puerto Rican, too, because we are already citizens."

As far as English went, writing was still easier than pronunciation. I had the thickest accent and couldn't seem to pronounce some words no matter how hard I tried—

particularly "literature," ironically enough. I couldn't go beyond "lit . . . litr . . . litreture." It took me a while to learn to pronounce the word correctly. But as my pronunciation of the spoken language improved, so, too, did my self-esteem. It was so embarrassing to see heads turning when I opened my mouth, you see; when language became less of an issue, it was easier to move on.

The language barrier is a trying transition for anyone migrating to a new land from any part of the world. Then it's about pursuing dreams, surviving, and breaking barriers. And for many of us who come to the United States from warm climates, getting used to the cold weather is just as challenging.

I bought the beautiful scarf and wore it out of the store, continuing on through the mall. Comically enough, I glanced at a children's store as I walked by and saw a book titled *I Want to Go Home*. I was touched by the title and felt compelled to read it, so I stepped inside, picked up the book, and did a quick scan through it. Just like the yellow bird who was the protagonist, I still wanted to go home; and I impulsively hugged the little book. A lady nearby laughed as she saw me do so. "It's the meaning that moved me," I said to her.

"That's sweet," she said. "Where are you from?"

"Puerto Rico is my home."

"Well, it's not too far—you could visit. I went there on a cruise with my family, and we loved Old San Juan. If I were you, I'd go every year," she said, smiling.

"Thank you," I said shyly. "I think I'll do that. Thank you."

I decided to buy the little book as a keepsake. Just the feeling I could freely talk with people now was thrilling, exhilarating. Back when I'd first arrived and people tried to speak to me, I'd have to say "no English" or "no" whenever

I wanted to avoid attention. Back then, I dreaded talking about myself, didn't like too many questions, detested rudeness, and was repulsed by what Father referred to as "two-faced" people.

When I wasn't interrogated too closely, I'd share my background with great pride; I was Puerto Rican, born in Ponce, raised in Jayuya, one of thirteen legitimate children. I was used to people's reaction of, "Oh my God, thirteen children!"

I then reflected on the old, cold feeling of watching out for familiar faces during my homeless days. This day, I'd be meeting a very familiar face—one of the faces I'd been on the lookout for and frightened of the most during a period of my life when I was finding myself again, when I was deciding who Doris was and how she would move on with her life.

As I approached our meeting spot, trying to keep hold of this blissful feeling of life created anew, wearing a mauve knee-length, hip-hugging dress, black heels, and the new burgundy scarf, clutching my little book, my eyes met Mother's.

I nearly froze, because she gave me one of those cold smiles, reminding me of those days when we used to arrive home from school—the same look she gave me while balancing a toothpick in her mouth. She looked old and tired, and the mean look hadn't changed one bit. My knees shook, but I smiled at my mother so she could see my joy and see I was okay. Her eyes pierced me, though, and didn't reflect back any emotion, so I decided to keep some distance. I did not ask her for the blessing I'd been accustomed to asking for as a child.

Naomi was there to mediate our meeting. In fact, she did most of the talking. I chatted with my mother, and although she appeared somewhat cheery as she listened, there wasn't much warmth there. She didn't ask how I was doing but kept a Mona Lisa smile on her face. It was too late for me to walk away. My feet felt glued to the floor, and the conversation seemed ready to die. Then Naomi picked up the frayed threads and went on to tell Mother I was working and had moved into my own apartment. Mother's black eyes pierced mine yet again, but she appeared just a little impressed.

I had hoped letting Mother into my life would work for once, but I only felt uneasy and extremely nervous. "We're a big family," Naomi said at one point. "I think we should all make peace. Let's just forgive one another and move on. We need each other." I nodded, hoping Mother would say something, but she remained silent. Naomi continued, "Because where are we going like this? First Veronica was gone, then Dori, then Franco, then Alejandro, and Jonas, and now Marcos."

I saw something in Mother's black eyes then; they looked somber, so I decided to take a chance. I took a step forward and extended my hand to her. "Mother, I'm sorry."

"It's all right," she whispered.

Naomi continued, "Yes, Franco and Jonas stayed local, but Alejandro and Marcos went to Florida. The only ones left are the three youngest kids. Everyone is gone."

I genuinely felt bad for Mother during this moment, but it was difficult to move forward because she didn't say much. I took her silence as a bad sign; silence was never good with her. The meeting stumbled to a conclusion shortly afterward, without much of a result. "Doris, can I give Mom your number so she can call you?" Naomi asked me.

"Sure," I said, while thinking, *for what and talk about what? We hardly spoke.* I was nervous, and just like on the day we'd first arrived from the island, the air felt strange.

Why couldn't she share *her* phone number? Could I trust her? Would she try to hurt me again?

Mother started calling me on Saturday mornings, and those calls were most unwelcome. She was quietly sarcastic on learning about my achievements, which made me insecure, or she'd keep silent and not offer any positive comment at all. Repeatedly, she'd ask, "How are you feeling? Did you sleep okay? I had a dream you came knocking on my door and asked for help."

I perceived sarcasm and answered in the same vague tone, "I'll tell you, I've had countless dreams . . ."

I left her comment in the lurch and didn't bother to share the nightmares. I knew her too well and knew where she was coming from.

I went back to my old vigilance whenever I stepped out of the apartment, constantly on the lookout for familiar faces. Father revived me with optimism. He believed in me. It was a good thing Father remained my pillar. Mother drained me and made me feel insecure.

It wasn't long before the inevitable steel-hard confrontation occurred between Mother and me. I didn't know what she wanted, and our talks just made me weak. Slowly, slowly, the sleepless nights returned. I hated nighttime again; oh, how I hated nighttime, how I cursed it. I'd vent by writing, "Oh you nightfall, you seem most mighty! May I tell you how much I despise your ugliness? If I could prevent your arrival, you dark haunting nights, I would! Why do you approach?"

Then came the confrontation during one of her calls— the moment had arrived, and I simply blurted out, "I hate the way you treated me, Mother! I wanted to make you proud! I wanted your love and trust—and you betrayed me!"

"Doris, don't start!" she said, breathing heavily. "You were the one who left."

"I'm glad I did. If I hadn't, I wouldn't be where I am today. The so-called new home for us was a lion's den. It was hell, where deceit was served in abundance."

"Hmmm." Mother was still breathing heavily.

"Mother, you tried to destroy me. It seemed like you enjoyed seeing me in pain. You were never kind to me—not since long before you abandoned us!"

Mother's nostrils made a horrific thick noise.

"Mother, did you know Arnaldo harassed me for months? Did you know I spent *years* having nightmares every night? Do you even care I was homeless? Not *once* have you asked me how I made it, or if I slept okay then. I'm glad I live far away from you."

"Yes, and you're living near your father now," she said nastily. "A *great* future awaits you."

There was the answer I was looking for; and now, I no longer cared what she thought of me, or what she wished for me. "Mother, you will never see me want—but thank you." I hung up.

I was angry at myself for being weak and allowing Mother into my life again. I should have known better. I was angry at Naomi for her fruitless attempt to make peace between us. This failed attempt changed me, reversing some of the progress I'd made, as my insecurity and fear of failure crashed down on me again. Suddenly I wasn't myself, and I committed myself to working extra hard, even when I was sick, so that I wouldn't fail. Once again, I became more guarded when interacting with people.

Several months later, in late 1993, Mother visited me. I was twenty-seven. Again, deep down, I was scared—but I had to try. Was I being weak? Was I letting Mother manipulate me? She arrived with little Uma in tow, and my sister loved my apartment. "Doris, this is your apartment? I love your furniture. I want to be like you," said Uma.

"Thanks," I told her. "You can achieve anything in life, but you have to work hard. As long as you don't let go of your dreams, no matter how hard it may seem, you'll get there," I said to my little sister, who was in middle school by then.

Mother looked around the place, saying nothing but listening to every word I said. She made a loud *Hmmm* once while I talked with my sister, interrupting our conversation. She appeared serious, not angry; I couldn't read her at all. I didn't know if she was happy for me, or if she didn't want me talking to my sister, or what. I began feeling very uncomfortable and said, "Look. This is all I wanted to do, Mother."

"Yes—but you left, Doris."

Here we go again, I thought. Talking with her felt like plunging into a muddy puddle. Something about her just drained me. I didn't want to argue, not on the first day of my Mother's visit, especially not in front of my little sister. I turned on the TV and sat Uma in front of it so she wouldn't hear our conversation. I whispered, "Mother, if I hadn't left, I wouldn't have made it this far. It was all too much—you wanted me to pay for things I never did. I kept my part of the bargain in caring for the kids, and you repaid me by beating me. I was about to have a nervous breakdown. When I was living alone with the kids, we were hanging by a mere thread of dreams and hope, but at least we had that back home. You destroyed our life by bringing us here—and for what?"

Mother kept her silence, maintaining a poker face, and the air was filled with an unbearable tension for a split second. Then it broke as I said, "Mother, I don't care anymore about the past. I'm not mad about it. Even though we didn't have much back in Puerto Rico, we were happy. Even though I was homeless for years, look at me now. It's time to move forward. I don't even talk about the past with Father. I don't want to live in the past." I looked straight into Mother's eyes and smiled at her.

She didn't smile back. I felt cold and nervous, vulnerable, her piercing eyes once again making me freeze, as if she had me pinned against the wall. I wanted the visit to be over; and I don't know how, but I managed to suggest to them both, "Would you like to go walk around?"

My little sister's eyes sparkled at the suggestion, and as I extended my hand to open my apartment door, Mother's muscular right arm intercepted it. At first, I thought she was going to hurt me, and I half-closed my eyes as I envisioned her fist flying. But it didn't, to my shocked surprise.

"I'm sorry," she said, her shoulders drooping. I remained frozen and didn't dare to hug her. I looked at her searchingly and saw that her black eyes looked sincere. "I'm truly sorry," she repeated.

I unthawed a little. "Don't worry, Mother. I'm at peace. The kids had the best time of their lives under my care; I'm sorry they're gone now. I gave up a lot because you said we had to come here, that we had a new home. None of us wanted to come here. This is all . . . horrific."

"You could have told me. I didn't know," Mother said.

"You didn't know? How could you not know? Mother, I called you about it. I told you I didn't want to leave. I even had a full scholarship to go to the university, a wonderful opportunity any high school graduate would love to have, and you made me give it up . . . but it doesn't matter anymore," I said.

Mother's tone seemed a little choked as she repeated, "I'm really sorry. I am."

I'd never seen Mother this way: her shoulders were

sagging, her voice calm, her black eyes tearful. Her face scared me as she whispered, "I have to tell you, Doris, when you left, I was the one who warned Naomi and Lorena not to help you. I told the younger kids not to talk to you if they saw you. I told Franco to drag you home if he found you. I gave away your belongings, and Naomi and Lorena and everyone else took most of your things. I don't know why I did it. I'm sorry. I'm really sorry."

I was devastated at the awful news and felt betrayed beyond words. Taking a deep breath, I tried hard to forget about what used to be my "belongings" and hoped my sisters appreciated my clothing, shoes, keepsakes, and jewelry, just as I had. Even the writings and quotes I'd collected—one in particular I had bought in a flea market with Dad and Veronica. It was a quote by President Ronald Reagan in a tiny frame: "Life is one grand song, so start the music."

We walked around outside for a while. I walked containing my tears and trying to let go of what I'd already lost. My little sister loved our walk and chatted away, enjoying the moment. By the time we returned, I felt drained and had a pounding headache. The visit concluded as Mother hugged me, then held my hands and again repeated that she was sorry.

Later, when I told Father what Mother had said, he let out a suspicious "Uhum," then continued contemptuously, "*Él que cría cuervos, le sacan los ojos.* When you raise crows, you get your eyeballs pecked out. Like crows, they picked through your things. Remember how we used to go to the flea markets on Sundays? I had a big stock of magazines and an entire collection of Donna Summer's greatest hits. I assume those don't exist anymore."

Aside from sharing with Father, I didn't know what I could do to get the help I needed to get through this ordeal with Mother. Luckily for me, my notebook and pencil helped me pour out my losses. I committed myself to forgiving everyone—but it took a lot of writing and rewriting to do so. Later on, Mother was most kind to give me a couple of my graduation pictures, a prom picture, and my favorite amber earrings. "I'm sorry, Doris. I had a jeweler change the hooks. But I can't keep them any longer. They're yours."

I very much appreciated receiving these few things from Mother, especially my earrings; but no one else came forward or said anything.

Father never liked me talking with Mother, and vice versa. The tension between Mother and I lasted for a while. I assumed she could tell I was happy living near Father, and I tended to talk too much, maybe, about our adventures in going to the flea markets and shopping trips to New York and, our favorite, the Spanish restaurant in Springfield—and how I simply enjoyed his peace.

Years later, Mother attended my college graduation, and our relationship slowly became more wholesome. Living with Father, staying close to him and receiving his instructions in life, served its purpose. He cared about me and would not rest until I was doing okay.

Father was happy to meet Roberto, my future husband, whom I met in my thirties. Father blessed him while expressing a look of happiness. I was almost unprepared for Mother's reaction upon meeting him; she blessed him while embracing him with warmth, calling him "son."

"Doris, the way your family has embraced me, I've never felt so loved," said Roberto. He enjoys spending time with my brothers in Massachusetts and Florida. He adores all of the kids and has expressed his admiration for how disciplined and well-spoken and special they turned out to be. He listens in awe as my siblings talk about our adventures in the little house back in Puerto Rico.

Finally, I feel I have achieved happiness and success— and I've been overwhelmed by the outpouring of blessings I've received from forgiveness. I especially thank all the good people of good faith who took a moment to care about me while I worked on my manuscript. Thanks to my father for everything, as I first knew happiness with him.

23. Mother

This is my mother's story, told to me in her own words: "I was born on June 29, 1939, right at home, north of Ponce. I'm the youngest of fourteen children. My parents worked hard selling coffee and other fruits and vegetables in bulk.

"My mother was like a general. From the time I was seven years old, Mother woke me up every morning at four to care for our animals. Your grandmother sent me barefoot to school, though my siblings didn't go barefoot. Honora got to wear brand-new shoes all the time. It wasn't like my parents didn't have the money.

"I wanted new shoes for church, but my mother had me wear whatever Honora discarded. On a few occasions, Dad told her to get me new shoes and clothes, but she resisted. My father was a sweetheart and treated me with love; he called me his little girl.

"The mornings were cold and dark. Every morning I'd walk barefoot on the cold grass, wishing I was still in bed. Mother didn't even bother to brush my hair."

Mother paused, looking away, onyx eyes clouded but relaxed. "I wouldn't call this a life, but a curse."

"A curse?" I asked.

Mother's eyes were serene, deep in thought. Her hands were crossed on her lap, and her bulky fingers seemed almost swollen. I looked her in the eye and said, "Thank you for giving me life, Mother."

Mother nodded, raising thin eyebrows, her back straight, her chin up. Her posture saddened me; it seemed almost as if my mother sat on a witness stand.

"Mom, do you remember the time we cooked outside on three rocks?" I asked.

"Yes, I do. The stove ran out of gas, and we cooked pasteles outside. We had the boys bring wood. Those were the best pasteles we ever cooked together!" Mother laughed.

She continued her story: "You know, my daughter, learning and going to school was my world. Against my father's will and my own, Mother took me out of school in the third grade. She wanted me to work hard at the farm. She'd say school was not for girls, that we were just exposed to learning perverse things. I remember how she'd say women with schooling were useless—that they didn't learn about real life. But I never stopped wishing I could go back to school one day. I'd stare at other kids on their way to school. It saddened me, and I tried to avoid conversations with them. I was embarrassed by my bare feet.

"I loved school, and preserved my notebooks. I hoped Mother would change her mind one day, but it never happened.

"My mother sent me by myself to deliver breakfast to my father every single morning. Our property was vast, so sometimes, I'd have to walk a very long way, and I was afraid. Many times I walked and walked, and he would find me first. He was kind to me, calling, 'Honey, I'm here.' He would eat his breakfast while I waited to bring the lunch bag back home, smiling with me. When he was done, he would tell me to go home and be a good girl. And so I would.

"Returning home was pure anguish. Any protest against performing my chores would carry a heavy punishment, so I had no choice but to follow Mother's orders. My father's voice didn't have any effect on my mother's decisions; they were final, no matter what.

"When your uncle Monserrate married, I wasn't allowed to attend his wedding. I wanted to go and kept begging Mother about it, but she wouldn't let me. I was very angry with her, and for the first time in my life, I felt I had to take revenge. Mother had a nice piece of fabric neatly laid down on a table, and I ruined it by cutting it straight across. Mother never knew I did it, but I'm glad I did. Everyone went to my brother's wedding but me. I was left at home. My father wasn't happy, but in our home, my mother was the boss—and her word was final.

"My mother despised how my father treated me. She assigned me the hardest chores to do, including going to the river to wash clothes by myself. The basket of laundry was too heavy to carry, so I dragged it and struggled with it until I made it to the river. Mother timed me, and if I took too long, she accused me of "playing around and killing time." She inspected the clothes piece by piece and made me rewash them if she didn't think I'd done a good enough job.

"While she inspected each piece, I'd swear to her all I'd done was the washing. She never listened and often hit me with a tree branch. She threatened me that if I mentioned that to Father, she'd do worse. I was tempted; I could feel her watching me when Father returned home from work. Father often noticed me acting differently and would ask me about it. 'What's wrong, my girl? You seem sad.'

"'I'm okay,' I'd reply. I knew Mother was listening.

"I only had one doll to play with. At one point Mother snatched it from my hands. '*Manganzona,* you are too old to play.' I loved my dolly. I was heartbroken when she took it, and I never saw it again.

I was fourteen when Father decided to send me to live with my sister Leonor in Philadelphia. I felt huge relief. My sister had children, you see, and needed help. When I came back and later met your father, my mother planned our wedding. I was seventeen. I did not want to get married yet, but my mother's reply was, 'You brought him here, so he is the one you are going to marry.'

"Your father began hitting me right after I had our first child, Lenora. I had barely turned nineteen when I had her.

"I'm sorry for the treatment I gave you. I didn't know better. You kids were too many. I was overwhelmed. By the time I had my first two kids, I knew I didn't want to be married anymore. I wanted something more, an education and a better life. When I told my parents I was considering a divorce, my father almost slapped me. He reminded me of the vows I took, that marriage was for life. I grew bitter. I really wanted to become an investor, you see. It's all I wanted to do. I thought investing was fascinating. It was my obsession.

"Your father took his revenge when he learned I didn't want to stay married. He never visited me when I gave birth; he just dropped me off in the maternity ward and I never saw him again until I returned home with a new baby. While other husbands visited their wives and held their new babies, he was never part of any of your births. The doctors kept suggesting surgery to have my tubes tied so I wouldn't have to be in the hospital almost every year, having a new child. They'd lay the papers before me, but I didn't have the heart to sign. I thought God might punish me with eternal damnation if I did. I'd hold the pen, ready to sign, and then shake my head and say, 'I can't do it.'

"The doctor, upset, would reply, 'Well, Mrs. Torres, we'll see you next year then.'

"I didn't want to have so many children. I was unhappy because of the way we were living; your father didn't earn enough. He wasn't ambitious enough. He grew up spoiled;

he was given everything, so he didn't know how to work hard and dream and hope. He was content with the little bit he earned truck driving.

"Things kept turning worse for me, because your father couldn't shake the fact that I wanted to divorce him. I guess he felt belittled. He began to mock me and make me suffer and laugh at the fact that I 'couldn't divorce him.' He refused even to build an addition to the house when we needed it. He told me, 'For you, I will never build anything.' He simply chose to torture me, because I had told him I wanted to divorce him from the beginning—but he told me I was stuck with him whether I liked it or not.

"My answer to him was, 'When they get bigger, I want nothing to do with you.' He laughed at me, telling me, 'A stupid woman like you don't know what she's saying.' I then became angry and responded to his insult with, 'I promise you I will take my revenge.' He kept laughing, but I knew I'd made my statement clear. His final words on the matter were 'We'll see,' to which I replied, 'You *will* see!'

"When all of you were small, his beatings were frequent. He broke my nose and a small bone below my collarbone. All my life I've been treated badly—like I'm nothing, no one. I feel like the black sheep. I'm sick of it.

"My parents left the property for us to live in, but your Aunt Honora's greed wouldn't let her see I had smaller children than she did. At that time, I thought, *Where will I go with my children?* One day, she asked me to see the deed. Without thinking, I handed it to her, and she took it away when she left. She said she would bring it back, but she didn't. When I went to her house to get it back, she told me, 'I'm keeping the deed because I think it's best to sell.' She had betrayed me. I reminded her about our parents' wishes that the property was for my children. My last statement to her was, 'If you think you can eat it, well, go ahead and eat it.'

"I'm glad we left for good. This is how I've always been treated, with inferiority—like my children and I were less than anyone else. I think I was born on a Friday the thirteenth. My whole life has been bitterness and suffering."

After she finished her painful story, I told my mother, "Well, thank you for having me, Mother. You can be happy now—there's no more raising kids, cooking, or housework to worry about."

"Now I'm tired and hate cooking," Mother said, laughing.

I chuckled. "It's okay Mother. Look at the beautiful children you brought into the world!"

"Thanks, my daughter, I knew you were good. Ever since you were very young, you've been a quick learner and insisted on helping. I love you all, you know."

"Well, Mother, now you can rest from so much cooking and housework and be happy," I sighed.

"I also wanted my own house," she mused. "I never had the house I dreamed of, you know. I didn't want to stay at my mother's house; I wanted my own house, where I could raise my children and see them run around and know we had something that belonged to us. Every single minute of my life was based on control. I'd bow down to my parents, even after I was a married woman, as well as to your father, for being my husband. My word and opinions did not count." She took a deep breath. "I was forbidden to express myself. I wanted to be free from this life of control and bitterness. My own life desires, my dreams—in my parents' eyes, they were vain and preposterous ideas."

After a moment of deep thought, Mother said, "My father, Teyo, stood six foot two, with very refined skin, an oval face, almond-shaped eyes, and brown hair. His hair was so fine that he used to comb it with his fingers. His ancestors were from Madrid, Spain.

"He was a comedian, but his anger—God help the man who provoked it! He was generous but had no tolerance for laziness or bad manners. Teyo died at the age of eighty-five—some say he was older, but I'm not so sure. I know he worked all his life. I remember the day he came to see me after working on the farm and asked me for a cup of espresso; after he drank the coffee; he started coughing, then went very pale and started sweating. When I asked him, 'Are you okay?' he threw himself at me. I put my arms around him, and we both fell to the ground. He died in my arms. I'll never forget that day, and never have I felt such agony ever since.

"He just took a deep breath, let it out, and his body slumped in my arms. His lifeless body was agonizing to see; if I could have revived him, if I could have given him my life, I would have. I just held him on my lap for a long time.

"I was pregnant with Franco then, and superstitious people kept telling me, 'One who died that way could be reborn.' I wished people would respect our mourning, without making it some prophetic thing, but they persisted. When Franco was born, even Mama Blas said, 'That child is Teyo the Second. He came back. Look at him.'

"I eventually resigned myself to people's superstitions and agreed that Franco has the exact temperament as my father. His eyes are identical, and so is his demeanor, especially when someone ticks him off."

"You know, Mother, Franco sharpened Mama Blas's machete every day when we were living there alone."

Mother took a deep breath, and then said, "Thank God nothing happened."

Doris Mercado

As I mentioned earlier, Mother attended my college graduation along with my siblings, and the Chanel No. 5 she wore reminded me of our happier days. Her manly hands were gentle that day. "I'm proud, my daughter. You are a rock."

I embraced my mother; I love her as I always have, unconditionally. "Well, Mother," I told her, "you gave thirteen of us the gift of life and sacrificed so much. To me, that's having real *cojones*."

Epilogue: In Their Own Words

I don't recommend that anyone, especially youngsters, be forced to keep secrets the way we did. If you're undergoing any form of pain, negligence, or abuse, reach out to someone. Don't be afraid to speak out for yourself, or for a friend, or even for someone you don't know, if that person is in obvious torment. Don't keep secrets, and most of all, don't suffer in silence—and don't let others suffer in silence.

There were times I wanted to reach out, but I was too afraid I'd lose Veronica and my brothers. After first Victor, then Diego, said we were too many, I didn't think anyone would be willing to help all six of us. Although we went through some times of dangerous poverty, we'd hang on while modestly thinking other children had similar or even greater needs. It was also a time when we discovered our inner strength and the great power of prayer and faith.

The six of us who were abandoned still reminiscence about those good days when we visited the river, the days when we laughed together and felt whole and free. We all agree that although we were abandoned, we shared a special love that kept our hope alive. Our humility and love for one another composed the great armor that strengthened us to go on. We joke every now and then about being gifted with two lives, about how we have risen from our own ashes and are able to look back and reflect on and admire such resilience. Hey, let there be light!

As for each sibling: well, Franco remains the great optimist. He's a business owner, doing just fine. Whenever any of us wants to get away and walk in the countryside, we visit Jonas. He took a little after Mama Blas and is a multitasking nature and animal lover. Marcos remains the chatterbox. His gift is no doubt his personality, and he has an awesome ability to be able to speak in front of a crowd. He's tactful and funny and writes poetry. Alejandro devoted almost a decade to studying martial arts and then made a major life decision. Now he leads a spiritual life, helping the needy, and he also writes poetry and inspirational tales. Veronica enjoys helping the needy as well. She paints, writes, and meditates, and like Jonas, she is settled in the countryside. As for me, the five are still my children and will be for all eternity.

I don't take a single moment for granted and have remained the same daughter who wanted to please my mother and do better. Writing a word or two every day, meditation is a must, and translating my creativity into vivid oil paintings is a special personal treat. Comically enough, and just as Doña Porfi predicted, I married a man from 'another land,' Italy. Porfi continues to reside in Springfield. Although she denies that she has retired from divinations, she has never lost her fame for sharing her predictions with strangers.

Over the years, I've conducted brief interviews with my siblings about our abandonment days. Other than that, they have their own life stories to tell. Alejandro was the first; I spoke to him once when he visited from Florida. He was in his late twenties. After sharing my writing with him, I asked him about his feelings regarding those days.

Alejandro laughed nervously. "But why do you want me to talk about it?"

"Well, I've been writing about my life and how we made it through the abandonment. Do you realize there are over one million homeless children in the country, many of whom suffer abuse or neglect?"

He laughed again nervously, eyes wide open. "Well, it's funny you should ask me about that. In fact, I was sharing about us recently at church. I think we share the same interests. I love to write, and I've been writing about those times as well. I think anyone who cares for a child should automatically take parenting classes, regardless of social status, age, or religion. Abused children suffer in a state of despair, and many of them can't survive such great pain alone.

"About us living alone . . . at first it was hard to keep the faith. All I felt was uncertainty. After Mother left, and then Dad, I couldn't help but feel there was little chance for us to make it. I'd go to school and church, but I couldn't foresee our future. I was haunted by the silence in the house, the waiting, the hoping—it was all too much to grasp. It felt almost like we were dying inside as we waited and waited. I was fortunate to spend time with Diego. I truly feel the one person who saved us was Mama Blas. Her prayers, and the spirituality she instilled in us, are what I believe saved us."

"I also write my own speeches for church. And I wanted to know, Doris, if you'd accept me?"

"Accept you? What do you mean, Alejandro?" I said.

"I've decided to pursue a religious life. I must know if you accept me."

"My God, Alejandro, of course I accept you wholeheartedly, how can I not accept you?"

I hugged him and saw a faded sadness in my brother's expression. His dark cinnamon face seemed relaxed, though, and he seemed to be at peace. Clearing his throat, he said, "I've traveled, you know. I've gone to different places, helping refugees in different parts of the world."

"I'm proud of you, my brother," I said, feeling blessed to be sharing in his peace and spirituality.

Doris Mercado

§ § §

Veronica visited me with her family when she was in her early twenties. The visit was emotional. I felt small, tired, and broken at the time, but my sister appeared happy at the turn my life had taken. "Wow, Doris, this is a cute place. You can buy your own house now, you know?"

"Not yet, Veronica, I'll know the time and place."

"Yes, Doris, but be aware renting is wasting money," said Veronica—as always, exercising her common sense.

"I'll keep it in mind, Veronica, thank you. Believe me, I know, but I don't want to rush into anything right now. One thing, though: I will never ever take a second of my life for granted. I feel I've lost too much already." I remembered our conversations at our precious little home on the island. I asked quietly, "Remember what you said before we came here? You said it was bad luck leaving home."

"Ugh, I still remember that day as if it were today," said Veronica.

"Listen—all along, I've been writing about my life, and I wanted to ask about your feelings about that time. How did you feel when we were left alone?"

"Oh, jeez, why are you reminding me of that awful past? I've written a little as well. I think one day I'd like to write about my own life. Living alone with no adults around—I've never felt so lost, out of place, or afraid in my entire life. I was afraid we weren't going to make it. Every day I wanted to fit in; I wanted to feel we had a home we belonged to, but I didn't feel we did. I felt as if the abandonment marked us, like we'd never have a normal childhood, or parents who loved us. Just remembering that past—not having much, the fear of being raped—I hate to bring back those haunting memories."

She sighed. "I wouldn't say I had a good time, except when I stayed at Naomi's or Victor's. I couldn't seem to let go of the memory of Mother and Dad leaving us. Then coming here . . . well, I'm just grateful we're okay now. I'm glad Dad tried to help us, and during that time he did tell me he loved me. Other than that, I didn't feel loved at all."

§ § §

When I visited with Jonas and Marcos, both were in their twenties. Both were married, both had children. Both married around age twenty-one. I was a little nervous to see them again, yet was astonished at how tall Jonas had grown. He turned out taller than Alejandro and is quite an attractive young man: at six foot two, he has a wide, muscular chest, golden-brown hair, a golden complexion, and a dimpled smile. Jonas's demeanor reminded me of Mama Blas's, and it seemed like he stopped time while he contemplated me as we talked. We reminisced about our old times and laughed together.

"Thank you, Doris," Jonas said. "It was scary, but we were safe—and that's the only positive thing I can remember."

I shared with both brothers that I had been writing about my experiences and asked them about their feelings regarding our childhood and subsequent abandonment.

Jonas cleared his throat and went on to say, "I don't know how we made it. Dad was a bastard—he didn't teach me anything. I'd feel so embarrassed when we went to school and church, always wearing old clothes and broken shoes. We didn't have shit, and didn't go anywhere. I felt like shit, like we were less than everyone else. That was fucked up. At the same time, though, I felt too young to worry much about anything.

"Thank goodness for Diego; we learned a lot from him and Don Franceschini.

"At a very young age, I could tell Dad had something wrong in his head and never gave a fuck. Everything was a joke to him; he didn't bring in much money from work, and Mother was too depressed to deal with it, with no one to turn to. She was also too ignorant to get help. She always said she was abused as a kid, so she passed it on to us. I don't even want to remember those days of feeling like we were nothing, like we were just leaves rolling along the ground in the wind, waiting to die. People even stepped on us and didn't care."

By then, Jonas was so upset that his honey eyes looked dim, as if he were in mourning for someone. Then he grinned and nodded, lifting his chin. "But we made it. And imagine what we'd have done if any of us had any idea we'd come straight to hell afterward. I never would have come here," he said, laughing.

The topic brought back the tension; and Marcos, who was listening, held a huge silence, his eyes watering. We looked into each other's eyes, in sympathy for our pain.

"Thank goodness for Mama Blas. She was our role model," said Jonas.

"Amen to that," Marcos said, chuckling nervously.

Marcos ended up being just as attractive as Jonas. He seemed fearless, and his face was open and expressive. I could read him like a book; I knew his answers to my questions before he voiced them. "Dear Mother of God, I don't want to remember those days," he told me. "I used to think that I wrote poetry as an escape—but I've been writing poetry ever since I relocated to Florida. I can't live without writing. I've shared my work with people, and some call me a philosopher, others an anthropologist. Writing sets me free, Doris."

He smiled. "I often think about Don Franceschini. He treated us with so much love; he'd take us to his house some afternoons. He was just too smart—I think he knew we were alone, but because we seemed okay, he let us be. And although we didn't have shit, I felt good because the hitting was over, and we didn't have anyone pestering us all the time. I remember playing with my friends and coming home from school and going to the river. I was happy. It felt good."

"Marcos, remember the witch, and your prayers at night?" I asked.

We laughed together. "Oh my God, how embarrassing," he chuckled. "You guys didn't believe me sometimes, but I *know* there was something prowling around the house at night. I'd hear things.

"Anyway, our time at the old house was the best time I ever had in my life. We'd venture in the woods and the river. I felt safe, and looked up to Franco, who never put down the old machete."

§ § §

I then had the chance to visit with Franco, who was in his thirties. His look was dark and exotic, with carefully trimmed hair and beard. He had happy almond eyes, masculine, clean hands, and well-pressed clothing. I felt safe around him, which reminded me of our old times. He did resemble our grandfather in many ways and walked as if spreading joy were his duty.

"I heard you had a car accident and hurt your back," I told him. "How are you feeling now?"

"For a while, it hurt like a son of a bitch. I went for a series of injections, which made the pain better, but only for a little while. Then it got worse . . . but I got used to

298

the pain. I'm still working—same job, same place." He chuckled. "At first, the doctor said I wouldn't be able to walk again. They did a bunch of tests, and I didn't have feeling in my legs. Days later, the feeling came back, and I got up."

"Oh my God, Franco, that's a miracle!"

Later, I said, "Listen, Franco, I've been writing about my life since we lived in Puerto Rico, and I wanted to ask how you felt about the turn our lives took—living alone, then coming here."

Laughing, he said, "Oh, I didn't want to come here, that's for sure. But here I am. As a teenager, with our parents gone, I wasn't thinking about much of anything. I was sad most of the time. I guess that's why I was always in a so-called happy mood, because I was in denial. I asked Victor to delay the plane tickets on three separate occasions, but he always said no. I was numb for a while. I felt no one cared. Just as we left, I was about to get a good job as a corrections guard. It was while I was waiting to learn whether I'd passed the test, but we received the fucking plane tickets.

"From that point on, something came over me, some strange feeling. This was the only time I felt any real fear. I tried to get Victor to delay the tickets, because I wanted to stay and work, but he said time and time again it couldn't be done. I kept feeling a strange fear and a terrible sense of trouble. I felt like something bad was going to happen after our move.

"We had family all over the place in Ponce and other towns—and no one bothered to visit us. I became determined to save the kids. I came really close to using the machete sometimes. Then, after a while, I just didn't care anymore. I was sort of lost and didn't know how I felt. Then it seemed that just when our lives were about to start, we were forced to move. I didn't want to leave. After we came here, it seemed like it all went wrong for every single one of us. I'm glad, however, that we fought for ourselves—and it's all over now. For a while, I felt like a fish swimming against the current, but I believe that in the end, we won."

"Franco," I told him, "I never had the chance to thank you for your protection while we were on the island, but thank you so much. You are my hero, my light. For you, I'd swim the Atlantic!" We laughed and hugged.

Franco and Jonas remain my confidants.

We had a harsh beginning, and for a while, we lost each other. Every time we get together these days, the six of us reunite like a lost puzzle. We connect as one and share in the same energy. Together, we revive our vow of dreaming together; we share our vulnerability, and our joy and passion for life and it feels right.

It's still hard when we part. It almost feels wrong. Sometimes it feels our journey is yet unfinished. We're still in the evolution and dream mode, sharing a special love, a bond that's never to be broken.

§ § §

Never in a million years did I imagine we'd leave my little home or that I'd become homeless and finally take on a crusade to save myself just as I reached the prime of my life—and that by forgiving everyone, I'd be blessed, as Father predicted, sevenfold. At the age of thirty-four, I decided to share my life and wrote the first manuscript version in two days, by pencil, as my preferred writing tool.

In May 2009, walking into Luz Muñoz Marin Airport in San Juan felt like walking right into my living room. I had visited before in the 1990s, when Mama Blas passed away, but this visit was most special because it was our honeymoon. My next challenge was yet to come, as I struggled to adjust to a new life, marrying a man of honor who took pride in taking me back home. Life then felt as if it was a continuous adjustment until I was able to reach calm waters.

"This is a paradise," said my husband.

"This is it," I said. "Welcome to my home, Mr. Cerasani, welcome to Puerto Rico."

I was joyous to stop by our first little home in Ponce and to retrace our steps in our bubbly and happy city. We drove around downtown, meeting with some of the Mercados in Ponce, and I shared some of our stories.

We then visited my heroine, Mama Blas, at her resting place—with white flowers, of course. She had passed away in 1993. "Here I am, Mama," I said out loud, in a loving, playful tone, as I'd do when I was ten years old. "Mama, this is my husband, Roberto." He wiped his tears away as I shared some of her stories.

A yellow butterfly flew around the cemetery, making little stops at her flowers. The warm air caressed my face, and I gathered it was a sign of approval.

I was then glad to head out to the high country and breathe the scent of freshly picked coffee once again, and walk into our old familiar surroundings. The aged cement house was still there and felt like my true home; it welcomed me as it always did, like a mother, with open arms.

"This is it? It's such a small house!" my husband exclaimed.

"Yes, this is it, welcome home," I said.

My husband proceeded to unseal the front door, and I felt my soul was released as he did so. In my heart, I said, *My precious, I take my soul; but our secrets, our agonies, and the echoes of our weeping are yours to keep. I have a new house, but you'll always be in my heart, my home sweet home.*

Everything inside the house had decayed, the floors were muddy, but the memories filled it still. Walking into our rooms and Mama Blas's bedroom, and looking at what was left of the herb garden, made me picture the little girl with bouncy long hair and happy brown eyes, running back and forth, helping Mother and longing for her acceptance. I walked into what used to be my tiny room and pictured the days we had lived in the house.

I could see them, the little faces that believed and dreamed with me. I could picture Marcos stomping around, Jonas collecting insects, Veronica playing with her doll, Alejandro racing wooden cars, and Franco keeping a watchful eye while sharpening the machete, its blade shining like white gold against the sun.

I took a last glance at the farm, including everyone's favorite spot by the old mango tree—and I pictured Father releasing the little owl he had rescued. For a second or two, our memories overwhelmed me like an ocean current. It all seemed too much and strange and dark, so much had happened, yet so fast. Then thinking about my siblings and wishing I could share the moment with them, I wondered how'd they feel and accepted that our destiny was as beautiful as we had dreamed it to be. It was almost hard to believe that we actually lived all these events. I frankly don't know how we got to endure so much and finally conquer.

I then blessed the land that witnessed my birth and the little home that gave six of us a hopeful sign of a blue morning sunrise—a humble home that had kept us together under a deteriorated little roof and guarded us against the elements, where we shared hope, dreams, teachings, and values.

I felt fortunate to revise the final version of the

manuscript in September 2012, while visiting my husband's homeland, Italy, while listening to one of my favorites, Wisin y Yandel, "Déjame Hablar." It was a very special moment as I finally gave closure to my story. I'll forever treasure the fondest memories visiting such a sacred land, the very land that saw my husband's birth.

My experience taught me a thing or two about abuse and neglect and the importance of a good support system. It taught me not to subject myself to walking the same road twice. I learned the importance of being surrounded by positive people.

By nature, I'm a caring person, a leader, a free spirit no doubt. I've been the child protector since day one, a tireless helper. My caring nature led me to forgive Mother over and over again, almost at the cost of my life, but my effort was well rewarded in the end. I thank Mother for encouraging me to continue doing the beautiful things I do.

Child abuse and neglect to me are just as bad as cancer; if left untreated, abuse kills. In our case, the cancer was Mother's pressure caring for us. Her ambitions to one day become successful made her ill, and we were the ones dying. Her dreams came and went, and this, plus the aftermath of her own life experiences, was a dangerous combination—not to excuse my mother, but that volcano erupted. Mother wanted to reach her goals, and she had the capability and intelligence and her own ideas, but she had no support.

As for us, following Mother's initial instructions while enduring the abandonment saved us. We pursued and achieved; it was hard work, but we never let go, plus we had each other. It was the same tactic I used to save myself during my homelessness.

Father and Porfi played the supporting role. I owe Father everything, as he took me on where he left off; he searched, he counseled me, he loved me and never rested until I did well and met my future husband. We share the most hilarious memories, taking off to New York City to the flea markets on Sundays, to different antique stores; we'd visit with Veronica and the boys, and we had much fun. His inherited electrifying energy made me happy. I am where I am supposed to be in my life, and for me, forgiveness, faith, love, and perseverance were the key to everything. Forgiveness gifted me with many blessings—and new beginnings.

Doris Mercado

The Great Wave

It seemed like I was a rock next to a great ocean. A huge wave came in full force, wrapped in darkness, horrifying and merciless, crashing down on me over and over, piercing and rattling my entire being. It almost broke me. I hung on, pleading for the storm to pass. The great wave is now calm water. The two of us have reached a balance; now there's peace. We are each other's keeper.
—*The author*

Acknowledgments

Mother, thank you for giving me the gift of life; Dad, thanks for being the great pillar; your love and guidance brought my tempest to an end. I love you. I feel most lucky and blessed and thank our Lord God for always being by my side and for saving me during the most vulnerable moments in my life. To my twelve siblings, Lorena, Victor, Naomi, Raquel, Uma, Josue, Sergio, and my heroes, Franco, Jonas, Marcos, Titus, and Vera, I'd like to shout out a grand thank-you for believing and dreaming with me during those days when you were most vulnerable. I'm honored and blessed to be part of your lives and to have embarked on a journey to lead and protect you. It's a great blessing to reminiscence about our times together. Our bond of infinite love can never be broken. Thank you, Franco, for your enthusiasm and support all along.

Roberto Cerasani, my husband, confidant, and best friend: when I lacked strength, you sustained me. When I dreaded the effort necessary to look back and recount my memories, you were my fortress. I couldn't have done this without you. Thanks for all your love.

A warm and very special thank-you to Jayuya's Department of Education—to all of our teachers in La Pica, Collores, and Josefina Leon Zayas High School, who, day by day, educated us with the ethics and values we hold high today. To all of our neighbors, and fellow students, thank you for being part of our journey—your friendship and kindness are most treasured.

Thanks to San Patrick's Catholic Church in Jayuya. Your Masses, retreats, and holiday celebrations revived our hope and kept us going.

Doris Mercado

To the Batistas, thank you for your deed in escorting me to prom. I also give my heartfelt thanks to the Reyes family, for your love and care, and for the rides to graduation and prom. There are several people I'd like to thank, friends, neighbors, and any person whom I came across and was somehow part of my journey. Jinnel D'Hereaux, Sarah Caratasios, Lisa Sanders, Debra Candelora, Jennifer Bellamy, Sheree Breeden, Yecenia Casiano. Thanks to the shelter volunteers and the other homeless women at the shelter for your kindness. To Luz M. Rivera, Bev Maldonado, and Professor Mark Burt, thanks for your encouragement to write.

Special thanks to my childhood friend and fellow athlete Mary Garcia: knowing that you settled in Connecticut as well, just a few miles away, and reuniting with you have been yet another gift. Thanks to Alice, the shelter volunteer, for giving me a ride to church on Sundays. You were one of my guardian angels.

I'd also like to thank my editors Maureen Brady, for working on my first draft, Floyd Largent, and finally Holly T. Monteith, for taking on the final editing task. Your professionalism, patience, mentoring, and confidence were yet another blessing. Your confidence was as brilliant as a new sunrise. I am most grateful to all of you.

About the Author

Born and raised in Puerto Rico, Doris, is one of thirteen children. She is an abstract oil painter and foster/adoptive family advocacy professional. Doris lives in Connecticut with her family. This is her first book.

Made in the USA
Charleston, SC
18 October 2014